NIVI CARGALLIS

D1395541

The Abyssinian Crisis

By the same author:

The Political Influence of the British Monarchy, 1868-1952

The Abyssinian Crisis

Frank Hardie

Le relais où les destins changèrent de chevaux

B. T. Batsford Ltd, *London*

To the Warden and Fellows
of St Antony's College, Oxford

First published 1974
© Frank Hardie 1974

Printed in Great Britain by
Willmer Brothers Limited, Birkenhead
and bound by Hunter & Foulis Ltd., Edinburgh, Scotland
for the publishers B. T. Batsford Ltd.
4 Fitzhardinge Street, London W1H 0AH.

ISBN 0 7134 2773 6

Contents

Contents

Foreword

My text is spattered with 'superior numerals', which direct the reader to the notes and references. For the sake of economy these have all been relegated to the back of the book. This should, however, make the pages of the text more pleasant for the general reader. The scholar should easily surmount the slight difficulty involved in checking sources, using the cross-references, and obtaining information of tangential rather than essential interest.

On Shavian principles I try never to use two letters where one will do and so I spell Tana rather than Tsana, Jibuti rather than Djibuti or Jibouti, and so on. On the other hand I write Abyssinia rather than Ethiopia (except when quoting from contemporary sources) because Ethiopia was commonly called Abyssinia in 1935. In the references I dispense with *Official Report, Fifth Series, Parliamentary Debates, Commons, Volume etc; Hansard,* the date, and the number of the column concerned is perfectly adequate. By the same token 1(35)1, as a reference to a Cabinet Conclusion ('minute' in common parlance) means that the reader is referred to the first Cabinet meeting to be held in the year 1935 and the first Conclusion. The Public Record Office serial number is Cab. 23 and all the references here are to Volumes 81, 82, and 83. Cab. 23, Vol. 81, or whatever, need not be repeated in every reference. The quotations from Crown Copyright materials in the Public Record Office appear by permission of the Controller of H.M. Stationery Office.

It seems to me unsatisfactory to distinguish between pacifism and Pacifism. Too much hangs thereby on the difference between a small and a capital letter. I prefer therefore to use Mr. A. J. P. Taylor's distinction between pacifism and pacificism: 'By "pacificism" I mean the advocacy of a peaceful policy; by "pacifism" (a word invented only in the twentieth century) the doctrine of non-resistance.'*

The name of a country, whenever it appears, refers only to its Government and not to Government and/or people unless there is an indication to the contrary.

The original suggestion for the writing of this book came from my old friend, Michael Balfour, now Professor of European History at the University of East Anglia. I am grateful to him for the encouraging interest which he has taken throughout.

The French phrase used as an epigraph I culled from an essay by Sir Lewis Namier on quite a different subject, but unfortunately he does not give its source and I have not been able to trace it. I should be most grateful for the attribution.

F. H.
London
1st November, 1973

*The Trouble-Makers, 47,n5.

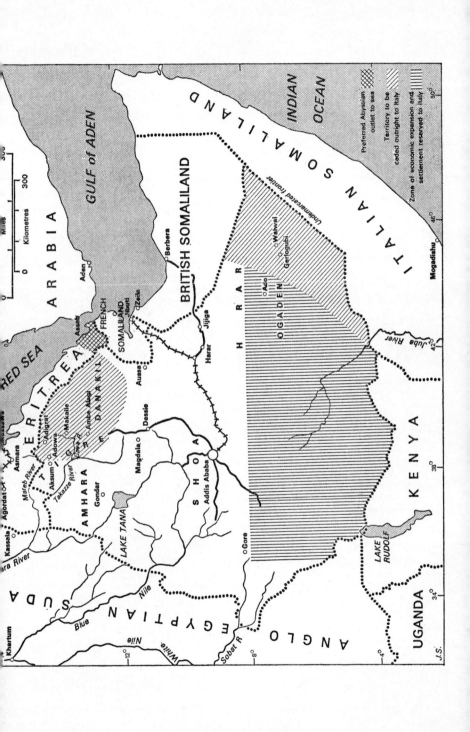

ARABIA

GULF of ADEN

RED SEA

Aden

ITALIAN SOMALILAND

INDIAN OCEAN

BRITISH SOMALILAND

Berbera

Zeila

Djibouti

FRENCH SOMALILAND

Assab

Mogadishu

Walwal

Gerlogubi

O G A D E N

Ado

H A R A R

Jijiga

Harar

Aussa

Juba River

KENYA

Undemarcated frontier

Preferred Abyssian outlet to sea

Territory to be ceded outright to Italy

Zone of economic expansion and settlement reserved to Italy

E R I T R E A

Asmara

Agordat

Kassala

Mareb River

Adigrat

Makalle

D A M A K I L

Amba Alagi

Adowa

Aksum

Takazze River

Mai C.

Atbara River

Khartum

S U D A N

Blue Nile

A M H A R A

Gondar

LAKE TANA

Dessie

Magdala

S H O A

Addis Ababa

Gore

LAKE RUDOLF

ANGLO-EGYPTIAN SUDAN

White Nile

Sobat R.

UGANDA

J.S.

300

Miles

300

Kilometres

0

Part One
Pieces and Positions

'I don't know if you have had the same experience,
but the snag I always come up against when I'm
telling a story is this dashed difficult problem of
where to begin it. It's a thing you don't want to go
wrong over, because one false step and you're sunk.
I mean, if you fool about too long at the start, trying
to establish atmosphere, as they call it, and all that
sort of rot, you fail to grip and the customers walk
out on you.

'Get off the mark, on the other hand, like a scalded
cat, and your public is at a loss. It simply raises its
eyebrows, and can't make out what you're talking
about.'

P. G. Wodehouse,
Right Ho, Jeeves, p. 9

I

Introduction

The outcome of the Abyssinian crisis was the first great act of appeasement; the second was Munich. The fires of controversy about both events, and especially the British part in them, which raged at the time, still burn. They seem less likely to be doused by any kind of, even provisional, historical judgment in the Munich than in the Abyssinian case. Perhaps for that very reason the former has hitherto been much more written about than the latter – but was it more important? First steps count more than second, especially down a steeply slippery slope. Moreover, the effective ending of the League of Nations was perhaps a more decisive turning-point on the road which led to the Second World War than the Anglo-French surrender of Czechoslovakia to Nazi Germany. If Abyssinia had been saved from Fascist Italy, the League would have been saved; if the League had been saved, Czechoslovakia might never have been surrendered; both Mussolini and Hitler might have been 'toppled' and European war prevented. Lord Vansittart, Head of the Foreign Office at the time, saw the sequence clearly. Referring to the Wal-Wal incident and Mussolini's wicked exploitation of it, he later wrote:

'Thus, because a few askaris had died by brackish water-holes in an African waste, was taken the first step to the second German holocaust. The pretext was more trivial than the murder of Franz Ferdinand.'[1]

The Abyssinian crisis was *the* turning-point of the thirties.[2] In between the Abyssinian crisis and Munich (with its echoes of the Hoare-Laval plan) comes the Spanish Civil War, beginning in 1936 just when the Abyssinian crisis ended and ending after Munich (coinciding, significantly, with the extinction of Czecho-

3

slovakia in March 1939). A civil war cannot easily be fitted into the normal categories of international events, but in this civil war Germany and Italy intervened on the one side, and the U.S.S.R. on the other. In these circumstances the Anglo-French policy of non-intervention was to Franco's advantage. Hence this policy could justly be called a third act of appeasement on the road to September 1939. On appeasement's altar three whole nations were sacrificed by Britain and France.

'Act of appeasement' is here defined as meaning not mere failure to resist an act of aggression but connivance at it, buying off the bully at someone else's expense, as opposed to just giving way to him oneself. (Lord Cecil defined appeasement as 'a policy of placating your enemies by sacrificing your friends'.[3]) Under this definition, failure to resist the series of Japanese acts of aggression against China starting in 1936 and the Anschluss of 1938 do not rank as 'acts of appeasement' but as acceptances, for reasons good or bad, of acts of aggression.

I have mentioned above the Anglo-French surrender of Czechoslovakia to Germany and the Anglo-French non-intervention policy in Spain. The policy of the League throughout the Abyssinian crisis was essentially an Anglo-French one. (In all three cases, moreover, Anglo-French, not Franco-British, is the correct hyphenated adjective, for it was Britain who took the lead, France who followed, very unwillingly in respect of Abyssinia, willingly, though with misgivings, in respect of Spain and Czechoslovakia). This is not surprising. In December 1934 when the curtain goes up on the drama of the Abyssinian crisis, though the reader must bear with a long overture, there was one Super-Power, not two. Britain and France were Great Powers, the two greatest European Powers; still wearing the laurels of victory in the First World War; founder-members of the League with Permanent Seats on its Council. (Britain, moreover, in 1934 still had a vast Colonial Empire and was the principal member of a Commonwealth notably more compact and cohesive than today's). Where Britain and France led, the other members of the League were, for the most part, content to follow.[4] It is too easily forgotten, however, that in 1935 Britain and France were not the Allies of 1919 and 1939, bound together by Treaty as they became in 1947.

Vansittart in a paper put up to Sir Samuel Hoare on 30 July

1935 refers to France as 'our eventual ally',[5] but Pierre Laval was going far in speaking to Hoare on 10 September 1935 of the 'entente with England' being 'an essential element' of French policy.[6] There was at that time more misunderstanding than understanding between the two countries over every aspect of foreign policy; Anglo-French relations were as bad as at the time of the French occupation of the Ruhr in 1923. However, where Britain led France had, in the last resort, to follow, if only because France was more dependent on Britain than Britain on France. For all the tragic events which are to be chronicled it is Britain, therefore, which bears more responsibility than any other State.[7] For this reason all chronicles of the Abyssinian crisis should revolve round British policy. That is the explicit object of this book.[8]

This crisis, however, was a Clapham Junction of crises: an astonishingly large number of lines crossed in it. A chronicle, therefore, written with special reference to and, one hopes, special knowledge of British policy and British opinion must take account of the policies of other States, most obviously those of Abyssinia and Italy, but also to an important extent those of France, Germany, and the United States of America. Histories of the Abyssinian crisis as seen from Addis Ababa, Rome, Paris, Berlin or Washington would undoubtedly show a more detailed knowledge of those policies than this book, but would, I trust, though by a different route, reach the same fundamental conclusions. Again, if the story were to be told primarily as an episode, the key episode, in the history of the League of Nations, the treatment would again be different. The League then had 53 members; the attitude and actions of each one of them would require discussion.

The starting-date of the Abyssinian crisis is usually defined as 5 December 1934 (the Wal-Wal incident), the ending-date as 15 July 1936 (the lifting of sanctions). Thereafter the League States continued feebly to concern themselves with questions of the recognition or non-recognition of the Italian conquest of Abyssinia and the credentials of Abyssinian delegations to Geneva. These activities, however, were the navigation of shoals and shallows; the tide, not taken at the flood, was never to flow again.

The crisis of the crisis, so to speak, occurred between 4 September 1935, when the League of Nations became fully seized of the

Italo-Abyssinian dispute (nominally arising out of the frontier incident of the previous December) and 18 December 1935, when the resignation of Sir Samuel Hoare marked the death of the Hoare-Laval plan for the settlement of the 'dispute' which was then in fact being settled by an Italo-Abyssinian war. In my own view the birth of that plan marked the death of the League itself. On that account I try to speed up the narrative thereafter. Reasons for that view will appear later.[9] For the moment I pray in aid Mr. A. J. P. Taylor:

'The real death of the League was in December 1935, not in 1939 or 1945. One day it was a powerful body imposing sanctions, seemingly more effective than ever before; the next day it was an empty sham, everyone scuttling from it as quickly as possible.'[10]

The Italo-Abyssinian War began on 3 October 1935, and effectively ended on 5 May 1936. In other words, this war was part of the 'crisis'. I must make it plain, however, that I shall not recount the course of the campaign nor make more than a brief mention of the massive military preparations which, on the Italian side, preceded it. (They were clear for all the world to see from mid-February onwards). These military events are treated as only the background, albeit they were the all-important background, to the political events which I shall describe. In other words this book is not concerned with the deeds of soldiers (and, on the Italian side, airmen) but the utterances of politicians and, to a lesser extent, of more ordinary people.

The Abyssinian crisis is perhaps, strictly speaking, misnamed. The war was fought on Abyssinian soil and the Abyssinian peoples were those who, initially at any rate, most suffered from the mishandling of the crisis which allowed the war to occur. Its primary importance, however, was not as an episode in the relations between European and African peoples. For that reason I do not discuss contemporary African reactions to it, though I hope that someone else will tackle that important and interesting subject. The primary importance of the Abyssinian crisis was as a catalyst of the disintegration of international law and order in Europe, leading to a European and so to a World War. Moreover, as it was seen from the start to be the supreme test for the League of Nations, it was from the start a crisis in world as well as

6

in European and African affairs. It was a crisis from which, in the long run, not merely the Abyssinians but countless millions of human beings suffered the whole world over. For Britain it had a special secondary importance. It clarified public opinion about pacificism; the same umbrella could no longer shelter the heads of pacifists and coercionists.

There is, in short, an inevitable element of confusion in speaking of an Abyssinian crisis when what is meant is primarily a European one. In the long history of Abyssinia the events with which this book is concerned, and the Italian occupation of 1936–41, now seem to constitute a short interlude. However, the European meaning of 'Abyssinian crisis' is widely understood and accepted and so I stick to it.

For the writing of history with these terms of reference someone of my generation has a double advantage, enjoyed by no previous comparable generation, to be enjoyed by many later ones. In the first place, if one was interested in public events at the time – and I was, deeply – one can remember their flavour. In the second place, to those memories (checked, as often as possible, against the contemporary written record) one can now add knowledge of what was going on 'at the top' as opposed to what was then known, or appearing, to be going on. In other words, one can add to knowledge gained then from what was published knowledge of what was then 'top secret', e.g. what was decided at Cabinet meetings, said in diplomatic despatches, and so on. This is because the Public Records Act of 1967, with rare exceptions, releases to scholars all material of this kind, provided it is more than 30 years old. This is the '30 years rule', which has replaced the '50 years rule' created by the Act of 1958. It follows that any historian who is the right amount older than the British public papers which he is studying has the double advantage of which I speak. (In the case of the Abyssinian crisis this double advantage becomes a treble one in that what one can remember, and indeed participated in, i.e. the movement of British public opinion in relation to the crisis, is an essential part of its history.) A young man or woman reading this book can easily see the worth of this double advantage if he imagines himself 30 years hence writing about a now contemporary public event and able to find out in the Public Records Office what went on 'behind the scenes'.

2

Abyssinian Background

On 27 September 1938 (the Munich Agreement was signed on the 29th) Neville Chamberlain, then Prime Minister, spoke in a broadcast of 'a quarrel in a far-away country between people of whom we know nothing'. C. E. M. Joad had not then come along to popularize, through the B.B.C.'s *Brains Trust*, the phrase 'It depends what you mean by....' 'Far-away' was an adjective open to rigorous scrutiny; so were the nouns 'we' and 'nothing'. And if 'we' meant the common people it was surely the duty of the Government, in such a crisis, to see to it that they knew as much as possible of Czechoslovakia and the possible effects of the 'quarrel'. But in 1934 Abyssinia was even further away and less was known of it by fewer Englishmen than was known in England in 1938 about Czechoslovakia. Interestingly Chamberlain's phrase of 1938 – famous for its infamy – echoes one which he had used unnoticed in 1935 about Abyssinia: 'a country remote and unfamiliar'.[1]

The principal physical feature of that country is a *massif central* constructed on a prodigal scale. Centrally placed on this plateau is Addis Ababa, the capital city since 1889, about 8,000 feet above sea-level. To the north and east of this mountainous area are torrid plains and then, respectively, the Red Sea and the Indian Ocean; to the south, tropical Africa; to the west, the basin of the Upper Nile. The Blue Nile issues from Lake Tana, 50 miles within Abyssinia, but then flows in an immense horse-shoe south-east, west, and north-west (a kind of African Grand Canyon) before leaving Abyssinian territory to join the White Nile at Khartum, still being fed en route by tributaries, notably the Atbara, with sources in the Abyssinian mountains. In the torrid plains between the central mountains and the Indian Ocean are situated the 'hundred wells of Wal-Wal'.

In 1934 Abyssinia was entirely surrounded by the Colonial possessions of three European Powers, Britain, France and Italy. (The Sudan was nominally an Anglo-Egyptian condominion, but Egypt itself was then a British Protectorate, which meant that it had no more real independence than India at that time). In this respect, more than any other, the 'scramble for Africa' had changed the map to Abyssinia's disadvantage. Until the nineteenth century she had always had a sea coast. Without one, she could have neither a Navy nor a merchant fleet. Nonetheless, because of American neutrality legislation, the U.S. President in a proclamation on 5 October 1935 scrupulously – or to ridicule the legislation? – warned American citizens that, war having broken out, they would travel in either Abyssinian or Italian ships at their own risk.[2]

The lack of a Navy hamstrung Abyssinia's defences against invasion. If hostile forces were to approach by sea, whether from the Mediterranean (via the Suez Canal) or the Indian Ocean, only some other country could stop them at sea. Moreover, without access to the sea she could not import the means of defence on land without some other country's permission. (A railway ran from Addis Ababa to the port of Jibuti on the Red Sea, but the railway was French-owned and the port in French Somaliland). Thus Abyssinia in 1934 had been landlocked by European imperialism and so rendered to an important extent defenceless against European imperialism. She retained, however, her ancient independence. The only other independent African state then in existence was Liberia, a small country dating back only to 1847, and to the extent that she depended on American protection perhaps more accurately described as only semi-independent.

Abyssinian history on the other hand was very long, not so dark as that of 'Darkest Africa' as a whole, but, before the nineteenth century, exceedingly obscure. The Red Sea has played an important part in determining its course. Across the Red Sea came the immigrants who founded, in the 5th century B.C., the first Abyssinian State known to history, the Kingdom of Aksum. Across the Red Sea, about a thousand years later, went Abyssinian Armies, who – in a brief imperialist period – conquered the Yemen. Mohammed is said to have been born in the very year (about A.D. 569) when an Abyssinian Viceroy reached Mecca. (His Army included an elephant; hence, the Year of the

Elephant). In due season back across the Red Sea came Moslems who conquered substantial portions of northern Abyssinia. Along it, eastward and westward, passed, for aeons before the opening of the Suez Canal in 1869, a trade between the Mediterranean and India which made Abyssinian shores an object of interest to Mediterranean countries, to Egypt, Greece, and Rome. But far more important in Abyssinian history than their trading plantations was the arrival of Christianity in the 4th century A.D., not direct from Palestine but, it seems, by a roundabout route through the Romanized Mediterranean. The Red Sea, in short, in early Abyssinian history, linked Abyssinia with Western Europe; the later presence of Islam on its northern shores cut that link. In Europe, however, the knowledge lingered of a Christian State, somewhere beyond Islam, and to Abyssinia, therefore, in the fourteenth century was attached, very naturally, the legend of Prester John.

Even if Islam had not been interposed between European Christendom and Abyssinia, little would have been known of peoples living in remote mountain fastnesses, with all that that implies in terms of bad communications and political disunion. As one seeks to peer through the mists of the distant past, those mists are specially heavy over the Abyssinian highlands. Infrequently they lift and then the first thing usually to be perceived is fighting. There is war between Christians and Moslems; Galla tribes invade from the south-east; for, historically, a brief moment, the Portuguese joined in from their Indian Empires in the east. Thereafter Abyssinia was as cut off from Europe as was Japan, and for as long. Internally, over-powerful monastic communities fought against their secular sovereigns; different 'tribes' were constantly at war with each other. English readers can gain some understanding of medieval Abyssinian history by thinking in terms of English history in the Dark Ages (the primitive conditions materially, the meagre culture, the absence of a central secular authority, the complications of foreign invasions, the presence of a Christian Church). They can gain too some understanding of the centuries of struggle by Abyssinian Emperors to build up their authority by thinking in terms of medieval English Kings trying to assert their authority over that of their over-mighty and unruly Barons. The Abyssinian equivalent of the English Baron was called a Ras. In Fascist Italy, long before the

Italo-Abyssinian war, that name was given to the local Party boss.

The whole of Abyssinian history until the nineteenth century is, in effect, one long Dark Age: 'A few main outlines, a few remarkable details may be discerned; the rest is all conjecture and ambiguity'. Reliable chronicling begins with the first modern ruler, the Emperor Theodore II, born in 1818 and crowned at Aksum in 1855.

Theodore won his crown by a series of battles against rivals and ruthless repression after each victory. His times saw the first contacts, not predominantly happy, with European Powers since the Portuguese interventions in the late fifteenth and early sixteenth centuries. The British were the first in the field. In 1847 a British Consul, W. C. Plowden, was appointed to Gondar by Lord Palmerston and two years later concluded a Treaty of Commerce (which proved a dead letter) with the local Ras. Gondar was captured by Theodore in 1854; Plowden was murdered on his way back to England in 1860; a successor, Captain C. D. Cameron, arrived in 1862. Theodore then wrote a letter to Queen Victoria, which the Foreign Office contrived to pigeon-hole. In 1864, no answer having arrived, Theodore (by now a kind of Ivan the Terrible) imprisoned Cameron and some other Englishmen in his fortress-capital, Magdala, and in 1866 imprisoned also a number of other Europeans. These events led to Sir Robert Napier's rescuing expedition. It took his force nearly a year, because of the physical difficulties, to march from a bay just south of Massawa to Magdala. The prisoners were released; Theodore committed suicide; the expedition retreated without any attempt at annexations. Disraeli said that he had hoisted the standard of St. George on the mountains of Rasselas. The defeat of Baratieri's expedition in 1896 must have been all the more galling to Italians because of the success of Napier's in 1868.

The four years following Theodore's suicide were a period of anarchy reminiscent of the period preceding his accession. Kassa, Ras of Tigre, fought his way to the top and was crowned Emperor John IV in 1872. European infiltration continued. The French had established themselves at Obock on the Somali coast in 1862, the Italians on the Bay of Assab in 1869. The Rubattino Shipping Company bought the port of Assab from the Ras in 1870 and sold it to the Italian Government in 1882. The British occupied Zeila and Berbera in 1884, the Italians Massawa in

1885. Thus were laid the foundations of the Colonies which were to cut off Abyssinia from the Red Sea under the names of Eritrea, French Somaliland, and British Somaliland.

The principal foreign threat to John IV's Abyssinia came, however, not from Europeans but from other Africans, at first the Egyptians and, later, Mahdist dervishes from the Sudan. Egypt began to push down the Western shore of the Red Sea in 1865 and in 1872 occupied Berbera and Harar. In 1875 a large-scale attempt, based on Massawa, at large-scale conquest was organized. This was defeated and Harar was evacuated in 1884. This marked the end of the Egyptian attempt at ascendancy, initiated and pressed, one should note, before the British took control of Egypt in 1882.

With the Anglo-Egyptian withdrawal from the Sudan (for the British reader the chief association is Gordon's death in 1885) Dervish raids on Abyssinia became increasingly serious. In the spring of 1889 John IV had to choose between striking at the Dervishes or his chief internal enemy, Menelik, Ras of Shoa. He marched on the former, but was himself killed in the moment of victory.

The Italians, frustrated in their Tunisian ambitions,[3] now took the place of the Egyptians and Sudanese as the principal foreign infiltrators of Abyssinia. As we have seen, their official occupation of what was to become Eritrea began in 1882 and they occupied Massawa three years later. (This Italian expansion was encouraged by Britain;[4] discouraged by France.[5]) The Italians, more or less in alliance with Menelik, while he was still a rebel against the Emperor, then proceeded to penetrate Northern Tigre. Menelik proclaimed himself Emperor on the death of John IV. At first Italian relations with him continued to be friendly and in May 1889 there was concluded the Treaty of Uccialli. Its text was in Italian and Amharic and, according to the Italian text of Article 17, Italy was given the right to establish a Protectorate over the whole country. Britain accepted this provision; France[6] – and Russia – did not. Crispi, the Italian Prime Minister, talked triumphantly of having wiped Abyssinia off the map.[7]

That summer the Italians occupied Asmara and Keren, and a Protectorate was established over what was to become Italian Somaliland. (Thus was Abyssinia cut off from the Indian Ocean as well as the Red Sea.) In 1890 the occupied places in the North were proclaimed to be the Italian Colony of Eritrea. This further Italian expansion made Menelik anti-Italian and this change of attitude was encouraged by France and Russia, who sent him personal gifts, military and religious missions, and arms.[8] Significantly too these Italian encroachments to some extent had the same effect on Abyssinia as had the English conquests in France in the fifteenth century, prompting a patriotism and a sense of national unity which hitherto had been notably non-existent. In February 1893 Menelik denounced the Treaty of 1889. That December an Italian force won a resounding victory over 10,000 Dervishes at Agordat. Further advances and victories followed under the command of General Baratieri. (Both he and Crispi, who became Italian Prime Minister for the second time in the same month, had been among Garibaldi's 'Thousand.') In November 1895 war with Abyssinia followed, but now Abyssinian victories resounded. On 7 December Baratieri's southernmost garrison at Amba Alagi (40 miles beyond Makalle) was overwhelmed. On 21 January 1896, after a siege of three weeks, the garrison at Makalle itself surrendered. Italian power in the Tigre crumbled.[9] The Italian Parliament voted an additional 20 million lire for the war and 20,000 more troops were sent out between mid-December 1895 and mid-February 1896.[10] Crispi ordered a victory (much as Napoleon ordered one from Villeneuve). Instead he obtained, on 1 March 1896, the most crushing defeat of all, Adowa.

The repercussions in Italy we shall observe later, but this battle was an event of world-wide significance, the first decisive defeat of a European by an African Power since Hannibal's victories over the Romans.[11]

3
Abyssinia on the Eve

It was during the Emperor Menelik's reign that the foundations of the Abyssinia of 1934 were laid. He greatly extended his country to the south and the siting of the new capital at Addis Ababa constituted a deliberate shifting of the centre of power from north to south.[1] European Powers began to be continuously represented diplomatically at the capital. The railway from there to Jibuti was begun in 1894 and finished in 1917.[2] However, the Abyssinian Empire remained a ramshackle affair: a poor and backward country, a temptation to any developer with an eye on the main chance. No state is completely civilized, but Abyssinia by any standard was only semi-civilized. Slavery, for example, had been abolished on paper, but remained a reality. The Emperor's writ did not run very far outside Addis Ababa. It is perfectly understandable that, before the war started, Sir Samuel Hoare should have said to Pierre Laval:

> 'His Majesty's Government has no particular sympathy with Abyssinia. They have had just as much trouble from the Abyssinians on the Sudan frontier as the Italians have had in Eritrea. Things have become perhaps a little better during the last few years, but there is no effective Government in Abyssinia and Abyssinia is a bad neighbour.'[3]

Professor Toynbee had asserted in 1934 that 'the spectacle presented by the one indigenous African state that has succeeded in retaining its complete independence is perhaps the best justification that can be found for the partition of the rest of Africa among the European powers.'[4]

Menelik died in 1913 and was succeeded by his grandson, Lij Yasu. When the European war broke out he was backed by

Germany and Turkey, while Britain, France and Italy supported
the pretensions of Tafari Makonnen (Menelik's great-nephew,
now the Emperor Haile Selassie) who had become Ras of his
native province of Harar three or four years previously. Yasu
flirted with Islam, despite the majority of the population being
Christian. A troubled reign was ended by his deposition in 1916.
Menelik's daughter, Zauditu, was then proclaimed Empress and
Ras Tafari Regent. In 1928 Tafari Makonnen assumed the title
of Emperor ('King of the Kings of Ethiopia, Conquering Lion of
Judah, Elect of God') and the name of Haile Selassie ('Might of
the Trinity'). The Empress Zauditu died in 1929. Haile Selassie
was crowned in 1930 and is still (1973) Negus, the longest-
reigning monarch in the world. Of his reign up to June 1935, the
Maffey Report remarked that '... there had been a sincere,
though unhappily only partially successful, attempt to improve
frontier administration, to eradicate slavery, brigandage, and
other abuses. Cruelty, crudity, and confusion can still be found
... but it does not appear reasonable or just to write off the
Ethiopian Empire as irremediably barbarous and uncivilized
without any hope of eventual reform'.[5] Haile Selassie had too
many titles and too little power, but he did his reforming best.

To the Maffey Report we also owe a succinct summary of the
attitudes of the three limitrophe Powers (Britain, France, and
Italy) to Abyssinia in the period between the latter part of
Menelik's reign and the first part of Haile Selassie's:

'The main and, indeed, almost exclusive interest of the French
has been the safeguarding of their interest in the Jibuti Railway. The main preoccupation of the United Kingdom has
been to regularize the position on the frontiers, to protect our
interest in Lake Tana, and to secure the abolition of slavery.
The Italians have constantly thought in terms of spheres of
influence and wide economic concessions'.[6]

The British interest in Lake Tana derived from the British interest
in Egypt and the Sudan and was in its possible use for the regula-
tion of the flow of the Nile.

We have seen that in the 80's Britain gave her blessing to
Italian expansion in Abyssinia. In March and April 1891, and
again in May 1894, Anglo-Italian Agreements were signed defin-

ing, on the assumption of the Treaty of Uccialli having given Italy a Protectorate over the whole of Abyssinia, the British and Italian spheres of influence therein. The Italian sphere was to cover the whole country except for a small area in the west and north. However, the post-1896 position clearly called for revised arrangements between all three limitrophe Powers and in 1906 a Tripartite Agreement between them was signed.

The preamble to this Treaty stated that it was in the interest of all three Powers to 'maintain intact the integrity of Ethiopia'. Nonetheless, not surprisingly in view of Menelik's age and ill-health, the disintegration of Abyssinia was envisaged and it was agreed that, in the event of a break-up, the three Powers should act together to safeguard their special interests, viz. those:

1. Of Britain (and Egypt) in the Nile Basin.
2. Of France in the hinterland of French Somaliland and the zone necessary for the building and working of the Jibuti Railway.
3. Of Italy in her two Colonies, their hinterlands, and a connection between them to the west of Addis Ababa.

In short, if Abyssinia broke up, or was broken up, the area in which each limitrophe State might expand its sovereignty was roughly defined and grounds for possible clashes of territorial interests thereby avoided.

This Treaty was typical of its times. Abyssinia was not consulted about it and it was scarcely in her interests. Britain and France, by re-defining and limiting their interests in Abyssinia, implicitly recognized as paramount the indefinite interests of Italy. Abyssinia certainly seemed to have lost the advantage of rivalry between the three limitrophe Powers.[7]

All this follows a familiar pattern. In the world of European expansion, States such as Abyssinia were seen, by the European Great Powers, as 'sick men'. From their point of view Turkey was the sick man of Europe itself in the nineteenth century, Persia and China were sick men of Asia in the early twentieth. The sickness was to be cured by surgery, sometimes an amputation or two, sometimes total dismemberment, sometimes a total transplant into another body politic (as in the cases of Egypt and Morocco). As already mentioned, the only other state in the whole of Africa to retain its independence was, with American support, Liberia.[8]

In the Treaties which have just been mentioned regard for the integrity and self-development of Abyssinia was not the dominant feature. The emphasis is on co-operation between the three Great Powers concerned rather than on co-operation between any one or more of them and Abyssinia. By 1906 she had already been dispossessed of much territory; further surrenders of sovereignty, by division into 'spheres of influence' or by outright annexations, were plainly contemplated. It was her misfortune to have survived, more or less whole, into an age when her kind of 'sickness' was ceasing to be seen as wasting and probably fatal, but nonetheless to become the last victim of the old-fashioned method of 'treatment' at its worst.

Until the coming of the Covenant, the 1906 Treaty was the sheet-anchor of British policy towards Abyssinia.[9] To it, however, Anglo-Italian footnotes were added. Thus in November 1913, Sir Edward Grey, then Foreign Secretary, told the Italian Ambassador in London that, in the event of Abyssinia breaking up, Italy should have a territorial connection between Eritrea and Italian Somaliland to the west of Addis Ababa, but this connection must be secured in such a way as not to impair British control of the waters of the Nile and their sources: 'We could not possibly consent to the passing of Lake Tana under any control but our own if Ethiopia broke up'.[10] In November 1919, an Italian Note referred to the ultimate delimitation of 'a *territorial* zone, to be recognized as pertaining to Great Britain in respect of [her] predominant hydraulic interests in that area'. In 1922 Italy again took a diplomatic initiative, offering her support to Britain for the building of a Lake Tana dam in return for British support to Italy in building a railway linking her two Colonies west of Addis Ababa. Neither of these two offers was taken up by the Foreign Office.

In 1925, however, it was decided that there should be a response. The result was another agreement of a Victorian type relating to Abyssinia, made by an Exchange of Notes, between Italy (now Fascist Italy) and Great Britain. (It is a relevant consideration that, at this time, Abyssinia was once again in a highly unsettled state, Ras Tafari being Regent only, not Negus). The significance of this agreement is perhaps to be found more in its evidence of the Anglo-Italian cordiality then current than in its contents in respect of Abyssinia. Under the 1925 agreement Italy was to support a British request for a concession to build a Lake Tana barrage – and a motor road to it from the Sudanese frontier – and Britain was, *pari passu*, to support an Italian request for a concession to build a railway linking, west of Addis Ababa, the two Italian Colonies. (They were separated by 780 crow's miles and much mountainous country.) If the Tana concession was obtained, Britain would recognize 'an exclusive Italian economic influence in the west of Ethiopia and in the whole of the territory to be covered by the above-mentioned railway. . . .'[11] Neither concession was in fact obtained.

In 1925 Britain, as Mandatory Power for Irak, was involved in a territorial dispute with Turkey about the ownership of Mosul.[12] It has been cautiously suggested that the British object in promoting the Anglo-Italian Exchange of Notes on Abyssinia was to obtain Italian support against Turkey by allowing Mussolini a grip on the throat of his intended Abyssinian victim.[13] The correctness of this idea is doubtful. Mussolini was still in trouble in Libya in 1925 and his Abyssinian ambitions were not firmly formulated till 1932 at the earliest.[14]

The Foreign Office's change of mind seems in fact to have had prosaic origins.[15] It was pushed by the Board of Trade, in its turn pushed by the Empire Cotton Growing Corporation. The Director of that Corporation (Sir James Currie) saw a Tana dam simply as a help to the cotton-growers of Egypt and the Sudan. The Foreign Office saw the deal as a means of securing Italian support, or lack of opposition to, a long-standing ambition (dating back to 1902). Tafari had, in the previous August, rebuffed an approach from Ramsay Macdonald (then Prime Minister and Foreign Secretary) on the same subject. Perhaps it was thought that Italian support would obviate a second rebuff; possibly at some point in these Anglo-Italian negotiations a link was made with contemporaneous negotiations about the Anglo-Turkish dispute.[16]

The whole calculation, on the British side, may well have been Machiavellian in the sense that the Foreign Office thought that a specific British imperial interest could be achieved by a pledge to Italy which would never have to be redeemed. On the other hand, it was scarcely Machiavellian simply to overlook, as was in fact done, the French interest. (In April 1926, Austen Chamberlain, after a gentle reproach from Briand on this point, asked his officials how he had come to negotiate with Italy about Abyssinia without first consulting France.) On the Italian side, Mussolini, when first approached by the British Ambassador in Rome (Sir Ronald Graham), said that he was always anxious to co-operate with Britain but was ignorant of this particular question and would need time to prepare an answer. His Colonial Office thought that the agreement might damage Italo-Abyssinian relations; his Foreign Office thought that Anglo-Italian relations were more important. At that time Mussolini himself thought the same and so the agreement went through. The two Notes were, somewhat arbitrarily, dated 14 and 20 December; the actual exchange was made on Boxing Day.

Thereafter, from the British point of view, everything went wrong. Both the British and Italian Ministers in Addis Ababa wanted the wording changed to minimize any affront to Abyssinian feelings and it took till May 1926 to agree a few slight alterations. Meanwhile no text of the agreement being available for Paris, Geneva, or Addis Ababa, suspicions grew about its contents. Tafari received the Notes on 9 June and, possibly on French advice, protested to Britain, Italy and the League.

France was the 'sated Power' in relation to Abyssinia. The Jibuti Railway made her Somaliland Colony a viable *entrepôt* on the Mediterranean-Red Sea route to her Far Eastern Colonies. The railway also gave France virtual control of Abyssinia's foreign trade. Because she had this control, Britain and Italy in 1925 were, in close co-operation, asking her to agree to a limitation on the import of arms. (This was finally concluded five years later.[17]) France, because she had 'no more territorial ambitions' in Abyssinia, was the most influential Power at Addis Ababa. It was France who promoted Abyssinian entry into the League in 1923. Britain opposed it.[18] The roles of 1923, of Britain as critic of Abyssinia and France as protector were, as we shall see, completely reversed in 1935. Britain became her friend (on the part of her Government by no means whole-heartedly), France the friend of her enemy.

The British Foreign Office does not come too well, whether in terms of morality or efficiency, out of the story of the 1925 negotiations, but its rôle was that of a naive and incompetent rather than a cunning and unscrupulous conspirator. In the next two years the story is one of double-dealing, indeed treble-dealing, on the part of Tafari and Mussolini. The latter advanced his interests at the expense of Britain and the former played Britain and Italy off against each other so cleverly that neither gained from him any concession other than, in the Italian case, three years later, a paper one. Menelik had been another expert player of this sort of game. Tafari is not to be blamed for playing it too in the circumstances of 1926. In June the Regent indicated to the British Minister that he was more suspicious of Italian intentions towards his country than of British ones, but a little later told the Italian Minister that Mussolini's honourable intentions and good faith were not questioned. On the same day he sent his letter of protest against the 1925 Agreement to the Secretary-General of the League of Nations. Mussolini thereupon questioned Tafari's sincerity, but his own would have seemed questionable in London if it had been known there that in March he had told Tafari that he would exercise a restraining influence on Britain. Early in 1927 Mussolini instructed the Italian Minister at Addis Ababa to give Britain as little support as possible and present Italy as a mediator and protector of Abyssinian rights. Early in 1927 also the British Minister opened negotiations for the building of the Tana Dam. In September Tafari said that Abyssinia would attempt to build the dam herself; if unable to do so, a Company would be formed for the purpose, whose shares British subjects could buy. About the same time the Foreign Office received from a secret source a report (which was not disbelieved, but taken lightly) that Italy had given detailed advice to Abyssinia for avoiding British pressure for a concession by a counter-proposal of just this kind.

In May 1927, the Duke of the Abruzzi (the King of Italy's uncle) visited Abyssinia accompanied by two high Italian officials, Gasparini and Guariglia. (The nominal object of this visit was to repay the one which Tafari had made to Rome in 1924.) It was probably then that negotiations were started for a concession to Italy for the building of a road inland from Assab to Dessie. Britain was not told of these negotiations by the other party to the 1925 Agreement and only learnt of them early the next year. In March 1928 Tafari said he would sign the concession for the road if, to disarm internal critics, he could simultaneously sign a Treaty of Friendship and Arbitration with Italy. Mussolini did then consult Austen Chamberlain, who made no comment on the road project (which he now for the first time heard of officially) and no objection to the proposed Treaty. Both agreements were signed on 2 August.

This Treaty, which will play a prominent part in our narrative,[19] thus originated as a by-product of negotiations for a road-building concession to Italy. The two documents taken together constitute the high point of Italian friendship with, and influence over, Abyssinia. The Anglo-Italian Agreement had failed of its purpose. Anglo-Italian relations had, in respect of Abyssinia, deteriorated. The Agreement had not secured Italian support for, or disinterest in, the building of the Tana Dam, nor had a concession for its building been obtained. The Italians had got their road on paper, but, to the chagrin of Mussolini, it was never built. Britain and Italy had reversed their Abyssinian positions between 1925 and 1928. In the former year it had been Britain which was pursuing a 'forward policy', in the latter it was Italy. Tafari, however, had maintained his position and even improved it on paper. Italy had obtained a paper concession; Britain not even that; he had obtained a paper which, if honoured, importantly circumscribed Italian expansionism, but he had given nothing substantial away.

Professor Toynbee sees the 'motives which led the Abyssinian Government to sign the conventions of 2 August 1928, and thereafter to adopt an obstructive policy which nullified their effect' as 'something of a mystery'.[20] The simplest hypothesis seems the best: Tafari did not want to see the integrity and independence of his country undermined by concessions, whether for a dam or a road, which would amount to cessions of territory to limitrophe Powers of whose further ambitions he had reason to be afraid. Probably this is why late in 1927 he opened negotiations with an American firm for the building of the dam. (The Rickett concession is thus foreshadowed.) A mission from the White Engineering Company of New York surveyed the terrain in 1930, but the project ceased to be viable with the fall in the price of cotton consequent upon the Great Depression.[21] Tafari, now Haile Selassie, revived the project, plainly for reasons of political expediency, in May 1935. He then invited British, Egyptian, and Sudanese delegates to a conference on the subject at Addis Ababa. Egypt voted £E 3,000,000 for the project; the Anglo-Sudanese reply was to ask for the postponement of the conference so as not to 'aggravate the present unfortunate controversy between Italy and Abyssinia. . . .'[22]

By the time of the last old-fashioned agreement in 1925 a new world was already taking shape. A League of Nations came into being in 1920 and Abyssinia, as already mentioned, became a member in 1923.[23] She was admitted by unanimous vote of the Assembly, but after a debate in its Political Committee in which her claims were espoused by France and lukewarmly backed by Italy, against the doubts of Great Britain, Norway, Switzerland, and Australia.[24] Sir Joseph Cook, the Australian delegate, expressed disdain for the idea that Abyssinia should be entitled to supervise and pass judgment on Australia's administration, under League mandate, of New Guinea, whose inhabitants, in his view, were at the same stage of social development as those of Abyssinia herself.

The 1928 Treaty of Friendship between Abyssinia and Italy can also be seen as a step towards a new post-imperialist world. Under this Treaty neither Government was, under any pretext, to 'take any action which may prejudice or damage the independence of the other'. Disputes not settled diplomatically were to be submitted to a 'procedure of conciliation or arbitration'. 1928 is also the year of the Kellogg Pact under which the signatories (who included Italy and Abyssinia) undertood to 'renounce war as an instrument of national policy'.[25] Resort to war in 'self-defence' remained legal.

In 1930 an Abyssinian Arms Traffic Treaty was concluded between Abyssinia and the limitrophe Powers. The object of this Treaty was to limit the transit of arms and ammunition to Abyssinia through the adjacent territories (and by what other route could they come?) to deliveries to the central Government. Anarchy and brigandage could not be put down, in a land flooded with arms of all kinds, without a Negus more strongly armed than his subjects. This quadrilateral agreement, unlike the tripartite Treaty of 1906, made a real contribution to Abyssinian interests.

The Franco-Italian Agreements of January 1935,[26] were, in their impact on Abyssinia, a reversion to a bi-lateral agreement between two European Powers at her expense. Mr. D. C. Watt sees them as 'best understood as an illustration of the interplay, visible even in the classic period of European imperialism, between European and "colonial" considerations'. He adds: 'In this barter of interest for interest without even any pretence of a relation to the views of the local inhabitants, they mark perhaps the last major example of classical imperialism in action in the Middle East'.[27]

Since 1928, Wal-Wal, an oasis in the Ogaden province of Abyssinia, had been occupied by an Italian military force. The immensely long frontiers of Abyssinia were at this time still substantially undefined. Local tribes often considered that they had grazing rights on both sides of them; raids and counter-raids were common; frontier incidents were frequent. Abyssinia considered (a glance at almost any map will show why) Wal-Wal, valuable for its wells, to be well within its boundaries, but made no complaint of the Italian military occupation.[28] Trouble came in December 1934, with the arrival of an Anglo-Abyssinian Boundary Commission, escorted by Abyssinian troops. Confronted by the Italian force (largely native) the Boundary Commissioners discreetly withdrew. On 5 December the Italian and Abyssinian forces exchanged fire, with heavy losses on both sides. Who started the fighting was never determined.[29] The Italian Government on 11 December put to Abyssinia 'a series of sensational demands for compensation, salutes to the flag, punishment of the guilty, and other somewhat humiliating forms of reparation.'[30]

In November, Abyssinia had agreed to an apology (including a salute to the Italian flag) and reparations for an attack on the Italian Consulate at Gondar, but for the Wal-Wal incident she was not prepared to take the blame. From Mussolini's point of view the incident, because of its scale, provided a particularly good pretext for picking a quarrel.

Such was the starting-point of the Abyssinian crisis. We can now perceive, far more clearly than could observers of the inter national scene in December 1934, that the Wal-Wal incident was important only for what Italy chose to make of it. Undoubtedly it could have been settled easily and quickly. However, we now know that Mussolini had long previously (by the autumn of 1933 at the latest[31]) decided on war with Abyssinia. Wal-Wal gave him a pretext for open preparation for it.

In 1925 the Duce had written to his Minister for the Colonies instructing him to study, and make good, the defensive deficien-

23

cies of Eritrea.[32] By the spring of 1932, however, Mussolini was discussing with another Colonial Minister, De Bono, 'a careful and decisive political action ... to abolish the vital inconveniences' suffered by Eritrea and Somalia, notably 'the absolute lack of good lines of communication'[33] between them. It seems, however, that in 1932 nothing definite was 'settled as regards the character and method of a possible campaign against the probable enemy'[34], indeed that the Duce did not then decide to take the offensive.[35] By the autumn of 1933, however, he had decided that 'the matter would have to be settled no later than 1936 ...'[36] Nonetheless the Italian Government, on 29 September 1934, publicly stated that it had no unfriendly intentions towards Abyssinia.[37] This assurance was repeated to the Abyssinian Chargé d'Affaires in Rome (M. Jesus Afewerk) by the King of Italy and Mussolini in mid-January 1935,[38] and was again repeated in mid-February[39] to M. Afewerk by Signor Suvich (Under-Secretary for Foreign Affairs, Mussolini then being his own Foreign Minister). On 20 December 1934, however, Mussolini had personally prepared a document headed *Directions and Plan of Action for the Solution of the Italo-Abyssinian Question'*.[40] On 26 February 1935, he wrote to De Bono (by then High Commissioner in Eritrea): 'In case the Negus should have no intention of attacking us we ourselves must take the initiative'.[41] On 8 March De Bono received another letter from the Duce in which he spoke of 'being obliged to take the initiative of the operations at the end of October or September ...'[42] De Bono commented in his book on the 'radical alteration of our programme' then taking place: 'From the plan of a manoeuvred defensive, followed by a counter-offensive, we were obliged to change over to the plan of an offensive action'.[43]

The obligation to take the initiative and attack was, self-evidently, not imposed by political or moral necessity, only by a military calculation of the best way to win a war. At the end of May Mussolini asked De Bono whether the Treaty of Friendship with Abyssinia should be denounced. De Bono, in consultation with Graziani (Governor of Somaliland) advised against this on the ground of possible delay to military preparations.[44] On 26 July, according to De Bono,[45] the Abyssinian Government ordered general mobilization by 17 September: 'The die was cast. It was impossible, save in deliberate bad faith, to accuse us of provocation'. By the end of August he advised the Duce that an attack on Adigrat could be mounted by mid-September.[46] It was, however, decided to stick to the original plan for an attack in October. On 28 September Mussolini asked De Bono to fix the actual day and he chose 5 October. He also asked if there should be a declaration of war.[47] Mussolini's reply, on the 29th, ran:

'No declaration of war. Before general mobilization which Negus has already announced at Geneva must absolutely hesitate no longer. I order you to begin advance early on 3rd. I say the 3rd October.'[48]

This last-minute bringing forward of an agreed date by 48 hours was the kind of interference by a remote civilian with a military man on the spot which is always most unwelcome to the latter. To the former only a small change of plan may seem involved, the latter finds himself involved in vast and complex logistical rearrangements. But all was re-arranged and the attack began at 2 a.m. on 3 October 1935.[49]

The banners of the advancing Italian Army (not that the soldiers knew) were the tattered remnants of torn-up treaties: the Treaty of 1906 with Britain and France, the Kellogg Pact, and, last but not least, the Covenant of the League of Nations.[50] The breach of the Anti-Gas Convention was still to come. Perhaps too much has been made of the fact that Italy was attacking a fellow-member of the League. The Covenant had its provisions for defending a non-member against the attack of a member (Article 17). It was the wanton quality of the aggression which constituted the moral outrage.

4

Italian Antecedents

The most important event in Italian history in the nineteenth century, and indeed the most glorious event in the whole of Italian history as such, was the very start of it, the Risorgimento, the re-birth of the country through its reunification in the middle of that century. There followed a long period of anti-climax. This is not surprising. 'Nations rightly struggling to be free' become obsessed with the struggle for national freedom to the exclusion of all other national problems and wrongly assume that they will all be quite quickly solved once self-government is obtained. The sense of anti-climax was specially great in the Italian case. This was largely because she was, by European standards, economically backward, appallingly so in the south. As industry developed, so did industrial unrest. (The sit-in strike may be claimed as an Italian invention.) Politically, Parliamentary government proved corrupt and ineffective. There were too many Parties, too many coalitions, too short-lived Ministries. (There were 29 between December 1869 and October 1922). It was a sign of political ill-health that so many of these Ministries had to resort to legislation by extra-Parliamentary decree. It is no accident that the most famous Italian political philosopher, Pareto, was an advocate of élitism.

Mussolini had his forerunners in 'Liberal' Italy, that is to say the Italy of 1870 to 1922. One was General Pelloux (Prime Minister, 1898–1900), a figure reminiscent of the French General Boulanger, but one who lost his nerve after, instead of before, gaining power. Another, and more important figure, was Francesco Crispi, the Prime Minister who talked of having wiped Abyssinia off the map and whose long public life was ended by the Italian defeat at Adowa.[1] Between 1919 and 1921 D'Annunzio was as likely a toppler of the régime as Mussolini. In

26

the end, in October 1922, the latter gave it a gentle push and it collapsed.

Liberal Italy, Government and people, tended to suffer from a national inferiority complex. The State which had obstructed Italian unification, Austria-Hungary, was defeated more by France in 1859 and Prussia in 1866 than by Italian arms. In the First World War Italy was heavily defeated by Austria-Hungary, at Caporetto in 1917, and had to be rescued by French and British Armies. She emerged from the war on the winning side, but with a feeling, strong but illegitimate, that she had been badly done by in the peace settlement.[2] It is possible to see the truly liberal Italy ending in 1915; the whole period, from 1915 to 1940, as one of progressive deterioration;[3] and the nation finding its soul again with the overthrow of Mussolini in 1943.

In the 'great game' of Great Power politics, Liberal Italy was the odd man out, a Great Power by courtesy title only and having to play a lone hand, diplomatically closer to Britain, though not very close, than to any other State.

Throughout the Liberal and Fascist periods there was little love lost between Italy and France. They fought on the same side in the First World War, but there was no real rapprochement. The drawing together in January 1935, as we shall see, scarcely lasted till that summer. A major turning-point was the French annexation of Tunisia in 1881. Italian sovereignty in Tunisia had been seen in Italy as ordained in heaven, so much so apparently that successive Italian Governments took no steps to bring it about on earth. The French move caused Italy, contrary to her own best interests, to ally herself with Germany and Austria-Hungary. One consolation was British friendship, which contributed to the creation of a modest Colonial Empire, not on the southern side of the Mediterranean but on the Red Sea.

Thus Italy, late in the race for national unity, was in consequence late also in the race for Colonies. In what proved to be almost the last lap of that race, when the European 'scramble for Africa' was at its most intense, Italy failed to wrest Abyssinia from Menelik, was beaten at Adowa, and then had to watch Britain add the Sudan to Egypt and France acquire Morocco as well as Tunisia. These were great humiliations. Libya, Eritrea and Somaliland were poor substitutes for Tunisia and Abyssinia proper. Moreover, the process of acquiring these poverty-stricken areas did little to build Italian military self-confidence. In 1887 a column of 500 Italians had been butchered by several thousand Abyssinians at Dogali. (The name of the square in face of the main railway station at Rome, Piazza dei Cinque-cento, recalls this 'Italian Thermopylae'.) Compensation for this defeat was indirectly obtained six years later at Agordat with the victory over the Dervishes already mentioned,[4] 'United Italy's first authentic military success'.[5] However, the road from Agordat led, three years later, to Adowa.

The battle of Adowa was not merely a military defeat for the Italian Army in Abyssinia, but a political defeat for Nationalist politicians and Parties in Italy.[6] The imperialist fever, however, recurred. In 1911 an entirely unjustified war of aggression against Turkey was fought and – not over-easily – won, for the express purpose of establishing Italian sovereignty over Libya. In 1915 there was again war against Turkey, *qua* ally of Germany in the First World War. The main consequence for Italy was an Arab revolt in Libya. Italian control was not fully restored until 1931.[7] Thereafter Mussolini was free to turn his attention, and much public money, towards East Africa. Adowa had still to be avenged. The desire to do so can be compared to the French desire for revenge for Sedan, but more nearly to the British desire for revenge for Gordon's death and the loss of Khartum. This was amply achieved by Kitchener in 1898, two years after Baratieri's defeat.

In the 1920's and 1930's Italy had, from her point of view and from the point of view of the standards of those times, legitimate grievances against Abyssinia. It was, for example, a 'legitimate grievance' that this independent African country was largely closed to European capitalism and completely closed to European settlement. It was too a bad neighbour, the lack of an effective central government breeding constant disorder in the border provinces. The more the two Italian Colonies were developed the more of a nuisance this became to Italy. Furthermore, according to the up-to-date standards of the League of Nations, especially those written into Articles 22 and 23 of the Covenant, it was wrong that in Abyssinia subject races should be cruelly treated and slavery tolerated. If it could be said that European Imperialism of the kind which had led to the British occupation of Egypt and the French occupation of Morocco (and both these countries

28

were still 'Colonies' in 1934) was now an anachronism, it could also be said that the continued existence into the twentieth century of such a State as the Abyssinia of 1934 was also an anachronism. It could moreover be argued that for countries such as Irak, Palestine and Syria, to be 'A' Mandates under the League of Nations, and for Abyssinia to be a member of the League was an affront to commonsense. There were even words in Article 22 of the Covenant, Sections 5 and 6, which could have been prayed in aid of an argument that Abyssinia should be a 'B' or 'C' mandate. The difficulty was that mandates had been awarded in respect of areas previously belonging to the losers in the First World War. Perhaps Italy in 1923 missed its chance in not opposing the Abyssinian claim to League membership and pressing a case for an Italian Mandate whatever the legal impediments.

All these points are related to the state of affairs in Abyssinia. There can be no doubt, however, that the primary motivation for Mussolini's adventure derived from the state of affairs in Italy. It lagged far behind Britain and France economically; it was an over-populated 'proletarian State'; there had been massive emigration, principally to the United States. Why should not Italians instead be settled in Italian possessions overseas and, incidentally, thereby contribute to the developing and civilizing of those areas?[8] The more temperate regions of Abyssinia were specially suitable for such settlement and development.

These social and economic considerations were, however, superficial. The basic motivations were psychological and, like most human mental activities, by no means wholly rational. There was the sense of grievance, already mentioned,[9] that Italy had not been properly rewarded for her contribution to the Allied victory in 1918. Her main gain was Trieste. True, over and above what she had been promised by the Treaty of London in 1915, the Tyrolean frontier was fixed, for Italian strategic convenience, at the Brenner Pass. (This flouted another people's nationalism in that 200,000 Germans were consigned to Italy, and without the protection of the Minorities Treaties to be administered by the League.) True too, in addition to Trieste itself, she was given most of the Istrian peninsula, with nearly all the strategic passes and 250,000 Slavs on the Italian side of their frontier. None the less it became a great grievance that she was not given Fiume (now Rijeka). D'Annunzio, a pre-Fascist Fascist, added to his reputation as a poet and amorist that of a man of action by seizing Fiume on 12 September 1919, i.e. two days after the signature of the Treaty of St. Germain allocating it to Yugoslavia. (It is significant that the first breach in the Versailles structure was an Italian one, just as it is significant that Italy was the first Great Power to flout, in 1923, the authority of the League.[10]) Only at the end of 1920 did the last major statesman of Liberal Italy, Giolitti, having made an agreement with Yugoslavia for the future of Fiume, find the will to topple D'Annunzio's régime. In 1924 Mussolini made a still better agreement with Yugoslavia and so obtained credit for doing better than either Giolitti or D'Annunzio. Fiume itself then became Italian, the suburb of Susak becoming Yugoslav. The Treaty of Paris of 1947 allotted the whole area to Yugoslavia.

In all these circumstances the Italian sense of national inferiority, deepened by its sense of grievance at the post-war settlement, fastened itself on alleged Colonial rather than European deprivations – all the more so because the vast Empires of Britain and France were further expanded at the end of the war, whilst the small and wretched Italian Colonial Empire was not. Moreover, from 1933 onwards, there was a chance that Hitler would regain the German Colonial Empire lost by William II. Was Italy once again to be left behind in the race, behind even Japan which between 1931 and 1933 had defied the League of Nations and 'got away with it' in Manchuria? Only in Abyssinia could a major Italian expansion be looked for. Hence there was a harking back to Crispi's policies and renewed cries for the revenge of Adowa.

Mussolini defined De Bono's task as that of settling, once and for all, 'the great account which had been left open since 1896'.[11] This was rhetoric. He also wrote that Adowa, Adigrat, and Makalle were 'names that from 1896 onwards were cherished in the unforgetful hearts of the Italians'.[12] So that was that. There had always been plenty of Italian anti-Imperialists. (They had included Mussolini himself. As a young Socialist leader, aged 28, he was sent to prison for five months for stirring up riots in his native Forlì against the Libyan War. The break in his lifeline came in October 1914, when, just a little later than the majority of European Socialists, he renounced the doctrine of working-class neutrality in the war and gave his support to it.) The doctrines of national aggrandizement, Colonial expansion, and revenge for Adowa were not in the minds of all Italians; they were the doctrines of the Italian Right.

This is not to say that the Abyssinian War, when it came, was particularly unpopular in Italy. British Fleet movements and sanctions together produced a patriotic reaction, not unaided by propaganda, but natural enough in itself.[13] To see oneself as a member of one nation resisting 50 stirred intense patriotic emotions. The women of Italy, in large numbers, gave up their wedding rings to help increase the nation's gold reserves. That great writer, Ignazio Silone, in his novel *Bread and Wine*, published in 1937, described peasant life in Central Italy at the precise moment of the outbreak of the war. The picture (painted by a dedicated anti-Fascist) is not that of a wave of opinion against it. The 1962 preface to this book speaks of 'the enthusiasm of many Italians for the conquest of the Empire, the passivity of most of the population . . .'. The only free voice in Italy in 1935 was that of the Pope (Pius XI) and on 28 August he said that 'a war which was only of conquest would evidently be an unjust war – something which is inexpressibly sad and horrible.'[14] However, the Italian Church was far from following this muted lead. There was no organized resistance to Fascism in 1935. Dino Grandi, who began his Fascist career as Ras of Bologna and played the leading part in the Fascist Grand Council in overthrowing Mussolini in 1943, had become something of an Anglophile by the 1930's, but as Ambassador in London since 1932 had more chance to influence Britain in a pro-Italian direction than Italy in a pro-British one: no doubt just what Mussolini intended in making the appointment.

The heart of the mystery (of the motivation for the 1935–6 war on the Italian side) is to be found somewhere in the heart of Italian Fascism (just as the heart of the mystery of British policy in the Abyssinian crisis is to be found somewhere in the heart of British Conservatism.)[15] The philosophy of Italian Fascism was virtually non-existent, its achievements meagre. Negatively it had much to its discredit: – the suppression of Parliament, of representative Local Government, of a free Press, of Trade Unions, of opposition of any kind (by the terrorist activities of the Italian equivalent of the Black and Tans), the 'reversal of working-class gains made in the pre-Fascist era';[16] the lowering of working-class standards of life. But on the positive side, domestically, what was there? 'Corporationism', presented as a new solution to the old problem of the ownership of industry, was a fraud.[17] The Lateran Agreements of 1929, later written into the present Italian Constitution, will probably last longer than any other of Mussolini's achievements. It is true that in making those agreements he achieved something which had eluded every previous Italian Government since 1870, but about this achievement there was nothing inherently Fascist. Domestically, Fascism was notable for the social and economic revolution it did not effect. Hence, the longer the régime lasted, the greater the emphasis on a 'spirited foreign policy', on asserting national, including imperialist, rights. Overall, Fascism became just a blown-up version of the Nationalism which had been a part of Liberal Italy at its worst; it failed to develop into anything fresh. It is somewhere in this inner logic of Fascism that the roots of the drive for an Abyssinian Empire are to be found.

So great and so inexorable was this drive that it took little account, fundamentally, of the European situation when the Abyssinian War was definitely decided on. With Germany under Hitler's control and plainly a threat to the Brenner frontier, to choose, at that time, to start a war, for no really worthwhile material gain, was, to say the least, risky. The threat and the risk were underlined, heavily, on 23 July 1934 when a Nazi conspiracy to subvert the independence of Austria came near to success. Dr. Dollfuss, the Austrian Chancellor, was on that day seized in his office and shot, and only several days later, and after heavy fighting, did the Austrian Government re-assert its authority. Mussolini on this occasion ostentatiously moved large forces to the frontier (thereby obtaining a diplomatic credit with Britain and France on which he was allowed to draw over-long). The preservation of Austrian independence was plainly an Italian interest; the threat to Austria had plainly been only temporarily removed. None the less, Mussolini did not seek to convert the drive against the remote peoples of Abyssinia into a drive for the protection of Italy herself. Perhaps he calculated that with a renascent Germany to the north of him this was his last chance of an independent assertion of Italian military might and the acquisition of an Italian Empire in Africa.

On the eve of his aggression against Abyssinia Mussolini said: 'I have reflected well; I have calculated all; I have weighed everything'.[18] His success showed that substantially he had indeed done so. For most of his career he was pushed around by events; only in the Abyssinian crisis did he control them. One may judge him in the long run to have miscalculated his interests; one cannot help admiring his calm and determination in his conduct of his Abyssinian policy between December 1934 and the victory of May 1936. Aided by an efficient intelligence he took the exact measure of the extent of Anglo-French opposition to it.

In the last resort Mussolini's personal motivation must be deemed the biggest single factor in the Italian precipitation of crisis and war. It was not that there was active opposition to him in Italy in 1933 and 1934;[19] it was rather that Fascism had, so to speak, run itself into the ground. Mussolini, therefore, did not *have* to resort to the Dictator's traditional device of diverting domestic discontent by resort to foreign adventure. He wanted personal glory; a new and startling move; a great and solid success, for all the world to see, achieved by Italian might.[20] He wanted war not so much for the fruits of victory as for its own sake.[21] (Yugoslavia might have been the enemy rather than Abyssinia.) He got his war and with it a bonus of a new lease of life, though short, for his régime.

Inevitably the writing of the history of a foreign country is always difficult. It is hard for an Englishman to understand an Italian, hard for an 'intellectual' to understand a Dictator. But it was hard for an Italian Dictator to understand the British people in 'one of their periodical fits of morality'. When Mussolini said that, before deciding on his Abyssinian War, he had weighed everything, he spoke in error. He had, despite mild warnings from the British Government,[22] ignored British public opinion. Neither he nor Laval[23] began to understand it. The British Government itself was far from ignoring it, up to a point deferred to it. Its sin of omission was of another kind.

5

British Approach

In Britain in December 1934, at the time of the Wal-Wal incident, there was what was called a National Government, but in effect a Conservative one. It had been formed in August 1931, as a coalition to surmount a foreign exchange crisis. Initially, therefore, and indeed until 1933, its attention was focused on home rather than foreign issues. The bulk of the Labour Party immediately went into opposition against this new Government and in September 1932 the Liberal Party parted company from it on the issue of the Ottawa agreements for Imperial Preference. Thus what had been genuinely intended as a National Government became a Conservative one enjoying the support of minority Labour and minority Liberal groups.

Between the formation of the National Government in 1931 and the departure of the Liberals in 1932, there was a General Election in October 1931. Conservative Members were returned for 473 seats; National Liberals for 35; National Labour Members for 13. Labour Members retained only 52 seats, Liberals 37. There were 5 'others'. This gave the Government a majority of 501 before the Liberal defection, 427 after it.

The Cabinet, in December 1934, had 15 Conservative, 3 National Labour, and 2 National Liberal members. The Prime Minister was Ramsay MacDonald; Stanley Baldwin was Lord President of the Council; Sir John Simon was Foreign Secretary. Outside the Cabinet, Anthony Eden, now Lord Avon, then only 37, was Lord Privy Seal. This was an honorific position, but his duties were the same as those he had been carrying out, since the Government's formation, as Parliamentary Under-Secretary at the Foreign Office. He was Chamberlain-trained, having been Sir Austen's P.P.S. from 1926 to 1929. Eden was told by Baldwin in 1931 that he saw him as 'a potential Foreign Secretary' in a

34

Conservative Government in about ten years' time.[1] He was destined, as a direct consequence of the Abyssinian crisis, to hold that great office only four years later.

MacDonald had been Leader of the Labour Party from 1911 to 1914 and again since 1922 when the Labour Party had become His Majesty's Opposition. In 1924 he became the first Labour Prime Minister as head, for a few months, of a minority Government. He combined this office with that of Foreign Secretary and he showed, then and later, a considerable flair for foreign affairs. In 1929 he again became Prime Minister of a minority Government (his Party this time, for the first time, the largest in the Commons). In 1931, when he agreed to head a Coalition Government, he carried, as already implied, only a small minority of his party with him. Nonetheless, Baldwin, the Conservative Leader, preferred to hold a nominally second place. As Lord President he had few specific duties and it suited him to pick and choose his subjects and put on other shoulders the inescapable Prime Ministerial burdens. In any event, his position as Leader of a Party which, with its 473 seats, had, by itself, so huge a majority in the Commons, ensured that he was the real holder of supreme political power. From the Conservative point of view, especially electorally, MacDonald, after October 1931, was dispensable. Baldwin, however, partly out of appreciation of MacDonald's part in the 1931 'crisis' (less of a crisis in retrospect than it had seemed at the time), partly out of personal loyalty to him, partly perhaps because of a streak of selective indolence, was more than content to remain Lord President. By December 1934, however, it was clear that he could not so remain much longer. MacDonald's physical powers, in particular his eyesight, were failing. A new election had, by law, to be held before October 1936. It seemed no advantage to the Government to fight it led by an ailing MacDonald who no longer commanded a significant following in Parliament or in the country. On 17 June 1935 Baldwin and MacDonald swapped places. Baldwin was then vigorous in comparison with MacDonald, but he was 68.

Other changes in the Cabinet were made in June 1935. The most important one for our present purpose was that Sir John Simon (Leader of the National Liberals) exchanged the Foreign for the Home Office. He had been Foreign Secretary since November 1931. He had been Home Secretary before, but had resigned in 1916 because opposed in principle to military conscription. (Few politicians have sacrificed office to conscience twice.) Thereafter he was out of office for 15 years. During those years he and his wife were leaders of the British anti-slavery movement and his views on Abyssinia may have been coloured by its tolerance of slavery. Simon's historical reputation as Foreign Secretary is unenviable. In the early stages of the Abyssinian crisis his policy can be correctly described as Micawberish.

As Foreign Secretary Simon was succeeded by Sir Samuel Hoare. From August 1931 until June 1935 he had been Secretary of State for India. The future of India was one of the great issues in British politics at that time. As the responsible Minister, Hoare laboured mightily at Indian problems, playing the principal part, on the British side, at two out of the three sessions, between 1930 and 1933, of the Round Table Conference (the second was attended by Gandhi); at the prolonged sessions of the Joint Select Committee of the two Houses of Parliament which, from April 1933, until November 1934, considered the resulting White Paper (he, personally, over a period of 19 days answered more than 10,000 questions from its 32 members[2]); and, finally, during the carrying through Parliament, against the fierce opposition of Churchill and his followers, of the Government of India Bill which resulted from all this. It reached the Statute Book in July 1935, as an Act containing 473 Clauses and 16 Schedules.

It is not surprising that these labours had left Sir Samuel, by his own admission, 'physically weak and mentally tired'.[3] For four years he had immersed himself in Indian problems. For weeks on end he could not find the time even to attend Cabinets. Asked by Baldwin whether he would prefer the Vice-royalty of India or the Foreign Office, he instantly and understandably plumped for the former. A day later, however, he agreed to take the latter.[4]

The new Foreign Secretary was far from *au fait* with the current problems of foreign affairs. He had not even the advantage of a fresh mind in seeking to master them. He needed a holiday rather than a new and infinitely exacting job. The kindest, but not necessarily the truest thing, that could be said about his record in the new job, from his appointment in June until his resignation in December, is that he never caught up with its problems.[5] Certainly throughout these few months he continued to be a sick man. Experience shows that a sick statesman can get through surprising quantities of work but can simultaneously make surprising errors of judgment.

The only other man considered for the Foreign Office in June 1935 was Eden. He was now well versed in foreign affairs and certainly their mastery, contrary to popular supposition, requires a long apprenticeship. It was, however, perhaps more important from the Government's point of view that he was, for a politician, young; he could not be easily identified with an 'old gang'; his was a fresh and handsome face. Moreover, his 'image', whether justified by his record or not, was that of a League of Nations man.[6] That institution was known to be strongly supported by large numbers of voters; the largeness of their number was in process of being decisively demonstrated by the 'Peace Ballot'.[7]

Eden was now made Minister for League of Nations Affairs and given a seat in the Cabinet. The title was new, but the position was not. Lord Robert Cecil, as Lord Privy Seal, had held the same position in Baldwin's first Ministry, and held it again, as Chancellor of the Duchy of Lancaster, and again with a seat in the Cabinet, in Baldwin's second Ministry, until he resigned in 1927. The arrangement was not a success, and so it is in a way surprising that Baldwin repeated it.

Eden himself argued with Baldwin and Hoare against the dangerous disadvantages of having in the Cabinet two Ministers with responsibilities for foreign affairs.[8] Perhaps he should have argued more strenuously than he did, but Cabinet Office at 38 must have been a dazzling prospect and it would have been difficult for a loyal Party man to have brought pressure to bear for a different arrangement. Hoare hoped that Baldwin would define the division of duties between himself and Eden. In fact, Hoare only received a pencilled note, passed to him at a Cabinet meeting, asking him to settle the details 'direct with the young man'.[9] The di-archy at the Foreign Office was presented as a temporary expedient; even as such it was criticised by Sir Austen Chamberlain and Churchill. The latter quoted in the House of Commons a saying of Lloyd George's, relating to unity of command in war: 'It is not a question of one General being better than another, but of one General being better than two'.[10] Neville Chamberlain on the other hand thought that the Hoare-Eden combination would be a powerful one.[11] Amery did not, taking the earliest possible opportunity to tell Hoare that his hopes of success depended entirely on 'pulling Anthony back by his coat tails'.[12]

Thus was formed the team which had to face the most difficult moments of the Abyssinian crisis: Baldwin, Hoare, and Eden. Of these three the first was the most prominent and powerful. For the decisions of any Government the Prime Minister always carries the final responsibility.[13] Moreover, custom rightly allots him a special responsibility in relation to foreign affairs. So at the time of the Abyssinian crisis Baldwin was the leading man of the leading European and League Power. His handling of that crisis turned out to be his biggest failure.[14] He became responsible for the flight of the Negus and the loss of Abyssinia to Mussolini in the same sense as Gladstone had been responsible for the death of Gordon and the loss of the Sudan to the Mahdi. In neither case was the personal responsibility direct, in both the political situation was complicated. But complexity is the nature of political situations. History has inexorably judged that these two men, great as were their virtues, bear the blame for these two disasters.

Both the career and personality of Stanley Baldwin were remarkable. His father was a Stourport iron-master and a back-bench Tory M.P. On this side Baldwin's ancestry was, so far as we know, wholly Shropshire English.[15] But his mother was a MacDonald and Lloyd George recognized in his great enemy a fellow-Celt. One MacDonald aunt married Burne-Jones, another Edward Poynter, later P.R.A., a third John Lockwood Kipling, Rudyard's father. These connections, as well as his own inclinations, gave Baldwin wider cultural and literary interests than those of most politicians. (He gave Presidential addresses to both the Classical and English Associations.) His Kipling first cousin said, 'The real pen in our family is Stan's'.[16] So very accomplished a writer as A. L. Rowse must have his opinion respected in saying: 'It must not be overlooked that Baldwin's essential impulses were literary; what he liked was words, and playing on them, like the master he was ...'[17] Hence the greatness, on occasion, of his mastery of the oratorical art he affected to despise. He spoke best in the House of Commons, whose moods he was an adept in catching; he was also one of the best broadcasters of the early broadcasting age.

Baldwin's mind throve on solitude rather than society. His favourite recreation was a long country walk, either, as with all passionate walkers, solitary or with the ideal walking companion. His intellect was ruminant and he knew that many a man had more brains: Churchill, for example, with, in Baldwin's own phrase, 'his hundred horse-power mind'. He has often been accused of laziness, but it seems difficult to make that charge stick. His exterior concealed an inner nervous tension and such men are often dubbed lazy by more plodding personalities who have not the same capacity for rising to a crisis. A few days after Munich he confided, wistfully, to a friend: 'I love a crisis'.[18] How many more ordinarily industrious mortals could say that?

Baldwin was not the first man to make little use of considerable intellectual gifts at school or university, Harrow and Cambridge in his case. At 21 he joined the family firm (its name survived until recently in that of a great iron and steel combine, Richard Thomas & Baldwin). Long slow years in industry followed; he had no technical qualifications but made a good fist of the mysterious but all-important work of general management. He was a humane employer. His wife 'brought him on'. Both were deeply religious. His father died in 1906 and Baldwin succeeded to many of his business responsibilities (though he did not become Chairman of Baldwin's) and to his seat in the House of Commons.

Long slow years followed on the back benches. Almost by chance, in December 1916, he became Parliamentary Private Secretary to Bonar Law, Chancellor of the Exchequer, and shortly afterwards Financial Secretary to the Treasury. In March 1921, he became a member of the Coalition Cabinet as President of the Board of Trade. The turning-point of his career came seven months later. He took a risk which might have ended it; a new and obscure Minister, he made a speech at the meeting of the Conservative Party at the Carlton Club on 19 October 1922 which, more than anybody else's, brought down the Coalition. Lloyd George was replaced as Prime Minister by Bonar Law. The leading Conservatives remained Coalitionists and would not serve under him, so Baldwin stepped into the second place, Chancellor of the Exchequer. In the spring of 1923 the new Prime Minister fell ill; on 17 May Sir Thomas Horder diagnosed incurable cancer of the throat. On 19 May Law resigned, declining, because he was ill, to advise the King about the succession. The choice was between Curzon, who had been in the front political ranks since the turn of the century and had held many high offices, and Baldwin who, even a few months previously, had hardly been heard of. The King made appropriate enquiries of appropriate people and, wisely, decided on the Chancellor. On 22 May 1923 Baldwin became Prime Minister for the first time. It was largely luck which gave him the first place, but it was his own qualities which ensured his retention of power in his Party, and in the country, for 14 years.

In 1935 when Baldwin became, for the third time, Prime Minister, his political attitudes had, understandably, been fixed many years previously. During his career as iron-master he had formed a mental picture of an England, mainly agricultural, with industry on a small scale administered in a fatherly fashion. The spirit of England thus pictured he sought to preserve in face of the great material changes taking place all round him. Hence he abominated class war and industrial strife, sought for points in common with Socialists (his eldest son became a Labour M.P.), strove to constitutionalize the Labour Party. He could rise above Party, though he sometimes sank with it. Churchill was right to call him a 'most formidable politician'[19] and Cripps in telling him, to his face, that he resembled Franklin Roosevelt, 'a very great gentleman and as clever as a cart-load of monkeys'.[20]

Forty-seven in 1914, Baldwin was deeply conscious of his good fortune in personal survival in contrast with the mass slaughter of younger men. Hence by 1918 he thought more in terms of patriotic duty than ever before whilst his feelings had become intensely pacifist. It is an absurd illusion, still widely held, that in inter-war England hatred of war was confined to the Left; both Baldwin and Chamberlain had a genuine, perhaps excessive, horror of it and this horror was a substantial, and not discreditable, part of the motivation of 'appeasement'.

Member of the post-war Coalition, Baldwin saw Lloyd George running his own foreign policy and did not like what he saw. (Did he, between 1937 and 1939, think that those bad old days had come again?) Year after year he spent his summer holidays at Aix-les-Bains, where his wife took the cure and he went for his long meditative walks. Geneva was only 30 miles away, but he never put in an appearance there. His principal essay in personal diplomacy was a visit to Poincaré in September 1923; his object was to make it clear that he was not Lloyd George and no doubt he achieved it. Baldwin, like his Sovereign, did not greatly care for foreigners. He understood the House of Commons; he thought that he understood the English people – and usually he did; he knew that his antennae did not reach across the Channel. (And yet, about India, he was right and Churchill wrong.) A tinge of anti-Americanism may have been due to his unhappy experiences as Chancellor of the Exchequer over the negotiations for the settlement of the British war debt to the U.S.A.[21] When Hitler and Mussolini came on the scene he realized that they had added a new dimension to the problems of foreign policy. He went out of his way to try to take their measure, but could only reach the conclusion that Europe was dominated by a couple of madmen, by definition neither open to reason nor to be counted on to pursue self-interest rationally. Meeting a devil on the way was not an encounter an elderly English gentleman was equipped for. Baldwin's best days, so far as foreign affairs were concerned, were those of his most successful Ministry, that of 1925–9. That was the Briand-Chamberlain-Stresemann era in European politics, the hey-day of the League as a *forum*, the hey-day also of the Locarno Treaties.

As early as the end of 1933, however, when, as we have seen, Mussolini was actively preparing his war, Baldwin had decided, in his own mind, on the need for re-armament.[22] An attitude acquired, however, ten years previously now did him a disservice. In December 1923, a Prime Minister of only six months' standing, he obtained a Dissolution in order to obtain a mandate for Protection, of the case for which he had become intellectually convinced.[23] The Election was lost; Protectionism was delayed until 1932; and Baldwin became excessively anxious about the amount of time needed to prepare the British people for any major change of policy.[24] In general his chief political talent was that of waiting on events and making them work for him, but this was easier and less hazardous in domestic than in foreign affairs.

Baldwin's 1935 Cabinet as a whole has been described as 'full of mild men' who did well, except in Europe.[25] But this was no time for mild men. One of them himself subsequently wrote: 'Men who have to play a weak hand against time need, at the very least, a reasonably offensive spirit and sound nerves....'[26] Baldwin and his Cabinet colleagues conspicuously lacked these two qualities. It is hard to believe that so temperamentally resolute a man as Churchill, not left to be the mere spectator of the events we shall have to describe, would not have stiffened their backs. In fact, these were the men content to drift under Baldwin's leadership and row briskly, in the wrong direction, under Chamberlain's.[27]

Lord Templewood recalls of the Foreign Office as he found it in June 1935: 'Everyone seemed to be over-excited. There appeared to be no generally accepted body of opinion on the main issues. Diametrically opposite views were pressed upon me, and sometimes with the intolerance of an *odium theologicum*'.[28] This is not surprising. The Foreign Office officials of that time could see clearly enough how important the main issues were and rightly cared, passionately, that they should be rightly faced. But the navigation of diplomatic seas is not a science at the best of times and the old land-marks had gone. As we have seen,[29] pride of place was now given to the commitment to the Covenant. Sir Robert Vansittart wrote in a letter of 7 November 1935 to Lord Wigram (undoubtedly intended for the King's eyes) of 'the principles of the League which form the backbone of the policy of this country'.[30]

One suspects this to have been as much of a shibboleth from the pen of the permanent official as on the tongue of the vote-conscious politician. Baldwin never went to see the League at work, Vansittart only once. He accompanied Sir John Simon on the occasion of the Council meeting immediately following the Stresa conference.[31] He remarked on 'the unreality of the Geneva atmosphere', but was impressed by Litvinov's awareness of the Nazi menace.[32] In his autobiography he remarked:

'Anthony and Cranborne were not only correct but straight-forward in pinning faith on the League. That was our rightful policy, but I could never see the League's components tackling an aggressor of weight. So I laboured under a dualism which might look like duplicity. Suspicion can be both unfair and justifiable. My real trouble was that we should all have to choose between Austria and Abyssinia, if Mussolini stuck to his mania for fame and sand'.[33]

The British Government bears the prime responsibility for British policy in the Abyssinian crisis, but the Opposition bears a not unimportant share. When in 1931 the Labour Party 'hived off' MacDonald's National Labour group, Arthur Henderson, who had been his Foreign Secretary, briefly became Leader of the Labour Party and Leader of the Opposition. He lost his seat in Parliament at the ensuing Election and was succeeded as Acting Leader by George Lansbury, who was a Pacifist. (Henderson came back to Parliament at a by-election in April 1932, but, partly through long absence abroad after February as President of the Disarmament Conference and partly through physical failure, lost influence with the Party and resigned the nominal leadership in October 1932. He died on 20 October 1935, shortly after the Italian invasion of Abyssinia.) The Deputy Leader was C. R. Attlee, an ex-Major of the 1914–19 war; an ex-Pacifist of the 20's; and now a believer in collective security, though not in re-armament or military sanctions.[34] The Second Lieutenant, so to speak, in the Parliamentary Labour Party in the 1931 Parliament was Sir Stafford Cripps, whose views on most political questions were highly volatile. True, he was new to politics, having only come into Parliament at a by-election in January 1931. In the new Parliament he spoke brilliantly in defence of the collective system and was mocked at by Tory Members for so doing. Thereafter he moved towards the view that as capitalism was, through the clash of conflicting imperialisms, the cause of war, only working-class action could be trusted to prevent it. On this ideological basis there was no particular merit in supporting a League of Nations which was a League of capitalist States. This remained his stance even after the U.S.S.R. had become a member and even after the start of the Italo-Abyssinian War.

Of these three men only Lansbury had been a member of the Labour Cabinet; Attlee and Cripps had both been Junior Ministers as Postmaster-General and Solicitor-General respectively. Except for Lansbury all the Cabinet Ministers who had stayed with the Party were defeated at the Election of October 1931. Among the seats which had slipped away from Labour in that colossal landslide was that of Hugh Dalton, Eden's predecessor as Parliamentary Under-Secretary for Foreign Affairs (under Henderson) and throughout the years from 1931 to 1939 consistently the most firm proponent on the Labour side of sane and sensible views about foreign policy and defence.[35] Dalton only returned to Parliament in the Election of November 1935.

It will be seen that from August 1931 onwards the leaders of the Labour Party in Parliament had deeply divided views on the fundamental issues of foreign policy. Furthermore, between the Elections of 1931 and 1935 the Parliamentary Labour Party was both qualitatively and quantitatively weak. This situation was not in the national interest. It was to some extent remedied in the 1935 Parliament. The fact, however, remains that, throughout the Abyssinian crisis, the Government was not 'kept up to the mark' in the handling of it by an effective Opposition.

At the first Party Conference held after the electoral defeat of 1931, at Leicester in October 1932, the Party concentrated on domestic policy and paid virtually no attention to foreign affairs, even though the Conference was meeting a few days after the publication of the Lytton Report on the Manchurian crisis. A year later, at Hastings, perhaps through over-reacting to the League's failure in the Far East, the Party Conference passed a foreign policy resolution of remarkable silliness. (A kind of political fever chart would show such a peak of muddle-headed Pacifism being recorded once before, at Margate in 1926,[36] and not recorded again until the Scarborough Conference of 1960.) The Hastings resolution pledged the Party 'to take no part in war and to resist it with the whole force of the Labour Movement and to seek consultation forthwith with the Trade Union and Co-operative Movements with a view to deciding and announcing to the country what steps, including a general strike, are to be taken to organize the opposition of the organized working-class movement in the event of war or threat of war . . .'.

This was Left-Wing 'intellectualism' run mad. In the first place, Sir Charles Trevelyan, who moved the resolution, and most of those who voted for it, knew perfectly well that the 'organized working-class movement', to which they so blithely were leaving the job of preventing war, had no intention whatsoever of organizing a General Strike against it. (The Trade Unions had no belief in a policy of 'mass resistance' to war and, in any case, had had enough of general striking in 1926 to last them several lifetimes. Nor would they have been prepared to *do* anything about that which intellectuals were only prepared to *talk*.) In the second, the logic of the resolution was muddled to a degree. It made sense only on the basis that the British Government was preparing an aggressive war (against Russia?) or to take part in an 'imperialist war' in which no issues of significance to common people would be involved and to which therefore neutrality was to be preferred. It made no sense at all in relation to the possible need for self-defence against an aggressor (Japan or Germany?) or possible participation in military sanctions to enforce the Covenant or some combination of sanctions and self-defence. In the world of 1933 Labour intellectuals were fighting war with the weapons which had broken in the hands of international Socialism in 1914, but had had, it is true, a limited success in Britain in 1920. It is almost certain that at that time the threat of a General Strike did prevent British aid to Poland in her war against Russia.[37]

A week after the Hastings Conference in October 1933 Hitler announced Germany's withdrawal from the League and from the Disarmament Conference. In 1934, at Southport, the 1933 policy was, in effect, repudiated.[38]

By October 1935, the situation had changed again. This time it was Mussolini who had been the educator of the British Labour Party. Since February he had been openly preparing for war against Abyssinia. When on 1 October Dalton asked the delegates in the Brighton Dome to vote for sanctions, including military sanctions, against Italy they knew well enough that war was imminent. The debate was long, on a high level, and highly dramatic. Cripps reiterated his view that the League was 'the tool of the satiated imperialist powers'; Lansbury preached the Christian Pacifist gospel. Bevin, who followed him, in no way deferred to the mood of super-charged emotion and sentiment engendered by this speech. On the contrary, he made a brutal attack on the aged and revered leader: 'It is placing the Executive and the Movement in an absolutely wrong position to be hawking your conscience round from body to body asking to be told what to do with it . . .'. Bevin spoke more than anything else as what might be called 'an angry Trade Unionist'; the General Secretary of the Transport and General Workers Union could not stomach what seemed to him the sheer disloyalty of Cripps and Lansbury. There was only a small minority against Dalton's motion. Lansbury resigned the leadership on 8 October; Attlee was elected in his place. Twenty-four hours before De Bono crossed the frontier the Labour Party stood fully committed to a full League policy.

At the time of the August 1931 crisis the Trade Union leaders had shown great good sense. It is fitting to pause here to pay tribute to the good sense they showed about the Abyssinian crisis. Bevin's decisive role at the Hastings Conference of the Labour Party has already been described. At Margate on 3 and 4 September 1935 the National Executive Committee of the Labour Party and the General Council of the T.U.C., at the request of the latter body, spent two days hammering out a declaration of policy on the issues involved. The key paragraph arrived at 'called upon the British Government, in cooperation with the other members of the League, to use all the necessary measures provided in the Covenant to prevent Italy's unjust and rapacious attack upon a fellow member of the League'.

This declaration was accepted at the ensuing meeting of the Trades Union Congress (which traditionally precedes the Labour Party's Conference) by 2,962,000 votes to 177,000. Lord Citrine (then Walter Citrine, General Secretary of the T.U.C.) was interrupted at the start of his plea for the declaration by a cry of 'It means war'. He answered:

> 'It may mean war, but that is the thing we have to face. We have to face that there is no real alternative now left to us but the applying of sanctions involving the possibility of war. But I say this, if we fail now ... war is absolutely certain.'[39]

Alas, the armaments policy of the Labour Party did not correspond with its foreign policy (as of October 1935), although it was on such a correspondence that, by tortuous logic, it was based. The armaments policy is exemplified in a resolution agreed by an international emergency conference of Socialist and Trade Union leaders held in London on 19–20 March 1936 (the draft was mostly Citrine's and Dalton's):

> 'Peace is indivisible. All must rally unhesitatingly to the support of any State attacked by an aggressor. Any would-be aggressor must be confronted by an overwhelming superiority of force. To this all nations must make an effective contribution, according to an agreed plan. National armaments should now be regulated with this end in view. The only hope of securing a substantial reduction in this oppressive burden lies in perfecting the system of collective security.'[40]

But how to agree such a plan against the background of a constantly shifting international scene? No practical attempt to do so was ever made or perhaps could ever have been made, even if computers (as yet uninvented) had been available to help calculate the almost infinitely complicated logistics. The policy smacked of a vague notion of getting both national defence and international security on the cheap. If the arms of all nations were to be used against one wicked one, no one righteous nation needed more arms than it already had – and hopefully fewer – since it could also rely, both for its own defence and the coercion of an aggressor, on the arms of others. But which nation was likely to be the wicked one 'to be confronted by an overwhelming superiority of force'; what was to happen if the one became two or more; what was to happen as and when wicked and righteous from time to time, they reversed their rôles? The whole policy was intellectually on the cheap.[41]

Eden, a little earlier, was vague but more intelligent and intelligible when he said:

'When I view the future of foreign policy I can see several different lines along which events may develop, but whichever course events may take one element which appears as essential for every course is that Great Britain must be strong.'[42]

The first Service Estimates of the National Government (although the sums involved were less than those submitted by the preceding Labour Government) were severely criticized by Attlee on 8 March 1932; a year later (with Hitler in power in Germany) criticisms were repeated from the Front Opposition Bench; in 1934, ditto. In July 1934 the first proposals for re-armament (for the expansion of the RAF by 820 aircraft by 1939) led to a Labour vote of censure, supported by Liberals. The modest proposals for re-armament, explicitly because of the German danger, set out in the White Paper of 4 March 1935, led to another vote of censure, again supported by the Liberals. In February 1936, a Naval Supplementary Estimate, almost all of it consequential upon sanctions against Italy, was voted against. So were the regular estimates in that and in the previous year. Only in 1937 did the Labour Party abstain instead of oppose. In the Spring of 1939 an increased Army Estimate, to provide for a British Expeditionary Force, was opposed. So too was conscription.

This summary statement of some basic facts is inserted here partly to indicate an Opposition attitude which changed little from 1932 to 1939, but mainly because of the profound effect the record of that attitude up to 1935 had on the mind of the man who then became Prime Minister. What grounds had he for believing that the attitude of men so irresponsible in opposition would change in responsible office?[43]

Public opinion about political questions is not confined to those with Party views or expressed only through Party organizations. Undoubtedly the mood of the great majority of the British people, of all Parties and of none, throughout the inter-war period, was, in varying degrees, profoundly pacificist. There was no reason why the mother-people of a huge Empire should contemplate aggression against anyone. Even defensive fighting on the North-West frontier of India upset many consciences. Long-held and well-tried doctrines about the defence of this island had become unpopular. What is now called deterrence, then called the Balance of Power, became the belief of a minority only. The Locarno Treaties of 1925, the basis of stability in Western Europe, had been received with immense rejoicing in Britain. A few years later their importance had been forgotten by public opinion. There was no voluntary society whose business it was to see that they were remembered. Many, if not most of those who took an interest in public affairs, saw something they called 'power politics' as the root of all international friction, as if politics had ever been separated from the exercise of power, whether domestically or internationally, or as if force could ever be replaced by a universal change of heart or universal good will. In short, there were plenty of people around who fancied that they were talking about politics but in fact were preaching the millenium. Indeed, to a great extent they spoke as if, unexpectedly early one must say, it had already arrived.

If millenarian Pacifists were a minority of the British people at this time, 'militarists' were as small or an even smaller group. There were few sharers of Mussolini's doctrine of war alone bringing up 'to its highest tension all human energy' and so on. (Similar nonsense had been talked by an Italian of the previous generation, Marinetti, the Futurist.) The trench warfare of 1914–18 had destroyed the romance of war for the inter-war British generation. There was, however, a large, but largely inarticulate, group, politically Conservative, which did not want war, but thought it could no more be abolished than revolution. Such people set little store by the idea of the League of Nations as a preventer of war or by the idea of international disarmament. They were fond of saying that human nature did not change and on that account were dubbed enemies of progress. When they quoted Luke XI, 21, it was thought to be a sufficient answer to quote Verse 22. The Latin tag *Si vis pacem, bellum para* (If you want peace, prepare for war), in fact dating back to the 4th century A.D., was thought a plainly preposterous paradox, enunciated in an enlightened age only by 'Blimps'. In the 'twenties, and late into the 'thirties, competition in armaments was widely thought to be of itself a cause of war, a view becoming all the more influential after endorsement by Lord Grey.[44] The French emphasis on security fell on deaf British ears. Long after Hitler had started the unilateral rearmament of Germany, unilateral disarmament had its advocates in Britain.

In 1935 the pacificist mood of the British people was expressed, in its varying shades, by a variety of voluntary societies, religious and political, old and new. (The National Peace Council sought to co-ordinate the work of pacificist and pacifist bodies other than those whose primary objects were Party or religious.) The Society of Friends (the Quakers) had a pacifist tradition dating back to the first half of the seventeenth century. The Peace Society, addressed by the Prime Minister at the Guildhall on the eve of the 1935 Election, was founded in 1816; the Union of Democratic Control in 1914. (The great days of both were over.) The No More War Movement stemmed from the No Conscription Fellowship of 1916. (Its international counterpart was the War Resisters International.) In 1937 it was to amalgamate with the Peace Pledge Union, which originated in a letter sent to the Press by Canon H. R. L. Sheppard on 16 October 1934.[45] Very different was the New Commonwealth Society, founded by Lord Davies in 1932, to propagate the idea of an International Police Force and an International Equity Tribunal. Churchill became President of its British Section in August 1936.

By far the most influential and respectable of the pacificist bodies was the League of Nations Union. It enjoyed the support of all three Parties, though rather more came from the Liberals and Socialists than the Conservatives. Fortunately for the Union, however, this imbalance was to an important extent redressed by the fact of its President, from 1923 onwards, being Lord Robert (later Viscount) Cecil, son of the 3rd Marquess of Salisbury (a Conservative Prime Minister) and himself a Conservative Parliamentarian of long standing who had risen to Cabinet rank. For good or ill, the L.N.U. was to a great extent moulded in his image.[46] Its history, and that of the country, would have been very different if, say, Austen Chamberlain had been President.[47] Almost as influential in the counsels of the L.N.U. as its President was Gilbert Murray (Regius Professor of Greek at Oxford), a Liberal in politics, who was the Chairman of its Executive Committee from 1923 to 1938.

The Union attracted a substantial measure of 'middle of the road' support. It appealed to those whose horror of war stopped short of Conscientious Objection and belief in Unilateral Disarmament; it seemed to offer a practical programme for the prevention of war by the action of the League of Nations; it did not exclude those who foresaw that in the last resort the League's Covenant could only be upheld by force.[48] It is impossible to understand the British attitude to the Abyssinian crisis without understanding how widespread and, still more, how passionate was popular belief in the League in Britain at that time. Lord Cecil was the leader of a crusade.[49]

The most important event in the Union's history was its promotion of 'The National Declaration on the League of Nations and Armaments', which came to be inaccurately known as the Peace Ballot. (Beaverbrook's appellation, Blood Ballot, did not stick.) This event took place in the summer of 1935, a few months before, that is to say, the start of the Italo-Abyssinian War (on 3 October) and the British General Election (on 13 November). This coincidence was by accident, not design, but British public opinion, as expressed in the Ballot, had a profound effect on the British Government's policy in the Abyssinian crisis. It must be remembered too in this connection that the Ballot followed a wave of pacifist votes by British university students in the Spring of 1933[50] and by a succeeding wave of pacifist votes in by-elections, notably the East Fulham by-election of October, 1933[51] There were no public opinion polls in Britain until October 1938.[52]

The original source of the Ballot seems to have been the mind of a Mr. C. J. A. Boorman, Editor of the *Ilford Recorder* and a leading member of the local Branch of the League of Nations Union.[53] In January 1934, with the help of 500 voluntary workers, he got some 25,000 answers to a questionnaire containing 5 questions. Three of these were virtually the same as those later asked in the Peace Ballot: Should Britain remain a member of the League? Should the Disarmament Conference continue? Should the private manufacture of armaments be prohibited? To these three questions there was an overwhelming 'Yes'. Mr Boorman's Question 3, however, involved more than the recitation of accepted ritual: 'Do you agree with that part of the Locarno Treaty which binds Great Britain to go to the help of France or Germany if the one is attacked by the other?' The answers to this question still startle: only 5,898 votes said 'Yes', 18,498 'No'.[54]

Lord Cecil was asked to declare the results and did so at the Ilford Town Hall on 2 February, 1934. Thus perhaps did Mr. Boorman's brain-child pass into Lord Cecil's fertile mind. On 1 March he put to the Executive Committee of the League of Nations Union the proposal that a similar questionnaire should be organized on a national scale. It was decided that this task should not fall upon the L.N.U. alone. On 27 March a delegate conference from many pacifist societies set up a National Declaration Committee under Lord Cecil's chairmanship. (This Committee received the official support of the Labour and Liberal Parties, but not of the Conservatives.) With the help, this time, of 500,000 voluntary workers, it got its five questions answered by more than 11,000,000 citizens, rather more than half of the votes cast in the General Election of November 1935.[55] The first answers were known in November 1934, and as later answers became known it also became evident that the voting was remarkably self-consistent. (It followed that the trend of opinion thus gradually revealed was easy for politicians to interpret.) The final results were declared by Lord Cecil at the Albert Hall on 27 June.[56]

The value of any referendum substantially depends on the precise form of the question(s) put. The form of those asked in 1935 has been much criticized. They, and the voting on them, can be set out in tabular form, as on the following page.

All five questions in this pot-pourri can be, and were, criticized for avoiding the real problems; e.g. how could the defects of the League (mentioned in only one out of five questions) be

	Yes	*No*	*Doubtful*	*Abstentions*
1. 'Should Great Britain remain a member of the League of Nations?'	11,090,387	355,888	10,470	102,425
2. 'Are you in favour of an all-round reduction in armaments by international agreement?	10,470,489	862,775	12,062	213,839
3. 'Are you in favour of an all-round abolition of national military and naval aircraft by international agreement?'	9,533,358	1,689,786	16,976	318,845
4. 'Should the manufacture and sale of armaments for private profit be prohibited by international agreement?'	10,417,329	775,415	15,076	351,345
5. 'Do you consider that, if a nation insists on attacking another, the other nations should combine to compel it to stop by				
(a) economic and non-military measures?	10,027,608	635,074	27,255	855,107
(b) if necessary, military measures?'	6,784,368	2,351,981	40,893	2,364,441

remedied; what was to happen if the desiderated international agreements could not, as already seemed extremely likely, be obtained; and what was to happen if the other nations did not combine to stop an aggressor. Question 4 can be criticized as raising a side-issue. Question 3 was, next to Question 5, the 'most controversial throughout the Ballot'[57] because there was no mention in the question itself, as opposed to the literature circularized by the National Declaration Committee, of the control of civil aviation (the airliners of 1934 were easily convertible into bombers). Question 5 was the only one with 'teeth'. It asked two questions the answering of which really mattered, at home and abroad, as evidence of the state of British public opinion. The future of the League and the obtaining of international agreements (about anything) did not depend on British opinion alone; British participation in sanctions did.

To advance these criticisms, however, is, and was, to be unfair to the Ballot's promoters. The League's failure in the Manchurian crisis had generated a mood of despondency about the League's future among its British supporters. The purpose of Lord Cecil and his colleagues was to put fresh heart into those worthy people and fresh life, therefore, into the Union and kindred organizations. This was a legitimate purpose and entitled the Ballot's promoters to ask the kind of questions likely to produce that result rather than stimulate intensive intellectual exercise about the fundamentals of foreign policy. In Dame Adelaide Livingstone's words,

'Early in 1934, it looked as if the cause of international co-operation was dying. The Disarmament Conference had reached a deadlock, and the possiblility of war in Europe was being seriously discussed. The campaign for isolation was being vigorously pressed in certain quarters. A demonstration of British loyalty to the League and the collective peace system was urgently needed.'[58]

What did the voting in the National Declaration really show? In the first place, that there was little popular support for the Imperialist-isolationist views pushed by Lords Beaverbrook and Rothermere in the newspapers which they owned[59] or the less root-and-branch but still severe criticisms of the League put by such Conservatives as Mr. Amery, who was an Imperialist but not an isolationist. In the second place that, quite the contrary, there was much popular support for the League of Nations and for the control, reduction, and in certain instances abolition, by international agreement, of national armaments. In the third place, and surely most important, that there was much popular support for the use of economic and even military force against an aggressor nation. It was significant that whilst, roughly speaking, the same number of people voted 'Yes' to Question 5(a) as to the previous four questions, Question 5(b) produced far more 'No' votes and abstentions than any other. Since, as Baldwin so often pointed out, sanctions were likely to lead to war, to vote for economic sanctions and against military ones, showed muddled or incomplete thought. The fact remained, however, of 6,784,368 votes in favour of 'military measures' against an aggressor; only

2,351,981 against; and more 'Yes' answers even to this question than 'Noes', doubtfuls, and abstentions put together.

For political Parties on the eve of an Election there could not have been a more convenient presentation of the state of public opinion on the issues raised by the Ballot. Both Government and Opposition became more than ever convinced that the League was electorally popular. The tragedy proved to be that no political Party – and few leaders of opinion – drew the conclusion that the great body of opinion in favour in principle of military sanctions was a foundation on which more opinion of the same kind could be built; that the 2,364,441 voters who abstained on Question 5(b) were plainly educable in the sense that they might well change their minds from abstention to affirmation if the case for military sanctions was persuasively and authoritatively put; that it was also possible that quite a large number of 'Noes' might, in the same way, be persuaded to change their minds from 'No' to 'Yes'. In other words, comparison of the voting figures on Questions 1 to 4 with the very different results on 5 revealed a great many people waiting for a lead on this most important, however difficult, of all the issues.

Such a lead can always best come from the Government. In this instance both Government and Opposition led from behind. Winston Churchill and those who joined with him to found the 'Arms and the Covenant' movement were wise in their time. Unfortunately this movement did not come into being until December, 1936, late in the day and at a time when the nation was distracted by the 'great irrelevance' of Edward VIII's abdication. In *The Gathering Storm* Churchill wrote (in 1948):

'The Peace Ballot seemed at first to be misunderstood by Ministers. Its name overshadowed its purpose. It of course combined the contradictory propositions of the reduction of armaments and forcible resistance to aggression. It was regarded in many quarters as a part of the Pacifist campaign. On the contrary, Clause 5 affirmed a positive and courageous policy which could at this time have been followed with an overwhelming measure of national support. Lord Cecil, and other leaders of the League of Nations Union were, as this clause declared, and as events soon showed, willing, and indeed

54

resolved, to go to war in a righteous cause provided that all necessary action was taken under the auspices of the League of Nations.'[60]

On 21 and 22 August 1935, shortly after, that is to say, the failure of the Paris conference,[61] Sir Samuel Hoare and Mr Eden had conversations with a number of eminent Parliamentarians about the increasing threat of war in Abyssinia. Sir Samuel interviewed Sir Austen Chamberlain; Eden, Lord Cecil. (Perhaps a significant choice of interviewer?) The two together interviewed (on separate occasions) Lansbury, Sir Herbert Samuel, Lloyd George, and Churchill. Notes on these conversations were written by the two Ministers and circulated at a meeting of the Cabinet on 22 August 1935, and copies were also sent to the British Ambassador in Paris, Sir George Clerk.

These conversations are in the first place interesting as throwing some further light on public opinion at just about the moment when single-handed Anglo-Italian war first seemed a possibility. Thus Sir Austen 'was most clear and insistent that, provided the action was collective and that we and the French were keeping in step, economic sanctions of some kind were inevitable. . . . If we edged out of collective action of this kind, a great wave of public opinion would sweep the Government out of power'.[62] Lloyd George similarly said that Britain must play its part in collective action and make it clear to Laval that it would: 'any failure on our part to go to this point would bring down upon our heads the overwhelming mass of public opinion'. Hoare here added:

'I must say that this view is confirmed by the Press Department, the foreign editor of the *Yorkshire Post* declaring that 75 per cent of the north of England is behind the Government, and even the *Morning Post* growing restive at Italian arrogance.'[63]

What is most important about these conversations, however, is that they reveal the unanimity of the interviewees in supporting a line of collective action by the League and opposing any idea of unilateral action by Britain. (As so often in British history, as a moment of international crisis approached, a mood of national unity was in the making. Lansbury 'seemed anxious to help the

c

Government . . .'; Churchill specifically said that 'he was anxious to cooperate with us'.) 'Neither he nor his followers, with very few exceptions,' said Lansbury, 'contemplated unilateral action and by collective action they meant in part Anglo-French action. If . . . in actual practice collective action failed, the time would then have arrived for scrapping the existing machinery of the League and for attempting some new plan of international co-operation. It was, however . . . essential that the League machinery should be tried out before we could admit any such failure.'[64] Most Conservatives would, at that moment, have said exactly the same.

The official summary of Lord Cecil's remarks reads that he 'stated that the League of Nations Union were in support of the Government in their action at Paris and in that contemplated at Geneva, but they hoped a definite declaration would be made that H.M.G. accepted their obligations under the Covenant, as soon as the French position made this possible.'[65]

Sir Herbert Samuel seems to have listened rather than talked. Lloyd George 'seemed relieved' to be told 'that there was no question whatever of unilateral action' by Britain. Hoare and Eden were relieved to find that Churchill had 'toyed with the idea of unilateral action' but had 'modified this view'.[66] He made it clear that by collective action 'he meant principally Anglo-French cooperation'.[67]

In his own account of this meeting, published 13 years later, Churchill wrote:

> 'We had an easy talk. I said I thought the Foreign Secretary was *justified in going as far with the League of Nations against Italy as he could carry France*; but I added that he ought not to put any pressure on France, because of her military convention with Italy and her German pre-occupation; and that in the circumstances I did not think France would go very far. I then spoke of the Italian divisions on the Brenner Pass, of the unguarded southern front of France, and other military aspects.'[68]

'All roads lead to Paris', seem to say the British politicians to whose views we have just been listening.

6

The French Position

The Third French Republic was proclaimed on 4 September 1870. This régime, which collapsed in 1940, had much in common with the Italian régime which also began in 1870 and collapsed, earlier, in 1922. Diplomatically, as we have seen, the two countries (though Allies in the First World War) were for the most part at odds between 1870 and 1940, in which year they went to war with each other. The German threat had brought them together, as we shall see, in 1935, but only briefly. Domestically, however, the Third Republic and Liberal Italy shared striking similarities, notably government by weak coalitions, government that was often corrupt, government that bred cynicism about parliamentary democracy, government by short-lived Ministries. Laval's second Ministry was preceded by one, headed by Fernand Bouisson, which lasted only one day (1 June 1935).

The Third Republic lasted for 70 years because it was the political frame-work 'which divided Frenchmen least'. It had endurance, but not vitality. Its period was one of great glory for France in art and literature; it was also, however, the nadir of French politics. There was, moreover, a nadir within the nadir, just before and during the period of the Abyssinian crisis. All the various discontents with the 'république des camarades' came to a head early in 1934; the régime itself was imperilled.[1] The politics of the Third Republic did not really return to their normal level (never a high one) until the victory of the Popular Front at the elections of 3 May 1936. The months between February 1934 and May 1936 were for France a time of exceptional and extreme political weakness.

There was extreme economic and financial weakness also. The worst consequences of the Great Depression, which began in 1929, did not reach France until 1933. Laval tried deflation in

1935; Blum was forced into devaluation in 1936. Amid the political and economic turmoil a sizeable number of Frenchmen lost faith in democracy. Across the Atlantic, from March 1933 onwards, the New President, Franklin Roosevelt, talked the American people into self-confidence and recovery. But in Europe the Fascist era had begun. Hitler and Mussolini had many admirers in France. Organizations of the extreme Right flourished, notably the Croix de Feu, and the threat to the régime from that quarter persisted until the 1936 Elections.

A National Government (a faint parallel with Britain here) formed on 9 February 1934, was headed by Gaston Doumergue, a somewhat bumbling ex-President of the Republic. His foreign Minister was Louis Barthou (who resembled Clemenceau in spirit, but Poincaré in appearance). His War Minister and the most influential member of his Government was Philippe Pétain, Marshal of France, the hero of Verdun. On 9 October 1934 Barthou was (along with King Alexander of Yugoslavia) assassinated at Marseilles. He was succeeded by Pierre Laval. Thus did the Petain-Laval combination make its first appearance in history.

When Doumergue departed on 8 November 1934, Laval (who had been Prime Minister once before, from January 1931 till February 1932)[2] was offered the succession, but preferred to remain at the Foreign Ministry. The French Prime Minister in the early stages of the Abyssinian crisis, MacDonald's opposite number, was Pierre-Etienne Flandin. Laval, however, in the midst of a financial crisis, became Premier also on 7 June 1935.[3] He continued to hold both offices until 24 January 1936. A Caretaker Government then took over, with Flandin turning up again as Foreign Minister.[4] The elections of May 1936 brought Léon Blum to power as Prime Minister on 7 June 1936. Throughout the early and most critical stages of the Abyssinian crisis Laval's was therefore the most powerful personality on the French side.

Baldwin in power on one side of the Channel, Laval on the other: no contrast could be greater and yet they have in common an element of mystery. In Laval's case the principal puzzle is how he attained the position of supreme power in France. He was not a good writer, not a notably eloquent orator; he had not the backing of a powerful Party; in spite of a Degree in Law, his formal knowledge seems that of an early school-leaver; his ignorance of many facts one would expect a successful politician to know has often been commented on.[5] He was, however, extremely knowledgeable about human nature, especially in some of its baser aspects, and his rise to power, wealth, and fame was based on his exploitation of this knowledge. He was charming and unscrupulous, above all a professional button-holer. He preferred the ante-Chamber to the Chamber; hence perhaps he came to prefer Pétain to Parliament. To manipulate one Head of State must have been less exhausting, to say the least, than to manipulate hundreds of Parliamentarians, constituents, newspaper proprietors, and so on.[6]

In 1935 Laval had climbed to the top of a pole even greasier than the corresponding British one. As Prime Minister he was carrying out Right policies in a Left Chamber (elected in 1932). None the less, his policies touched something in the national mood.[7] It was on domestic issues that he was most criticized by the Left[8] and on them that he finally fell, after saving the Franc all over again. He had also, characteristically, avoided a 'showdown' with the Fascist Leagues whilst effectively restraining them. In a Parliamentary debate on foreign policy late in December 1935 he won by a majority of 43.[9] The new Foreign Minister, Flandin, on taking office in January 1936, said that 'he agreed with the foreign policy of M. Laval except in some details. . . .'[10]

The principal object of Laval's foreign policy throughout 1935 was to secure, and maintain, an Italian alliance. There were highly-placed and honourable people in Britain who thought, as he did, that it was more important to preserve peace in Europe than in Africa;[11] more important to preserve the independence of Austria than the independence of Abyssinia; more important therefore to have Mussolini as an ally against Hitler than to defend Haile Selassie against Mussolini; more important to use the League as an anti-German than an anti-Italian instrument. In the French case, however, there were geographical factors which made an Italian alliance far more valuable to her than to Britain. (These factors had been clearly perceived by that great and consistent friend of France, Churchill.)[12] France had a very long frontier to defend against Germany; she also had a frontier to defend against Italy. An Italian alliance might, in the event of war with Germany, add Italy's strength to France's, but would in any case add to France's own strength inasmuch as French forces could be withdrawn from the Italian to the German frontier. The equation was not merely that to the x of France's forces might be added the y of Italy's, but that the z of French forces needed to defeat Italy, hitherto subtracted from the x, could now be part of it. In short, an Italian Alliance meant for France that at least 10 Divisions could be moved from a watch on the Alps to the watch on the Rhine. Another seven Divisions could be withdrawn from French North Africa to Metropolitan France.[13] (In the first six months of a war with Germany, two Divisions were the most France could hope for in terms of military aid from Britain.[14]) Furthermore an Italian Alliance meant for France removal of the possibility of Franco-Italian war on French soil. An Anglo-Italian war would be fought mainly on the waters of the Mediterranean, in the air above, and quite certainly not on the soil of the British Isles.

Thus it came about that Laval, having become Foreign Minister on the assassination of Barthou in October 1934, fundamentally carrying on his predecessor's foreign policy and carrying out one of his predecessor's engagements, visited Mussolini in Rome in the first week of January 1935. Fear of Germany now brought France and Italy together to settle their differences, just as fear of Germany had been responsible for the Anglo-French agreement of 1904. In both cases what was important was not so much the actual content of the agreements as the indication of attitudes to a third Power. The 1935 French-Italian agreements were in substance about Europe but in content principally related to Africa.[15] A minority holding of 2,500 shares in the French-owned Addis Ababa-Jibuti railway were transferred to Italy, along with a thin slice of French Somaliland. There was also a territorial concession to Libya. It was further agreed that in Tunisia, 'an Italian Colony with a French Government', (more precisely put, a French Colony with more Italian than French residents) Italian children born before 1945 should retain Italian nationality and those born in the ensuing 20 years shoud have a right to choose between French and Italian nationality. Only after 1965 would all be legally French.

On the face of it these agreements were in France's favour. The surrender of the railway shares did not modify the French character of the railway; the ceded territory was small and valueless; the agreement on nationality in Tunisia meant that all Italian nationals there would eventually lose their Italian nationality. This was an important concession to France. What Mussolini in return obtained from Laval in January 1935 was his pledge that France would not stand in the way of Italian expansion in Abyssinia. This was in spite of the fact that Laval had been made aware of the possible importance of the Wal-Wal incident on the same occasion in mid-December as Eden had been.[16]

Later there were different interpretations in Paris and in Rome of this most important, and most secret, part of the January agreements. Laval asserted in the French Senate on 26 March 1935 that 'nothing in the Rome Agreements tampers with the sovereignty, independence, and territorial integrity of Ethiopia'.[17] *Au pied de la lettre*, this was true. In Rome on 24 June 1935 Mussolini contested Eden's view that France had only given Italy a free hand in Abyssinia 'economically'. Eden's record of this runs:

'Signor Mussolini replied that ... since he had yielded to France the future of 100,000 Italians in Tunis and received in return half a dozen palm trees in one place and a strip of desert which did not even contain a sheep in another, it must be clear that France had disinterested herself in Abyssinia. ... He was quite clear that the implication, if not the written word, was that Italy was free in Abyssinia so far as France was concerned. I contested this, telling Signor Mussolini that when M. Laval had described in Geneva his interview with Signor Mussolini he had insisted that France had only given a free hand to Italy in economic matters. ... At this Signor Mussolini flung himself back in his chair with a gesture of incredulous astonishment.'[18]

By this time, one must note, the January agreements had been followed by secret air and military conventions, signed in May and June, immensely in France's interest, so that Laval was now well and truly in Mussolini's pocket.

No doubt the exact truth about what passed between Laval and Mussolini in Rome in January 1935 about Abyssinia can never be known. An Italian Foreign Office report written at the end of 1935 speaks of 'Laval's verbal assurances'. On the other hand the French Ambassador in Rome, Comte Charles de

Chambrun (not Laval's son-in-law, Count René de Chambrun), attended the meetings between Mussolini and Laval, and in his memoirs maintains that the two men were never sufficiently alone for a private agreement to have been made. However, not much time or privacy is needed for a wink or a nod. Indeed, as Mr D. C. Watt well and shrewdly observes:'One is led even to wonder whether the question was not tacitly left in that grey and cloudy limbo where one assumes one has been understood for fear that direct inquiry may show that one has not.'[19] As we shall see, a miasma of just the same kind hung over the conference chamber at Stresa in April, so that Mussolini mistook British silence on the subject of Abyssinia for a disinterest in line with Laval's.[20]

The only votes in the French Chamber of Deputies against the ratification of the Rome Agreements were nine Communist ones. Léon Blum, Leader of the Socialist Party, said: 'In spite of our hostility towards the Mussolini régime, we voted for the ratification of the Rome agreement, because we believed this to be in the interest of peace. . . . We could not refuse to approve a diplomatic act which we should have carried out ourselves had we been in power'.[21] Herriot confided his uneasiness to his diary (on 10 and 12 January 1935), but not to the French people. Just after the Hoare-Laval negotiations in December, sitting next to Vansittart at lunch, he 'expressed his disgust at our actions but not with his country'.[22]

It must be noted that in May 1932, the Socialist Party Congress, meeting in the Salle Huyghens and drawing up a programme which came to be known as the Cahiers Huyghens, had made one point in it the reduction of French military expenditure to the 1928 level. In 1935 the Party opposed the law for the increase of military service from one year to two. At the Congress of the Radical Party that autumn Pierre Cot, who had prepared a speech advocating military sanctions against Italy, was persuaded by Herriot, the Party's 'elder statesman', not to deliver it. Herriot himself made pro-English and pro-League speeches, but clung to his position as Minister of State under Laval until the end of his Premiership.[23] The Communists started, but dropped, a campaign for closing the Suez Canal. In short, the French Left, in its own way, was as impractically pacifist as the British Left. The French Right was pacificist in the same simple sense as were British Conservatives; they were strongly against war. The minority of positive admirers of Hitler and Mussolini was larger in France than in Britain, but it was love of peace (or fear of war) and neither love nor fear of Italian Fascism which mainly motivated the French Right. All in all there was no significant movement of French public opinion against Laval's foreign policy.[24] (It was carried on, after all, by his successor, Flandin, though allowance must be made for his being a 'care-taker' Foreign Minister awaiting the elections for the new Assembly in May, 1936.) The criticisms of Laval were almost all, as already said, of his home policy.

Mussolini has been much praised by many for securing, after some 60 years of total rupture, an agreement with the papacy. Laval is entitled to some praise for securing, after some 70 years of strained relations, an agreement between France and Italy, short-lived as it turned out to be[25] and however much to be criticized for the loop-hole which fortified Mussolini's resolve to attack Abyssinia. If the agreement had been Barthou's, he would have been praised for it. Laval thought he saw the problem clearly; in fact he saw it narrowly, short-sightedly, and superficially.[26] His British counterparts had a wider but a more confused vision. It was a bitter fate for Laval to have at Geneva to watch, and reluctantly assist, the erosion of his work at Rome.

7

The other Great Powers

In 1934 there were four Great Powers in Europe (Britain, France, Italy and Germany); one astride Europe and Asia, the U.S.S.R.; one wholly in Asia, Japan; one in the New World, the U.S.A.; none in Africa or Australasia. Of these the first three (Britain, France and Italy) were members of the League of Nations; the U.S.A. had never been – and never became – a member, but her absence was to some extent made up for by the U.S.S.R. becoming a member in September 1934 (she was to be expelled in December 1939); Japan had been a founder-member, but in March 1933 had announced her withdrawal; Germany joined the League in 1926 but left it (and the Dis-armament Conference) in October 1933.

In the Abyssinian crisis the role of Japan and Germany was that of watchers in the wings, but watchers who might at any moment make a decisive and malevolent intervention. (One of them, Germany, did just that, in March 1936, though in another area, from the European point of view the supremely sensitive one.[1])

Japan at this time was not as fully engaged in attempting to conquer China as she had been from 1931 onwards. In the war which began with the Mukden incident on 18 September 1931 there was a lull from the Tangku Truce of 3 May 1933 until the Lukouchiao incident of 7 July 1937. Just because of this lull there was considerable fear in London that Japan might strike south-westwards, as in fact she did in 1942. This possibility was, as we shall see,[2] a major pre-occupation of the British Admiralty.

On 9 March 1935 Goering announced the existence of a German Air Force (Luftwaffe); on 16 March Hitler announced the re-introduction of conscription. Even under the preceding Weimar régime there had been breaches, albeit on a small scale,

64

of the disarmament provisions of the Treaty of Versailles. Since Hitler had come to power re-armament had been started on a big scale. The fact of German disarmament had given a greater sense of security to other European states than all the signatures on all the Treaties. The fact of German re-armament, now openly admitted, was far more menacing than the gesture of leaving the League in October 1933 (in any case substantially off-set by Russia joining). From now on it was as if a wolf was known to be prowling outside a hen-run: the nearer the wolf came, and the more powerful and ruthless he was seen to be, the more did the terrified hens tend to lose their heads and scatter. In other words, German re-armament became the great catalyst of European politics. The question was whether it would promote the union or the disunion of the other European states. Either way, all their decisions on foreign policy were now to be made with one eye on the particular question at issue, but with both eyes turned towards Berlin and Berchtesgaden.

For a year after March 1935 Hitler was on his best diplomatic behaviour. He had everything to gain by so being; an important move made before the outcome of the Abyssinian crisis was clear might prove a false one. His attitude, as the crisis developed, was therefore one of correct neutrality on the surface. Nonetheless fear of Germany and fear of Japan, encouraged timidity in face of Italy. This indirect help given by Germany and Japan to Italy would have been importantly offset by direct help given to Abyssinia by the U.S.A. But that was not on the cards.

As the First World War had worn on, many minds, especially Anglo-American minds, turned towards the idea of preventing a repetition of its horrors by what came to be called a League of Nations. In the U.S.A., as early as June 1915, ex-President Taft and President Lowell (of Harvard University) took the lead in setting up 'The League to enforce peace', to campaign for the creation of an institution with that name and purpose. The proposed League was to provide procedures for the settlement of international disputes by law or by conciliation, but Taft and Lowell and their colleagues went much further than that and wrote :

'The signatory Powers shall jointly use forthwith both their economic and military forces against any one of their number that goes to war, or commits acts of hostility against another of the signatories before any question shall be submitted (to conciliation or judicial procedures) as provided in the foregoing.'[3]

Thus does the idea of economic and military sanctions, imposed by an international agency on an aggressor, first take the stage.

Woodrow Wilson, President of the U.S.A. since 1912, did not seriously study these particular proposals.[4] However, in his address to Congress on 8 January 1918, setting out his peace terms, the fourteenth of his Fourteen Points read: 'A general association of nations must be formed under specific covenants for the purpose of affording mutual guarantees of political independence and territorial integrity to great and small states alike'. With this declaration by the most politically powerful and morally prestigious man in the world at that time, the idea of a League of Nations (indeed of a Covenant and what became its Article 10) entered 'practical politics'.[5]

The President proposed and the United States Senate disposed. The President, that is to say, obtained his Covenant at the Paris Peace Conference of 1919; the Senate exercised its constitutional right to reject the Versailles Peace Treaty in which the Covenant was embodied. The League of Nations came into being primarily at the bidding of the United States, but the United States did not become a member; the arch had to stand as best it could without the intended keystone.

At first the American reversion to isolationism was complete. Charles E. Hughes, Secretary of State to Wilson's successor, President Harding, refused even to read communications addressed to the United States by the League of Nations. There was, too, obstruction of its attempted interventions in Latin America.[6] Gradually, however, this attitude gave way to an undefined and half-hearted co-operation. Unsuccessful attempts were made to join the Permanent Court of International Justice (the last in January 1935).[7] The U.S.A., however, did in 1934 join the International Labour Organization. The Nine Power and Four Power Treaties expressed a policy for the North Pacific Ocean and for China which was by no means isolationist. Technical assistance was given to two Reparations plans (named after their American authors, Dawes and Young). In 1928 the United

States made its own peculiar (in both senses of the word) contribution to the attempted framework of world peace. What began as an initiative by Briand, French Foreign Minister, for a Franco-American Non-Aggression Pact was taken up by F. B. Kellogg (who had succeeded Hughes as Secretary of State, under Coolidge, in 1925) and turned into a universal Pact of Peace.[8] Abyssinia and Italy were among the 63 signatories.

Cooperation between the U.S.A. and the League reached its peak at the time of the Manchurian crisis of 1931. For about a month a U.S. representative sat with the League's Council. There was an American member of the League's Commission of Enquiry (headed by Lord Lytton) into the Manchurian situation. On 7 January 1932 Secretary of State H. L. Stimson (Hoover was now President, Stimson succeeding Kellogg in March 1929) proclaimed his famous doctrine of non-recognition in an Identic Note to China and Japan; the United States did 'not intend to recognize any situation, treaty, or agreement which may be brought about by means contrary to the . . . Pact of Paris of 27 August 1928. . . .'

Unfortunately, however (unfortunately for the whole world, including the U.S.A.), as the European situation deteriorated, the U.S.A. withdrew again into its shell. This was not a deliberate decision on the part of President Roosevelt and his Administration. The new President (inaugurated in March 1933) had been Assistant Secretary of the Navy under Wilson and the Democratic candidate for the Vice-Presidency in 1920, campaigning in support of the League of Nations. The new Secretary of State, Cordell Hull, urged legislation giving the President power to impose a ban on the export of arms and ammunition wherever their sale would, in the Presidential judgment, encourage the use of force in international disputes. This would have given the President a discretion to ban the export of arms to an aggressor and allow their sale to his victim. Congress, however, instead moved towards the 'new neutrality' which amounted to a policy of keeping out of war at almost any cost (including the understandable, but abject, abandonment of any idea of insisting on the neutral rights hitherto always insisted on). The attitude of Congress undoubtedly expressed the predominant national mood. The nearer war came in Europe the more did the American nation want simply to stay out of it. The popular drive for neutrality was even stronger than in 1914–17.

Roosevelt and Hull found themselves obliged to carry out a policy in which they did not believe. They believed that a valid distinction could be drawn between an aggressor and a non-aggressor State; that if the United States abandoned its rights it might assist the aggressor; that so doing might only postpone a war of self-defence to 'a day more dark and drear' on which the United States might stand alone in a World dominated by an aggressor or alliance of aggressors. Congress on the other hand did not want to give the President a discretionary power to hinder an aggressor or help his victim.

In August 1935 Congress (despite the virtual certainty of an Italo-Abyssinian war in the near future) passed Senator Pittman's resolution making it mandatory on the President, in the event of war, to ban the export of arms to all belligerents, with no distinction between attacker and attacked. Roosevelt reluctantly signed the Joint Resolution, though expressing the opinion that a mandatory measure of this kind might do more to drag the country into war than keep it out. 1936 was an Election year.

In the case of this particular war, however, the embargo on the export of arms and ammunition, proclaimed by the President, in accordance with the Neutrality Act, on 5 October (two days, be it noted, before the League of Nations came to grips with its comparable problem), enured to the advantage of one belligerent, Abyssinia. This was because the U.S.A. had a large trade with Italy, scarcely any with Abyssinia. The more, therefore, that American supplies to Italy were cut the more Italy would suffer, whereas Abyssinia would not suffer because she could not lose what she had never had. Indirectly therefore the U.S.A., while maintaining neutrality under the Act and duly imposing the mandatory embargo on exports to both belligerents was able to injure the aggressor and therefore sustain his victim. This situation, moreover, enabled the U.S.A. to co-operate with the League in deed, if not in words, to the important extent of not thwarting its sanctions when the time for them came. The more the scope of the embargo could be increased, the greater the injury to Italy and, correspondingly, the indirect aid to Abyssinia. But the Neutrality Act made illegal any positive American help for her. In this situation the U.S. Administration did its part to extend the mandatory embargo on the export of the instruments of war to both belligerents to cover also a ban on the export of the materials for war. Such a ban, however, could only be imposed by exhortation as opposed to law.

Wilson's Fourteen Points had been made largely as an attempt to outbid the propaganda of Soviet Russia. The U.S.S.R., like the U.S.A., though for very different reasons, adopted a post-war isolationist policy. For one thing it could still play an active part in international politics through the Third International (the Comintern). However, as the European situation deteriorated, Communist Russia felt the menace to itself of Fascist Germany. She felt also, therefore, the need for powerful and self-interested Governments as Allies rather than the ideological support of minority Communist Parties. The Comintern game ceased to be one the U.S.S.R. could afford to play. Accordingly the Comintern was hustled off the stage and the Soviet State stepped on. The last Comintern Congress was held in 1935, though the Comintern itself was not dissolved till 1943.

At the first Congress of the Comintern, held in Moscow in March 1919, the League of Nations had been denounced as 'The Holy Alliance of the bourgeoisie for the suppression of the proletarian revolution'.[9] The manifesto of the Sixth Congress, held in 1928, described the League as 'the product of Versailles, the most shameless robber treaty of the last decade', cloaking 'the warlike work of its members by working out projects for disarmament'.[10] (This was in spite of the fact that Russia had joined the Preparatory Commission for the Disarmament Conference at the end of the previous year.) In 1932 the U.S.S.R. obstructed the work of the Lytton Commission, refusing to allow Soviet officials to give evidence to it.[11] Within the next two years, however, the U.S.S.R.'s attitude to the League was completely reversed. In January 1934 Stalin himself said to an American journalist, Walter Duranty:

'We do not always take a negative attitude towards the League. . . . Despite the withdrawal of Germany and Japan from the League – or perhaps because of it – the League may well become to a certain extent a brake to retard or prevent military actions.'[12]

On 10 September 1934 the League Council agreed nem. con. (Argentina and Portugal abstaining) to Russian membership; the first appearance of a Soviet delegation in the Assembly was made on 17 September.

New Bolshevism was, in many ways, old Tsarism writ large. The negotiations for the entry of the U.S.S.R. into the League were intertwined with those for the revival of the pre-1914 Franco-Russian Alliance. In 1930 Stalin had said:

> 'The most striking representative of the bourgeois movement towards intervention against the Soviet Union is the bourgeois France of today, the fatherland of Pan-Europe, the cradle of the Kellogg Pact, the most aggressive and militaristic country, among all the aggressive and militaristic countries of the world.'[13]

This was, to say the least, a 'through the looking-glass view' of a country, admittedly then the most powerful in military terms in Western Europe, but bled white by the 1914-1918 war, supremely anxious to avoid another such blood-letting, spending millions on the defensive Maginot Line, a country which in the same year as Stalin's strident speech reduced the period of military service to a single year.

Hitler's accession to power made Russia realize that her interests were anti-revisionist.[14] *Mein Kampf* had made it plain that one of his major ideas was German expansion at her expense. It now became a Russian interest, therefore, to make an alliance with France and to join a League seen, as her enyclopaedists had done a decade previously, as an anti-revisionist bloc. The first official overtures to France were made in November 1933.[15] In May 1934 the then French Foreign Minister, Barthou, who had no illusions about Hitler's ambitions, formally suggested to Litvinov, Soviet Commissar for Foreign Affairs, that, as an indispensable pre-condition for a Franco-Soviet Pact, the U.S.S.R. should join the League.[16] In September 1934, as we have just seen, she did so.

Barthou was assassinated a month later. His successor, Laval, signed a Franco-Soviet Pact in Moscow in May 1935. He delayed its ratification for a year and, when it was at last ratified, late in February 1936, the event was exploited by Hitler as a justification for the most decisive of his blows against the European order established in 1919.[17]

On the Soviet entry into the League, Professor Beloff comments that by virtue of it and 'its pacts with France and Czechoslovakia, the Soviet Union definitely took sides in the political struggles dividing the non-Soviet world, and became less and less like a unique and unprecedented apparition in the world and more like a Great Power among Great Powers. . . .'[18] Stalin and Litvinov, in other words, succeeded easily, where Roosevelt and Hull had failed, in completely reversing an isolationist policy. The capacity to make so sudden a reversal of policy is one of the short-term advantages of dictatorship over democracy.

Thus on the very eve of the Abyssinian crisis the League had a new and powerful member. Unlike Britain, France and Italy she had, in 1934, no direct interests in Africa. On the other hand she had signed a Non-Aggression Pact with Italy a year previously. While wanting to take a line compatible with the anti-imperialist gospel she had been consistently preaching since the Russian Revolution of October 1917, she was mainly concerned to use the League as a means of protecting her vital interests in Europe. Russia, in short, had her problems, just as Britain and France had, if she were to give the Covenant her undeviating support throughout the Abyssinian Crisis. When, however, Litvinov in his first speech in the 14th League Assembly in September 1934, said that a new assault on the Covenant would, if successful, 'put it completely out of action'[19] his warning was more than justified.

8

The League of Nations up to the crisis

The creation of a League of Nations was, as we have seen, the fourteenth of President Wilson's Fourteen Points, tabulated in public on 8 January 1918. The Armistice with Germany was signed on 11 November 1918; the Peace Conference assembled in Paris on 18 January 1919; the text of the Covenant of the League of Nations was adopted by it on 28 April 1919.

This was quick going. The speed with which the Covenant was concluded was partly owing to the pressure put by Wilson on the Conference for its speedy conclusion, partly due to the fact of much preliminary discussion of its possible provisions whilst the war was still raging. Nonetheless, the comparative haste with which the Covenant was put together is revealed by its form. Wilson himself took the chair at the meetings of the drafting committee; scant attention was paid to a French draft, still less to an Italian one; what emerged was an Anglo-American document, based on drafts prepared by Cecil Hurst, Legal Adviser to the British Foreign Office, and David Hunter Miller, legal adviser to the U.S. delegation. Even so, the document was an ill-arranged hotch-potch of quite different ideas for the achievement of the League's central purpose, the prevention of war. It combined fundamentally unrelated notions about arbitration, adjudication, conciliation, disarmament, mutual guarantees, open diplomacy, and law enforcement.

Jurists were quick to see the existence of the so-called 'gap in the Covenant', related to the procedures prescribed under Articles 12 and 15. In theory, under Article 15, Clause 7, a situation could arise in which Members could go to war after observing the three months delay in so doing laid down in Article 12, Clause 1 [1] The real gaps, however, went deeper than these juridical ones. They sprang, naturally and probably inevitably, from the human tendency to draw lessons for an open-ended long run from a short run which has just ended. In this instance that tendency was reinforced by the fact that the 1914–18 war had spread destruction on so mammoth a scale that, unlike most man-made events, it had made a real impact on the human imagination.

The lessons drawn from Armageddon, by the statesmen assembled in Paris, about how a League of Nations could prevent its repetition may be summarized thus:

1. Because Europe had been at peace on 27 July 1914 (the date of the Austrian ultimatum to Serbia) and was at war by 4 August, it was all-important to prevent international disputes 'escalating' (not a 1919 word) into war by hasty and hot-tempered decisions. Hence the concept of a needed 'cooling-off' period (though not then called that), of the League therefore as a shock-absorber (a term which came quite quickly into use in that context), and of the procedures designed to equip it as such. But wars do not always begin because of an over-quick resort to force. The Italo-Abyssinian dispute, which ended in war in October 1935, began in December 1934. The cooling-off procedures which occupied the intervening months played into Italy's hands because she had no intention of being 'cooled off' and used those months to hot up her preparations for war. Only when war itself began was the League's machinery galvanized into real action against the aggressor. The Covenant did not provide machinery for curbing open preparations for war over a long period of time by a State obviously bent on aggression; the League, by its very constitution, was tied to inaction until the aggression actually occurred.

2. Because the war of 1914 resulted, on the face of it, from an international *dispute* it was assumed that international wars would always result from *disputes*. But this did not provide for the case of a State, such as Italy, bent on expansion ever since its foundation or a State such as Germany, bent from 1933 onwards (some would say from even earlier) on expansion beyond the Bismarckian boundaries. The German-Polish dispute was the occasion for, not the cause of, the 1939 war. To overcome the tremendous international tensions, extremely likely to erupt into war, created by expansionist attitudes and policies, the League was armed only with Article 11, Section 2,

and Article 19 of the Covenant. Article 10 was a more powerful weapon against revision than there were weapons for it.[2]

3. Because the Austro-Hungarian dispute with Serbia was
resolved only by a European war, which became the first
World War, it was too easily assumed that any international
dispute was likely to involve the whole world in war. Hence the
Covenant provided a system of universal guarantees against
aggression. But if two Great Powers went to war with each
other, the mice (the Small Powers) were not likely to try to bell
the cats (the Great Powers) whatever their commitments
under the Covenant, and so the danger of war continuing –
and spreading – remained; if, on the other hand, two Small
Powers went to war with each other those not immediately
concerned were not likely to put themselves out, and run risks,
in trying to stop such a war so long as it seemed safely 'local-
ized'. The universal provisions of the Covenant in fact needed
to be supplemented by regional arrangements likely to be effective in terms of immediate self-interest.

4. Because the blockade of Germany had played an important
part in the Allied victory, and effective inter-Allied machinery
had been evolved to operate it, Article 16 defined with some
precision the economic and financial sanctions to be used
against a Covenant-breaking State. On the other hand
Germany had not been beaten by an international military
force (unity of command on the principal Western front had
only been established in 1918) and the Covenant had nothing
precise to say about the operation of military sanctions.

Great as were these defects of the Covenant, it can be said, here
and now, that it was not because of any one or more of them that
the League in 1935 snatched defeat out of the jaws of victory.
The founding fathers, with their pragmatic Anglo-Saxon
approach, built better than they knew. The rules they drew were
loose, but for that very reason the institutions they created (an
Assembly, a Council, and a Secretariat) had much greater
powers of growth than they would have had under a more
detailed constitution. The way in which these institutions grew or
were stunted, the extent and manner in which they were used or
ignored, depended on the collective will of the member-States.
Strictly speaking, there was no *League*; the word in this instance

described a severality (association, Wilson's own original word, was the right one) of sovereign States which had chosen to act, or refrain from acting, in certain defined ways. 'The League' had no governmental, let alone supra-national, powers.[3]

The term League of *Nations* was even more of a misnomer. It was a League of Governments. Yet it was a second great strength of the Covenant that it could be 'readily understanded by the people'. The document had the merit of being short. (Its 26 articles are, in this respect, to be favourably compared with the 111 articles of the Charter of the United Nations.) In Great Britain in particular (a country with a long tradition of Biblical quotations) the work of the League of Nations Union created a large body of public opinion well educated in the chapter and verse of the Covenant. Moreover, precisely on the eve of the Italo-Abyssinian War much further education in the general principles involved was, as we have seen, given by the Peace Ballot. On the other hand, the tendency of many publicists, whether for or against the League, however understandably, to speak and write of it as if it had an existence independent of its members did disservice to the cause of understanding its possibilities.

Before briefly tracing the history of the League up to 1935 a special word must be said about the Italian attitude to it. We have seen that an Italian draft for the Covenant was brushed aside. Both France and Italy saw the proposed League as an instrument for securing justice, but whereas for France that meant upholding the existing law for Italy it meant 'equity'. Thus, while the Italian draft concerned itself with the settlement of disputes, and indeed specified 17 varieties of sanctions, it also proposed an international legislature. It proposed too, for every independent political community, a guarantee, not of integrity or peace, but of growth. One of the fundamental principles of this guarantee was to be 'the international distribution of foodstuffs and raw materials required to sustain healthy conditions of life', international trade being regulated in such a way 'as to secure to every country what is indispensable to it in this respect'. To achieve these ends Economic and Labour Commissions were to be set up under the Council.

In other words the Italian concept of the League placed a special emphasis on economic growth for 'proletarian' States. This concept sprang naturally from the Italian situation in 1918 and to this concept Italy adhered, in spite of many rebuffs, throughout the League's life. Italy raised the question of the distribution of raw materials at the first Assembly in November 1920, and was severely rebuffed by Canada for so doing. The Italian workers' delegation raised the same question at the first International Labour Conference held in Washington at the same time. In short Fascist Italy's attitude to the League was based on the pre-Fascist one.[4] The difference was that Mussolini showed his indifference to and indeed contempt for it. The contempt was made manifest for the first time over the Corfu crisis of 1923. Mussolini, however, stayed in the League for the sake of whatever he might be able to get out of it. It was a final manifestation of his contempt for the League that he did not trouble to leave it when declared an aggressor by it in October 1935. The departure was delayed until December 1937.[5]

The League came into existence on 10 January 1920. The Peace Conference was over; three Peace Treaties had been signed and a fourth was to follow.[6] A Supreme Council of the Allied and Associated Powers had its life extended to tie up the remaining loose ends and generally preserve order in Europe. Some of its powers it delegated to a Conference of Ambassadors. These two bodies had faded out by 1924 and in that year both the British and French Prime Ministers (MacDonald and Herriot) for the first time attended the annual meeting of the League Assembly. Thereafter League meetings, especially Council meetings, became the regular and principal occasions for gatherings of the foremost European statesmen (though we have noted that Baldwin did not think it worth his while to break his annual holiday at Aix to attend a single one).[7] This role as a rendezvous increased the League's prestige; the demise of the Supreme Council and Conference of Ambassadors removed a dangerous source of confusion in international authority. International Conferences *ad hoc* continued, of course, to be held from time to time, but the great age for frequency of international meetings of that kind was the period from 1920 to 1923.

In its central task of checking aggression and settling international disputes peacefully, the League was notably unsuccessful in its early years. This was substantially the result of the combination of continued disturbance in some parts of Europe with the war-weariness of the victors. In 1919, as in 1945 (Russia then excepted), they proceeded to reduce their armed forces with great rapidity. They also proceeded to fall out with one another. In these circumstances a dissatisfied and adventurous State ran little risk in resorting to force to remedy what was felt to be a grievance. Sometimes the force was unofficial as when D'Annunzio seized Fiume in September 1919.[8] The next year a certain General Zeligowski, allied with and paid by Poland, forcibly occupied Vilna (the historic capital of Lithuania, though with a preponderantly Polish population). The efforts of the League to end this illegal Polish occupation were fruitless and in February 1923 the Conference of Ambassadors gave Poland an official title to the town. In January the Lithuanians, noting no doubt how crime had paid, invaded the town and territory of Memel. This port, at the mouth of the Niemen, was destined by Nature to be Lithuania's principal port, but it had a German population. In 1923 it was administered on behalf of the Allies by a French High Commissioner and garrisoned by French troops. The French, having just started their occupation of the Ruhr, had no troops to spare to throw out the invader. Again the Allies accepted the *fait accompli* and awarded to Lithuania sovereignty over Memel, slightly modified subsequently by a measure of local autonomy suggested by a League Commission in 1924. But Memel remained an object of German irredentism.[9]

The League came out of an earlier brush with Poland rather better than in the Vilna affair, though not extremely well. A plebiscite held in 1921 to determine the future of Upper Silesia produced, from the Polish point of view, the wrong answer (i.e. a majority vote in favour of union with Germany) and in 1922 a rising against the return of the territory to Germany broke out under the leadership of the Polish plebiscite Commissioner. As in Vilna and Memel, the Allies lost control of the situation. The Supreme Council referred it to the League, which suggested a partition. A 'judgment of Solomon', if adopted, is always a second-best solution of such a problem (one thinks today of Germany, India, Ireland, and Palestine), and this particular partition represented 'the easiest compromise between justice and the interest of the stronger. . . . Poland was certainly not penalized, and probably gained, as a result of her tactics'.[10]

Another boundary dispute, long drawn-out, between Turkey and Irak, was settled by the League, not by partition, but by the

77

award of the disputed territory, the Vilayet of Mosul, inhabited by the Kurds, to Irak.[11] This award was confirmed in 1926 by a tri-partite Treaty between Turkey, Irak, and Great Britain, which had held the League's mandate for the government of Irak. It does not seem that the League's award was made because of any fear of the Great Power involved, but rather because of the severe Turkish repression of a Kurdish revolt within Turkey, which scarcely boded well for the welfare of the Kurds of Mosul if placed under Turkish rule.[12]

The first clash between the League and a Great Power was, significantly in relation to what was to follow in 1935, with Mussolini's Italy. In 1923 an Italian General and three other Italian members of an International Commission engaged in the delimitation of the boundary between Greece and Albania were murdered on Greek soil. Italy sent Greece an ultimatum (reminiscent of that sent by Austria to Serbia in 1914 and foreshadowing that sent by Italy to Abyssinia in 1934) and answered a submissive Greek reply by bombarding and occupying the Greek island of Corfu. Greece appealed to the League, but Italy refused to recognize its authority in the matter. The League to some extent saved its face by drawing up a plan of settlement which was accepted by the Conference of Ambassadors. It was this body which imposed the settlement, one which included the payment by Greece to Italy of a fine of 50 million lire. This was a twentieth-century form of Danegeld; Greece paid Italy to evacuate Corfu.

Another Great Power, and a greater, defied the League in 1931. The League sent a Commission of Enquiry to the spot. Its findings (the Lytton Report) were in general condemnatory of Japan. The Assembly adopted the Report and Japan thereupon, in 1933, gave notice of resignation from the League. The League's defeat was total, but there were excuses for it. There was a Japanese case; the two Great Powers nearest to the scene of action, the U.S.S.R. and the U.S.A., were not League members; the leading League Powers, Britain and France, were far away and wrestling with acute economic problems. One can sympathize with the Chinese delegate's remark that his country could not be 'expected to admit that the operation of treaties, covenants and the accepted principles of international law stops at the border of Manchuria'.[13] It was, and is, however, difficult to see what, in practical terms, could have been done. It was clear, however, in 1933 that another such defeat would effectively end the League's essential work.

It was in relation to the Manchurian crisis that American membership of the League was most spectacularly missed. It was missed continuously in Europe, particularly in the sense that American absence made France feel constantly apprehensive of the inevitable German recovery, whatever form it took, and therefore pursue a solitary search for security. It was, however, in Latin America, for the first few years at any rate, that American isolationism did the League most harm of a positive kind. Renewed isolationism brought with it a renewed reliance on the Monroe Doctrine, which in its latter days had had its original meaning (U.S. determination to prevent European interference anywhere in the New World) warped to imply the right of the U.S. to play a dictatorial role in Latin-American affairs. This being so, the Latin-American countries welcomed, and hastened to join, the League as a neo-Canningite means of calling in the Old World to redress the balance of the New. When in 1920, however, an old tri-partite territorial dispute (over Tacna and Arica) between Chile, Peru and Bolivia was revived and the League's aid being invoked by all three, Peru had her knuckles so smartly rapped by the U.S.A. that she withdrew her application. In 1921 when Panama complained to the League of aggression by Costa Rica, the U.S. Government was stimulated to an even heavier-handed rap. One net result of all this was that Argentina, Bolivia, and Peru effectively withdrew from the League (the first members to be lost) and Costa Rica withdrew formally in 1924. Things became different after Roosevelt's promulgation of his 'good neighbour" policy and in 1934 the League scored a distinct success in settling a boundary dispute between Peru and Columbia. On the other hand, the League failed to stop the long 'Chaco War' between Bolivia and Paraguay. It was ended by an age-old, but now old-fashioned, method, the victory of one side over the other; in June 1935 Bolivia won the war.

Africa provides a little-known example of co-operation, not consistently happy, between the U.S.A. and the League and also an example of a problem and an attempted solution strikingly similar to some aspects of the problem presented by the Abyssinian admission to the League in 1923 and the attempted settlements of August and September 1935.[14] As already remarked the only other independent African State in 1935 was Liberia, 'a poor and neglected step-child of the United States'.[15] Contrary to British and French wishes it was admitted to founder-membership of the League. Britain and France would have preferred an American mandate, but the U.S. Senate's rejection of the Covenant ruled that out.

By 1929 Liberia was in a sorry state: 'A few thousand educated men, dwelling on the coast, kept all power in their hands, while the original tribes of the interior were left in primitive ignorance and poverty, knowing nothing of their government except that it forced them to pay taxes and supply labourers and gave nothing in return.'[16] The conditions were not as bad as in the Congo of Casement's time, but bad they were.

All this became known when League-American Commissions of Inquiry and a League-American Liberian Committee produced a Plan of Assistance. The principal obstacle to the Plan being carried out was the obstruction of the Liberian Government. In May 1934 the League Council resolved that Liberia had rejected the Plan and that its offers of help were therefore withdrawn. Eden told the whole story in public and threatened the expulsion of Liberia from the League for failure to observe Article 23(b) of the Covenant.[17] It is surprising that this story and this British threat were not exploited by Italy for anti-Abyssinian propaganda purposes the next year. But one can see traces of the Plan of Assistance for Liberia in that proposed for Abyssinia by the Committee of Five in September 1935, shortly before the start of the Italo-Abyssinian War.

It is generally agreed that it was in 1925 that the League gained its greatest success in preventing war. A 'frontier incident' led to a Greek invasion of Bulgaria on a considerable scale. In this case Greece was again penalized, to the tune of a fine of £45,000 paid to Bulgaria. But the League's diplomatic record as a whole, on the eve of the Abyssinian crisis, was not impressive. There had been one signal failure (in the Far East) and otherwise a mixed record of successes and failures, with the latter out-numbering the former and the successess attained only where Small Powers were involved. Nontheless, as the year 1934 drew to a close, there was a 'sudden rise of the League's stock'.[18] There had been the settlement of the Columbia-Peru dispute in May and by December the Saar crisis (remembered now as the occasion for the first international peace-keeping force) and a Yugoslav-Hungarian crisis (long since forgotten) were well on the way to peaceful settlement. Mr. Eden said, at Newcastle-on-Tyne, on 4 January 1935 (Laval was due in Rome for his conversations with Mussolini that evening):

> 'The closing weeks of the old year saw a definite, even a startling improvement, in the international outlook ... 1935 will be the most challenging year in post-war history. Its passage will show whether we can make the League – the collective system – effective, or whether nations are determined to pursue a selfish course.'[19]

Mr. Eden's prophecy proved correct.

Part Two
Opening Moves, Middle Game

'In my opinion it is the beginning of a long, and,
if we must judge from what has gone before, one of the
bloodiest and cruellest periods the World has ever
known.'

> General J. B. M. Hertzog,
> Prime Minister of the Union of South Africa,
> on the Abyssinian crisis, 4.9.35. (quoted
> Toynbee, 84).

'Mussolini has begun his conquest of Abyssinia. . . .
The Wilhelmstrasse is delighted. Either Mussolini will
stumble and get himself so heavily involved in
Africa that he will be greatly weakened in Europe,
whereupon Hitler can seize Austria, hitherto protected
by the Duce; or he will win, defying France and
Britain, and therefore be ripe for a tie-up with Hitler
against the Western Democracies. Either way Hitler
wins. The League has provided a sorry spectacle, and
its failure now, after the Manchurian débâcle,
certainly kills it. At Geneva they talk of sanctions.
It's a last hope."

> W. L. Shirer, Correspondent in Berlin,
> *Berlin Diary* (1941), 4.10.35.

'I dare say there are many honourable Members
here who know how to sail a boat. They all know
what a gybe is. It is a manoeuvre which in a strong
wind requires no little nerve and determination.
Incompetent or irresolute handling of the tiller may

easily lead to that most unpleasant of all experiences
– double gybe – when the boom swings right over
one way and back again. I have seen such a proceeding
result in an important member of the crew being sent
flying overboard. I have known it strain the whole
fabric of a vessel from main-mast to keel.'

L. S. Amery, House of Commons, 24.2.36.
(*Hansard*, c.103)

9

The League's machinery in operation (December 1934 to August 1935)

Fighting broke out at Wal-Wal on 5 December 1934.[1] The Italian Note of the 11th was 'crossed' by one from Abyssinia invoking the arbitration prescribed by the Italo-Ethiopian Treaty of 1928. The Italian answer to this said, in effect, that there was nothing to arbitrate about. On the 15th there was a telegram from Addis Ababa to Geneva alleging Italian air raids near Wal-Wal since the incident and drawing the Council's attention to the gravity of the situation. Thus was the League seized on a dispute in which one side had asked for arbitration, the other refused it. The matter was not, however, discussed at the December meeting of the Council, mainly occupied with the Saar plebiscite and a Hungarian-Yugoslav dispute.[2] Behind the scenes, however, M. René Massigli, Permanent Head of the French Foreign Ministry, went out of his way to invite Mr. Eden to listen to the Abyssinian delegate's tale of woe. 'It smells bad to me', said M. Massigli, 'like Manchuria'.[3]

The Abyssinian telegram of 15 December 1934 had not specifically asked for action by the League. On 3 January 1935, however, another telegram complained of Italian aggression at Gerlogubi (some 30 miles south-west of Wal-Wal) and specifically appealed for the application of Article 11 of the Covenant to the dispute. (This was the article under which hitherto all the League's actions in settling disputes had been taken.) The League Council met for its 84th session on 11 January. Britain was represented by Sir John Simon (initially) and Mr. Eden (throughout), France by Laval. There was Anglo-French pressure on the Abyssinian delegate, Tecle Hawariat, not to insist on the inclusion of the dispute in the agenda adopted on that day. Intensive secret negotiations followed and on the 19th the Secretary-General[4] announced to the Council an Italo-Abyssinian agreement to

85

negotiate directly (a procedure usually beneficial to the stronger of two Powers). Letters from Baron Aloisi, the Italian delegate, and M. Hawariat both expressed the intention of their respective Governments to prevent fresh 'incidents'. (The Abyssinian delegate was induced, most improperly, to forgo his right to take part in the Council's meeting.[5]) Baron Aloisi's letter stated that his Government did not regard the dispute 'as likely to affect the peaceful relations between the two countries. . . .' The naive could read into this a pledge by Italy not to let it do so.

At first sight this agreement seemed a genuine compromise. Abyssinia had dropped her right to insist on the Council discussing the dispute; Italy had dropped her previous contention that the dispute was not one to which the 1928 Treaty applied. However, the negotiations which followed, at Addis Ababa, showed that neither party was prepared to compromise on the substance of the dispute. Abyssinia's view was that the first question to be settled was that of the ownership of Wal-Wal, for – if it was Abyssinian – her forces were only acting in defence of Abyssinian territory on 5 December, no matter who fired the first shot. The Italian view was that Abyssinian aggression at Wal-Wal was clear and that, therefore, the reparation demanded for it on 11 December must precede the definition of the frontier. Moreover, until mid-March, Italy was insisting on the establishment of a neutral zone, although (as Eden told the Foreign Secretary on 26 February) there was 'nothing about a neutral zone in the letters of either party to the Council, nor in the terms of the Council resolution itself'.[6] This issue was finally, and usefully, disposed of by an Italo-Abyssinian agreement of 13 March for the creation of such a zone, six kilometres deep, in front of the Italian forces along a line Gerlogubi–Ado–Wal-Wal.

During February Abyssinia more than once suggested the setting-up of a Commission of Conciliation and Arbitration in the manner prescribed by Article 5 of the 1928 Treaty,[7] maintaining that this suggestion was in accordance with the Geneva agreement of 19 January 1935. On 8 March a Note to Italy made it clear that Abyssinia considered that direct bi-lateral negotiations had failed. To this Note Italy replied on 18 March, maintaining that the 1928 Treaty provided for resort to Article 5 only in the event of the complete failure of direct negotiation and that there had been no such failure. Abyssinia, however, had sent the previous day a further appeal to the League. This time the appeal was to Articles 10 and 15.

The Abyssinian Note asked the Council for 'full investigation and consideration, as provided in Article 15, pending the arbitration contemplated by the Treaty of 1928 and the Geneva agreement of 19 January 1935.' Moreover, a promise was made 'to accept any arbitral award immediately and unreservedly, and to act in accordance with the counsels and decisions of the League of Nations'. The Italian reply of 22 March denied that Abyssinia had 'vainly demanded arbitration' or that 'the phase of direct negotiations' was at an end, but went on to say that Italy had not, and never had had, any intention of evading resort to the procedure laid down in Article 5 of the 1928 Treaty. If direct negotiation broke down Italy was therefore willing 'to take steps forthwith with a view to the constitution of the Commission provided for'. In these circumstances Article 15 of the Covenant did not apply.

On 29 March Abyssinia pointed out that this attitude might prove 'the occasion of fresh delays in the pacific settlement of a very simple dispute. These delays must not be utilized for the continuation of military preparations and of despatches of troops and war munitions, as had been the case hitherto. Otherwise, once these preparations had been completed, nothing would be easier than to create incidents and, with the help of a press campaign, to find pretexts for aggression. Ethiopia possesses no military force comparable with that of her powerful neighbour. She has no newspapers, no means of propaganda to influence public opinion and to present all the circumstances, whatever they may be, in a light favourable to herself. To defend her rights, her only remedy is appeal to the League of Nations. She cannot therefore renounce this last resort for protecting her independence and the integrity of her territory'.[8]

Abyssinia therefore suggested, first, a time limit of 30 days for the constitution of the Arbitration Commission and, second, an agreement for the halting, throughout the whole period of negotiation and arbitration, of all military preparations. On 10 April (the day before the Stresa Conference)[9] Italy notified Geneva of her readiness to implement Article 5 of the 1928 Treaty, but made no mention of these two Abyssinian suggestions. On 15 April the League Council met again, but declined to

D

discuss the Italo-Abyssinian dispute until its next meeting in May, on the ground that both parties had agreed to adopt a procedure for peaceful settlement.[10] (There had been press reports that Italy would not be represented at this meeting of the Council if the dispute with Abyssinia were placed on the agenda.)[11] Laval said that Italy's agreement to activate Article 5 of the 1928 Treaty was, of itself, a guarantee that she would not use force. This was legally correct inasmuch as Article 5 proscribed it. The Abyssinian delegate pleaded in vain for an Italian promise to undertake no more military preparations pending the results of arbitration. Baron Aloisi dodged this question. Sir John Simon tried but failed to secure an agreement that the Arbitration Commission should be appointed and its terms of reference fixed before the Council meeting due on 20 May. By 17 April it was clear that Abyssinia and Italy had entirely different views about the terms of reference for the Commission. Abyssinia still maintained that the first question to be settled was that of the ownership of the Wal-Wal area, the responsibility for the fighting the second.

In the ensuing weeks difficulties arose about the appointment of arbitrators, two on each side. Only in mid-May did Italy nominate its two representatives and it then refused to accept the Abyssinian nomination of an American and a Frenchman. (Abyssinia argued that these two nominations were proof of her willingness to accept an impartial verdict.) When the Council met on 20 May the Commission of Conciliation and Arbitration had still not been constituted. The five weeks since the last meeting had been wasted.

As at the January meeting Britain and France 'leaned' on Abyssinia, not this time to prevent the Italo-Abyssinian dispute appearing as an item on the Council's agenda (that could not now be stopped) but to accept an agreement before that item was reached. Again, as at the January meeting, a compromise was reached. Abyssinia agreed to the Council once more postponing any discussion of the dispute; Italy agreed to waive her objection to the appointment of non-Abyssinian representatives to the Arbitration Commission and to the fixing of a time-table for its work. (Italy, however, refused a proposal that the Council should appoint a committee or *rapporteur* to follow the course of events and side-stepped a suggestion that the Council should decide itself to handle the dispute in the absence of any agreement on the completion of the time-table.) Accordingly on 25 May the Council decided to let the arbitral procedure go forward, but to meet again on 25 July if by that date the four arbitrators had agreed neither on 'the settlement of the dispute' nor, in that eventuality, on the appointment of a fifth arbitrator. On the other hand the Council was not to meet on 25 July if the four arbitrators had meanwhile agreed on the extension of the period of time allowed them to make their recommendations, but was to meet on 25 August if by then no settlement by means of arbitration had taken place. Italy again evaded an Abyssinian plea for the limitation and control of Italian military preparations in East Africa. 'By accepting the arbitration procedure', said Baron Aloisi, 'we have demonstrated our determination to respect the undertakings entered into by our two Governments.'[12] The next day Rome announced that the agreement at Geneva would not affect the mobilization and despatch of troops. The massive scale of Italian military preparations was increasingly obvious. It seemed decreasingly likely therefore that nothing would come of them even if the dispute arising from the Wal-Wal incident was peacefully settled. Meanwhile, Nature would ensure that the rainy season in Abyssinia would make war, but not preparations for it, impossible. Still, it was a gain that, as Professor Toynbee was to put it: 'The machinery for arbitration was now set in motion, and if it did not produce results within a given time the Council had bound itself to take action'.[13]

The Italo-Abyssinian Commission of Conciliation and Arbitration met for the first time at Milan on 6 June and the next day adjourned for three weeks for the collection of documents. It met again at Scheveningen on 25 June, but deadlock was announced on 9 July. The cause of the failure was a complete difference of view about the Commission's terms of reference. The issue involved was making a third appearance. The Abyssinian representatives argued that Baron Aloisi on 25 May had agreed that the interpretation of the treaties relating to the frontier was within the Commission's competence; the Italian representatives argued that all that was within its competence was the question of responsibility for the Wal-Wal and kindred incidents. The Abyssinian representatives thereupon proposed the appointment of a fifth arbitrator, but the Italian representatives argued that this could not settle the point at issue, which related to the Commission's terms of reference. Its failure to agree upon the appointment of a fifth arbitrator brought into play the League Council's decision of 25 May that, in the event of such a failure, it should meet again on 25 July.

The Council did not in fact meet till 31 July. Before the meeting Anglo-French pressure was again put on Abyssinia to moderate its demands and again Abyssinia was conciliatory, not to say compliant, agreeing:

1. to give up her previous insistence on the Commission's right to consider the line of the frontier;
2. to give up her request (made to the League on 19 June and hitherto ignored) for the posting of neutral observers in the frontier areas, and
3. to refrain from any formal request that the Council should discuss Italo-Abyssinian relations in general at the coming meeting.

When the Council met on 31 July it adopted its agenda and then adjourned for informal, i.e. secret, negotiations. These lasted for three days and nights and Litvinov, delegate of the fourth Great Power with a permanent seat on the Council, took part in them.

Two resolutions were adopted on 3 August. The first finally settled the long drawn-out difference of opinion about the terms of reference which had bedevilled Italo-Abyssinian discussion (whether by direct negotiation or by the Commission) of the Wal-Wal incident. It declared that 'the two parties did not agree that the Commission should examine frontier questions or give a legal interpretation of the agreements and treaties concerning the frontier'. The Commission was therefore not to found 'its decision on the opinion that the place at which the incident occurred' was 'under the sovereignty either of Italy or of Ethiopia'. It was, however, declared to be 'open to the Commission to take into consideration, without entering upon any discussion on the matter, the conviction that was held by the local authorities on either side as to the sovereignty over the place of the incident'. The resolution also noted that the two parties now agreed that the four arbitrators should choose a fifth and invited the two parties to report the results of the Commission's work to the Council not later than 4 September.

By the second resolution the Council decided 'to meet in any event on 4 September 1935, to undertake the general examination, in its various aspects, of the relations between Italy and Ethiopia'. This was an improvement on the decision of 25 May.

The first resolution was accepted by Italy; on the second, Aloisi (as on 25 May) abstained from voting.

The secret negotiations at Geneva, between 31 July and 3 August, also produced an agreement for a conference in the near future between the three signatories of the 1906 Treaty. This idea had first taken shape, not in a League context, but in a conversation between Hoare and Grandi on 5 July.[14]

Italy insisted on the exclusion of Abyssinia from this conference and on its not being held under the aegis of the League. Abyssinia accepted her exclusion under protest. Britain and France undertook to keep both the Council and Abyssinia informed of the course of the conference. It met in Paris between 15 and 18 August.[15] It could later be seen as a sinister foreshadowing of the conference held at Munich in September 1938, in that at neither conference was the country most concerned represented.

At Geneva on 3 August Italy again avoided any undertaking in any way to curb its military preparations. Professor Toynbee wrote (1936):

'Thus the upshot of the Council's meeting was an agreement for the resumption of arbitral procedure, on Italy's terms, for the settlement of a minor issue – the Wal-Wal incident; an agreement that the major issues should be handled outside the League framework by negotiation between France, Great Britain and Italy; and an agreement, which was neither accepted nor explicitly rejected by Italy, that the League should take up the dispute at a definite date, whatever stage it might have reached by then. The terms in which this last agreement was couched appeared to rule out the possibility of any further postponement of the Council's discussion after the 4th September, and on this point the Abyssinian representatives expressed great satisfaction. Monsieur Jèze declared that the Ethiopian Government hailed the Council's decision "with joy and gratitude", in the hope that a "full and general examination would enable the Council to establish, once and for all and on a solid basis, permanent, friendly and trustful relations between Ethiopia and Italy" '.[16]

10

The League's machinery in operation (August to October 1935)

The ground had thus at last, and very late (by 3 August 1935) been cleared for a settlement of the original occasion for the Italo-Abyssinian dispute, the Wal-Wal incident (of 5 December 1934). On 8 August 1935, M. K. Politis ('an ingenious Greek advocate, well versed in international affairs'[1]) was appointed as the fifth member of the Commission for Conciliation and Arbitration. On 19 August it met in Paris and on 3 September it rendered a unanimous award. It is clear that, had there been goodwill and reasonable expedition on the part of all concerned, the dispute about the Wal-Wal incident could easily have been settled before the end of January 1935, rather than at the beginning of September.

On 3 September 1935 it was found that neither Government was responsible for the incident on 5 December 1934; that the incidents which followed that at Wal-Wal 'were of an accidental character'; and that 'no international responsibility need be involved' in respect of other incidents unconnected with the original one, which 'were for the most part not serious and of very ordinary occurrence in the region in which they took place'.

The whole Wal-Wal affair was thus relegated to the dustbin into which it could, and should, have been promptly put. The Council of the League of Nations now had to honour its obligation 'to undertake the general examination, in its various aspects, of the relations between Italy and Ethiopia'. (It was the first item on its agenda for its meeting on 4 September). In other words, the League ostrich had now to take its head out of the sands of the Ogaden desert and direct its attention to the fundamental reality of the situation, the plain imminence of unprovoked Italian agression against Abyssinia. It is impossible to point to any precise date by which this fundamental reality had become plain. There is evidence that it was more than plain to Sir John Simon as early as January;[2] the first large-scale military preparations by Italy were certainly known in London by mid-February.[3] The 'ostrich' epithet had become justified long before September. And, if epithets of this kind are to be bandied, it is fair to describe the attitudes of Britain and France to Italy's diplomacy and military preparations throughout this first period of the crisis, until May at any rate,[4] as reminiscent of monkeys (not stupid animals) closing their ears, eyes, and tongues to the possibility of evil.

On the other hand, some allowance must be made for the fact, already mentioned,[5] that the League's machinery was not geared to operate against an expansionist State superficially involved in a dispute but in reality bent on aggression. Allowance must too be made for the skill with which Italy had played its diplomatic cards between 5 December 1934 and 3 September 1935. In the course of events at Geneva during that period a regular pattern can be discerned. Before each meeting of the League's Council an intransigent attitude was struck, at each meeting a seemingly conciliatory one. One cannot help admiring the diplomatic technique, the combination of dalliance and duplicity which spun out the politicians' proceedings whilst the soldiers' preparations went ahead. This was, however, the kind of diplomacy which in the long run gives diplomacy itself a bad name. The net result of Italian diplomacy during all this period had been effectively to keep the whole affair away from the League, but – be it noted – in this endeavour they had been aided by Britain and France.

On 4 September the Italian mask was suddenly (from a propaganda point of view too suddenly) thrown off. Aloisi made it clear that the settlement of the Wal-Wal incident had no significance for Italy. He put before the Council a very long memorandum in which it was argued that Abyssinia was a barbarous State, unquestionably Italy's enemy, with a signature not to be trusted, a State which should never have been made a Member of the League and was no longer entitled to rights as such or as a signatory of the 1928 Treaty. In particular it was argued that:

1. Abyssinia had broken treaties;
2. had committed outrages against Italians;
3. was no longer a State as she had been under Menelik.
4. His Empire, however, had been a cruel and oppressive

94

colonialism imposed on a majority, whose liberation was a duty for civilization.

5. Abyssinia's promise to abolish slavery and put down the slave trade had been broken, the Emperor himself being a large-scale slave-owner.

6. Contrary to the 1930 Treaty arms sold to him had been retailed to his followers.

It was also said that Italy was 'in most urgent and recognized need of colonial expansion'.

The presentation of this document was another clever diplomatic move, in that Abyssinia had come to the meeting as an accuser, but at once and without warning found herself the accused. Moreover, her delegates (in all such technical ways she was inevitably and always weak) were unable to produce a prompt defence to so many and so complex charges.[6]

On the other hand, whatever the propagandist merits of the document, it was easy to see the fundamental flaw in it. Even if all its charges were true, it was not for Italy to put matters right on her own and by force of arms. On 3 September Abyssinia asked the Council explicitly for prompt action under Article 15, Section 3, of the Covenant, as well as under Article 10. On 6 September, despite strenuous Italian opposition and Italian abstention when it came to the vote, the Council appointed a Committee of Five 'to make a general examination of Italo-Ethiopian relations and to seek for a settlement'.[7] It was a considerable advance that the Council had completely dropped the fiction that it was concerned with a 'dispute' arising out of an 'incident'.

Mention must be made of a speech made at the Council's sitting on 5 September (the only speech in addition to that of M. Jèze for Abyssinia) by the Soviet delegate, Litvinov. He had been in the chair at the Council's meeting in May and August and took, as we have seen,[8] a principal part in the negotiations leading to the compromise agreement of 3 August. Now he made the first open criticisms of Italian policy to have been uttered by a delegate at Geneva since the opening of the crisis. His statement was supported, in obscure language, by a Mexican delegate at the Council's sitting on 6 September, the first instance of any expression of view on the crisis by a delegate from any Power other than a Great one. The Russian sentiments would have aroused more attention if they had come from some other source and, in any event, Litvinov's speech was quickly over-shadowed by another, making no overt criticisms of Italian policy but no less firm in upholding League principles.

The scene at Geneva now shifts from the Council to the Assembly, which met for its sixteenth regular annual session on 9 September. It elected M. Benes, Foreign Minister of Czechoslovakia, as its President.[9] It was a wise choice. He managed the important and complex business of this Assembly with great skill. His first move was to dispose of routine business briskly and on the morning of 11 September he called for the opening of the customary general debate. The first delegate presenting himself at the rostrum was the chief British delegate, Sir Samuel Hoare, His Britannic Majesty's Principal Secretary of State for Foreign Affairs. Early in August he had been immobilized by acute pain in one foot and had retired to bed in Norfolk.[10] There he began to meditate about the speech he was now to deliver. He decided that a fresh approach was needed and to try, therefore, by an appeal for free access to raw materials (in ways discussed by the World Economic Conference of 1931) to move the issues from political to economic realms. He thought, not unreasonably, that Italy's real needs were economic. He decided also to base upon his fresh approach through economics 'a revivalist appeal to the Assembly. At best, it might well start a new chapter of League recovery; at worst, it might deter Mussolini by a display of League fervour. If there was any element of bluff in it, it was a moment when bluff was not only legitimate but inescapable'.[11]

That cannot be accepted; Mussolini was not a man to be deterred by 'a display of League fervour'. He was, as Lord Avon writes, 'a man to practise bluff, not to be its victim at faltering hands'.[12] It is hard to believe that he would have gone to war with Britain over an oil sanction or even a British cutting of his communications with Abyssinia; he made Hoare – and Laval – think that he might. If Hoare intended to deter Mussolini he had to make it clear that force, economic and military, would be used. He was not obliged to make a speech creating a false impression that it might be.

There was a measure of collective responsibility for this speech. Walter Runciman, President of the Board of Trade, had given his approval to the paragraph about raw materials; Sir Robert Vansittart, Permanent Under-Secretary at the Foreign Office, had helped with the first draft of the speech as a whole; Neville Chamberlain, Chancellor of the Exchequer, helped throughout with the text.[13] Baldwin and Chamberlain dined with Hoare on 5 September and it seems unlikely that its main lines were not discussed at that dinner party.[14] Hoare submitted the final text to Baldwin at Chequers and it was there, rather casually, approved by him.[15] But did Hoare confide to any of these gentlemen his thoughts about revivalism and bluff?

On 9 September Hoare flew to Geneva in a 'military machine with devices that made it possible for me to keep on my back during the flight'.[16] Only on that day was the speech read by the Minister for League of Nations Affairs and his Parliamentary Under-Secretary (Lord Cranborne).[17] Most of the next day was spent in discussions with Laval, whom Hoare now met for the first time. In due course more will be said about these important discussions,[18] but for the moment only one point need be recorded, i.e. Hoare's opinion that Laval had said nothing 'to make me change my carefully prepared speech'.[19] One or two minor amendments were made to meet criticisms from Eden and Cranborne.[20] So the next morning the orator hobbled towards the rostrum, limping on one leg and supported by a stick. 'As I proceeded with my speech', he wrote later, 'I became conscious of the fact that I was interesting my hearers'.[21]   What interested his hearers was not, as he had originally intended, the economics in the speech but the politics. The key passage proved to be the peroration. Its effect was further deepened by the calm, deliberate, and precise mode of utterance. It ran:

'In conformity with its precise and explicit obligations, the League stands, and my country stands with it, for the collective maintenance of the Covenant in its entirety, and particularly for steady and collective resistance to all acts of unprovoked aggression. The attitude of the British nation in the last few weeks has clearly demonstrated the fact that this is no variable and unreliable sentiment, but a principle of international conduct to which they and their Government hold with firm, enduring and universal persistence.'

These were the words which most interested the audience to which they were addressed; these were words which rang round the world; these were words which made at any rate one statesman of great experience in international affairs (Paul Hymans of Belgium) say: 'The British have decided to stop Mussolini, even if that means using force'.[22] They were widely interpreted as meaning just that. The impression thus made was heightened, and the correctness of M. Hymans' interpretation confirmed, by the arrival at Gibraltar on 17 September, detached from the Home Fleet, of two battle cruisers, three cruisers, and six destroyers.[23]

It is true that in the passage just quoted from the speech of 11 September, Sir Samuel put, in the phrase 'collective maintenance of the Covenant', particular emphasis on the word 'collective' by pausing and repeating it.[24] It is true also that in another key passage he said:

'If the burden is to be borne, it must be borne collectively. If risks are to be run, they must be run by all. The security of the many cannot be ensured solely by the efforts of a few, however powerful they may be. On behalf of His Majesty's Government in the United Kingdom, I can say that, in spite of these difficulties, that Government will be second to none in its intention to fulfil, within the measure of its capacity, the obligations which the Covenant lays upon it.'

This passage importantly qualifies preceding ones and later, as we shall see, it became the burden of the British Government's song that, whilst it was ready to play its part, others were not. We shall see also that that was not true. Moreover, 'second to none in its intention to fulfil' is an unsatisfactory substitute, in the case of the leading League Power, for 'will be found to take the lead in fulfilling' or some such phrase. Nonetheless, Lord Avon, in 1962, by then deeply experienced in international affairs, after quoting M. Hymans' summation of this historic speech, adds: 'To this day I consider that this was the only possible interpretation of the speech, if words meant what they said.'[25]

This seems to go too far. The words themselves cannot be interpreted to mean that Britain had decided to stop Mussolini by force. The fact remains that members of a sophisticated audience took them to mean that and that many people all over the world, sophisticated and otherwise, took them to mean that.[26]

Churchill, who was on holiday at the time, later wrote: 'I remember being stirred by this speech when I read it in the Riviera sunshine. It aroused everyone, and reverberated throughout the United States. It united all those forces in Britain which stood for a fearless combination of righteousness and strength. Here at least was a policy. If only the orator had realized what tremendous powers he held unleashed in his hand at that moment he might indeed for a while have led the world'.[27] Gilbert Murray thought Hoare's speech magnificent and that it could not have been better. He wired his congratulations and gratitude.[28]

Sir Samuel, in 1954, by then Viscount Templewood, put himself on record as puzzled by the effect his speech had had and is concerned to play down that effect. (Neither he nor his colleagues were thus concerned at the time.) He describes how: 'Wondering what it was that had so greatly excited [his audience] I read it through again and again later in the day, and could find nothing in it, except the passages about free access to raw materials, that I had not said time after time in the House of Commons without creating any notable reaction.... Was there ever a better example of the fact that in nine cases out of ten it is the occasion that makes the speech and not the speech the occasion...? When I spoke to a tired House of Commons at the end of the session, my words about real collective security made no great impression. When I repeated them at Geneva, before a cosmopolitan audience faced with an international crisis, they reverberated over the whole world. Even so, only Simon amongst my colleagues seemed to realize the impression that they had made.'[29]

It seems that we must forgive Sir Samuel Hoare for not knowing what he said. But that is hard to believe. Words are the stock in trade of experienced politicians. No one knows better how to choose words to create an impression which cannot be confirmed by a careful study of a text. Was not this precisely what Hoare did when he set about making 'a revivalist appeal'? It is at any rate patent that he executed very complicated figures on very thin ice; it is remarkable that it held for as long as it did.

In the general debate initiated by the British Foreign Secretary, his line received whole-hearted support from the representatives of Czechoslovakia, Finland, Greece, Haiti, the Irish Free State, the Netherlands, New Zealand, Norway, Portugal, Rumania, South Africa, Sweden, Turkey, and Yugoslavia. More

99

cautious support came from the representatives of Australia, Belgium, Canada, and, last but not least, France. Litvinov 'followed a separate road to the same destination'.[30] There were also some significant failures to participate.

The debate in the Assembly closed on 14 September. On the 18th the Council's Committee of Five made its recommendations. They amounted to a scheme for international assistance to Abyssinia under League auspices plus an Anglo-French offer to give her, out of their own territory, a port on the Red Sea. This scheme set out a rational solution of the realities of Abyssinia's problems at that time and would have met Italy's real needs in Abyssinia as opposed to Mussolini's dreams of war, conquest, and glory.[31] In a world of rational men this Report would have been instantly accepted. It was accepted in principle by Abyssinia on 23 September, but had already been rejected by Italy as 'quite unacceptable' on the 19th. That rejection was as quick and brusque as the Italian rejection of the Anglo-French proposals of August. In these circumstances the Committee of Five announced on 24 September the failure of its work. Mussolini, we may note, giving his views on its proposals to *The Daily Mail* had already commented:

'In the scheme of an international administration and gendarmerie it seems that Italy is not to be represented at all. The suggestion apparently is that all the 200,000 Italian troops in East Africa should be brought home and told that they have been sent out there for an excursion trip. That certainly will not be done in any case.'[32]

On 26 September the Council appointed a Committee of Thirteen, that is to say of all its members with the exception of the one, Italy, which was a party to the dispute, to draft the report called for by the application of Article 15, Section 4. The Italian forces moved more quickly than this Committee. They violated the frontiers of Abyssinia on 3 October.

11

The League's machinery in operation (October to December 1935)

On 5 October it was agreed that a vote on the report of the Committee of Thirteen would be taken two days later and that before then a Committee of Six would report on the latest developments. All this was in a private session. In a public session on the 5th Aloisi claimed that the Italian invasion was 'within the framework of the Covenant' as it was 'merely an immediate and necessary reply to an act of provocation', that is to say Abyssinian general mobilization on 28 September. M. Hawariat, for Abyssinia, claimed that Italy's resort to war had *'ipso facto* brought about the consequences laid down in Article 16, paragraph 1'.[1]

Aloisi's argument had been anticipated by an Italian message to the same effect sent to the Council on 3 October. The argument was double-edged; if it was right for Italy to go to war in response to Abyssinian mobilization it would have been right for Abyssinia to have done the same at any time since the start, at the beginning of the year, of the massive Italian preparations for war.

The Council met again on 7 October, now having before it the reports of both the Committee of Thirteen (mainly on questions of fact and law) and the Committee of Six. The latter document ended with a succinct statement: '. . . the Committee has come to the conclusion that the Italian Government has resorted to war in disregard of its obligations under Article 12 of the Covenant of the League of Nations'.

Both reports were adopted unanimously, the sole adverse, but not valid, vote being Italy's. (She had hoped for an adverse vote from Poland, always something of the Council's rogue elephant).[2] The Assembly, which had merely adjourned on 28 September instead of closing its session in the normal way, now met again on 9 October. In the debate which ensued on the 10th and 11th the only dissents from the Council's findings of the 7th came from Italy herself and three client-states, Austria, Hungary, and Albania. These three States announced their refusal to take part in sanctions against Italy. The other 50 members represented at this Assembly accepted the Council's findings, either explicitly or tacitly. 'Fifty nations against one' became Mussolini's propagandist slogan for domestic consumption, and as such not unsuccessful.

The Assembly adjourned on the 11th, having the previous day voted for the creation of a Co-Ordination Committee which was in effect a standing conference of the 50 States which had agreed that Italy had violated the Covenant. It now fell to these States to implement the provisions of Article 16, Clause 1. The new Committee's title expresses exactly the function which it was to perform, the co-ordination of the sanctions now to be imposed on the Covenant-breaker. The Committee met for the first time at 10.30 a.m. on 11 October. It appointed what was in effect an executive committee, which met for the first time at 3.00 p.m. on the 12th, and came to be known as the Committee of Eighteen or Sanctions Committee.

This Committee's Proposal No. 1, for the raising of any arms embargo against Abyssinia and the imposition of one on Italy, was adopted the same afternoon.[3] Proposal No. 2, for financial sanctions, was adopted on the 14th. Proposal No. 3, for the prohibition of Italian imports; No. 4 for the prohibition of certain exports to Italy; and No. 5, on the organization of mutual support, were adopted on the 19th. In nine days the Committee had created, in outline, a new world of international sanctions; now it was to rest from its labours, adjourning until the 31st to await the response to these specific proposals of the States which had agreed to sanctions in principle.

At 6.00 p.m. on the 31st the Chairman of the Co-Ordination Committee was able to report to his colleagues that 'fifty Governments had prohibited, or were about to prohibit, the export to Italy of arms, munitions, and war material, in conformity with Proposal No. 1 . . . forty-nine Governments had already taken action on Proposal No. 2, or had declared their readiness to take such action. With regard to proposals Nos. 3 and 4 for the prohibition of imports from Italy and the embargo on certain exports to Italy, the replies received from 48 Governments already warranted the conclusion that these proposals had met with very extensive agreement on the part of Governments. Lastly, thirty-nine replies had been received to Proposal No. 5'.[4] On 2 November the Co-Ordination Committee voted for Proposals 2, 3 and 4 being put into force on the 18th.

We must note that the passing of this resolution was followed by a general discussion to which important delegates found it worth their while to contribute. First came Laval, who changed the subject:

'We have all – and I should like to emphasize this point on the very day on which we are taking an important decision – another duty to fulfil, one that is dictated by the spirit of the Covenant. We must endeavour to seek, as speedily as possible, an amicable settlement of the dispute. The French Government and the United Kingdom Government are agreed that their co-operation shall be exerted also in this sphere. This duty is particularly imperative for France, which, on the 7th January last, signed a treaty of friendship with Italy. I shall therefore stubbornly pursue my attempts ... to seek for elements that might serve as a basis for negotiations ... without the slightest intention, however, of putting the results into final shape outside the League.'

Hoare spoke second, giving 'full approval' to these words. Van Zeeland, from Belgium, then, as Professor Toynbee puts it, 'made haste to say his transparently appointed lines'.[5] These amounted to a suggestion that the League should entrust to Britain and France the task of seeking 'the elements of a solution which the three parties at issue – the League, Italy, and Ethiopia – might find it possible to accept'. The Committee 'took note of the desire expressed by the Belgium delegate'. Thus – the Election campaign in Britain already under way – it had been announced on 18 October – did Britain and France obtain from the League what mandate they had to continue doing what they had already been doing.[6] This mandate had no legal validity, but it did correspond with the realities of the situation.

On 6 November the Sanctions Committee arranged for an experts committee to study the working of sanctions. This committee reported on 12 December. Its statistical findings on the operation of the five Proposals (as at 11 December) can be set out in tabular form:

No. of Proposal	No. of Governments accepting	No. of Governments enforcing
1	52	50
2	52	47
3	50	43
4	51	45
5	46	Does not apply

Three Members (Albania, Austria, and Hungary) were taking no action under Article 16. (The Peace Treaties in any case prohibited the export of arms from Austria and Hungary.) Three Members not represented at the sixteenth Assembly were nonetheless taking action : Dominica was co-operating fully in the application of sanctions, Guatemala had accepted the Proposals in principle but had not yet implemented them, and Salvador had implemented Proposal 3 which alone had any relevance in her case. Luxembourg and Switzerland were operating embargoes on arms exports to Abyssinia and Italy alike because, in their view, this followed from their position as permanently neutral States. The dependent territories of sanctionist States were all applying sanctions with the exception of Spanish Morocco and Spitzbergen, ice-bound in December in any case. The first State to put into force (on 30 October) all the sanctions proposed by the Committee of Eighteen was South Africa.[7]

Only one non-member State, Egypt, applied against Italy the same sanctions as were applied by Members.[8] Germany had not effectively been a Member of the League since October 1933, when she gave notice of withdrawal (technically her membership only lapsed on 19 October 1935),[9] but was unexpectedly helpful to its purposes at this juncture.[10] Germany had, like Luxembourg and Switzerland, imposed an embargo on arms exports to both belligerents. Mr. Alexander Loveday, Director of the Financial Section of the Secretariat, who was acting Secretary to the Co-Ordination Committee, told the Committee on 6 November of information orally and unofficially communicated about the attitude of the German Government, viz., that it was 'at the present moment troubled by the fact of a number of private persons – German and foreign – purchasing all sorts of material in Germany apparently with a view to exporting them at a profit to the belligerent countries. The Government did not wish this to happen' and would 'in the very next few days issue laws with a view to controlling and, if necessary, stopping such purchases and exports for the purpose of preventing private profiteering'.[11] This was done on 9 November.[12]

Such was the system of sanctions on 12 December 1935, a date not only significant in their history but significant also, alas, in a parallel chapter of history which was to render them futile. If, however, we consider the efficacy of sanctions as such at that date, the first point to note is that they were not in full accord with Article 16, Clause 1. This read:

'Should any Member of the League resort to war in disregard of its covenants under Articles 12, 13, or 15, it shall *ipso facto* be deemed to have committed an act of war against all other Members of the League, which hereby undertake immediately to subject it to the severance of all trade or financial relations, the prohibition of all intercourse between their nationals and the nationals of the covenant-breaking State, and the prevention of all financial, commercial or personal intercourse between the nationals of the covenant-breaking State and the nationals of any other State, whether a member of the League or not'.

Working backwards through this text, the League's members had obviously done nothing whatsoever to prevent 'all financial, commercial or personal intercourse' between Italians and non-Italians, whether nationals of a League Member or of a non-Member.[13] Moreover, the sanctionist States had done nothing whatsoever to prohibit all intercourse between their nationals and Italians. Their nationals were still free, for example, to take holidays in Italy. More important and more significant, although Italy had, according to Article 16, committed an act of war against all other Members of the League, not one of them had declared war on, or even severed diplomatic relations with, Italy or, apparently, even thought of doing so. Finally, and most important, such severance of trade and financial relations as had been effected could only be called 'immediate' by stretching the ordinary meaning of the word, and had certainly not been complete.

The sanctionist States, however, cannot be seriously blamed for thus falling short of action in accord with the letter of Article 16. At the very start of the League's history it had been realized, by the second Assembly, that this would be impossible. That Assembly, therefore, passed, in October 1921, seven resolutions (not legally binding) to serve as 'rules of guidance' in the implementation of Article 16, Clause 1. The purpose of these resolutions was to give the Council a discretion in the implementation of Article 16, Clause 1, similar to that expressly conferred upon it by Article 16, Clause 2. Specifically it was contemplated that:

1. A Co-Ordination Committee would be set up.
2. While some Members would be expected to impose a range of economic sanctions others would be exempted from this in whole or in part.
3. Sanctions would be imposed by stages.
4. The recommended plan of economic action might stop short of the complete severance of economic intercourse prescribed by the text of Article 16, Clause 1.

In the event, the procedure followed in October and November 1935 in imposing sanctions, and the system of sanctions then set up, owed more to the 1921 resolutions than to the text of the Covenant itself.

In assessing the efficacy of sanctions as at 12 December 1935, the second point to be made, in allowing for their inadequacy, is that nothing of the kind had ever been attempted before. There were 'rules of guidance' dating from 1921 (one should pause to pay a tribute to the foresight of those who devised them), but there was only one piece of guidance from past experience, the organization in 1934 of an embargo on the export of arms to the two belligerents in the Chaco War, Bolivia and Paraguay. The theory of this embargo was that, as neither belligerent manufactured any arms, its imposition would bring the war to an end. In practice, it did not do so.[14]

In the light of these considerations the sanctionist States deserve retrospective congratulations on what they achieved

between 10 October, when the Co-Ordination Committee first
met, and 12 December, when the experts reported on the results
of its activities. Still more are they to be congratulated on what
they achieved between 11 October and 18 November, on which
latter date Proposals 2, 3 and 4 came formally into force. They
could hardly have moved more quickly. We have seen how the
Co-Ordination Committee first met the day before the Assembly
itself adjourned; how its executive committee, the Sanctions
Committee, first met the day after the first meeting of its parent
body; how its first recommendation was made the same afternoon; how the initial structure of recommendations was complete
by 19 October. There had been some very efficient 'contingency
planning' and the contingency planners deserve their fair share of
praise.

We must, too, give credit to the States concerned for adopting
and enforcing the Co-Ordination Committee's recommendations
for economic sanctions at a time when the world was recovering
from the greatest of all economic depressions. This meant that the
economic sacrifices to be made, in any case great, would be
greater than if made in times economically more normal. (The
British Cabinet minutes of the time show a constant pre-occupation with the adverse effects on the South Wales coal-mining
industry of the banning of coal exports to Italy.) These sacrifices,
moreover, were bound to be greater in some cases than in others
and to an extent which no scheme for mutual support could fully
redress.

There can be no doubt that the speed and effectiveness of the
Co-Ordination Committee's work owed much to strong convic-
tions, on the parts of Governments and peoples, of its righteousness. A spirit of devotion to the principles of the League was
active in the world, if only because the consequences of a second
'Manchuria' were all too clear. It is still distressing to read the
speeches of British Ministers which showed no recognition of the
sacrifices made in the League's cause by other countries or even
implied that our support of the League in this supreme crisis of its
history was held back by the unwillingness of others to help.[15]
On the other hand, it can be recorded that Eden was the pace-
setter in the work of the Sanctions Committee. In the Assembly
debate in mid-October he had said: 'Since it is our duty to take
action, it is essential that such action should be prompt'.[16] He

held this principle clearly at the front of his mind at the first meeting of the Committee of Eighteen when he extricated it 'from the rut of a judicial debate'[17] and put forward what became Proposal 1. At the second meeting he initiated what became Proposal 3 and successfully resisted a suggestion that it should go to a technical sub-committee. He maintained that that might mean a long lapse of time before it came back to the full Committee and that what was required was not 'any technical elaboration whatsoever' but an 'admittedly very difficult political decision'.[18] At the third meeting he proposed the date of 31 October as that on which the Committee's recommendations should be put into operation.[19] At the sixth meeting he again suggested a date (29 October)[20] for the reassembly of the Co-Ordination Committee itself. (The Sanctions Committee in fact voted for 31 October.) In these activities anyone who has knowledge of any committee's proceedings sees the character of a man who wants 'to get things done' and knows how to set about it.[21]

Praise of Eden's leadership of the Sanctions Committee and of its work is not to say that it could not have pulled the noose tighter or that its own members did not at the time realize this. On 19 October Madariaga of Spain raised the question of extending the list of commodities forbidden, under Proposal 4, to be exported to Italy. He argued that it was illogical for that list to include iron ore and scrap iron, the raw materials for iron and steel and not include the finished products, iron and steel themselves. To this it was answered by other members of the Committee that the idea had been to include only products controlled by members of the League. It was for this reason that iron ore – and raw rubber – had been included and iron, steel, and the products of rubber excluded. Mr. W. A. Riddell, of Canada, supported Madariaga's argument.[22] For the sake of expedition the list was, on 19 October, voted as it stood, but on 2 November Madariaga raised again the question of adding iron to the list. Mr. Riddell again intervened and formally proposed the addition of coal, iron, steel *and* petroleum and its derivatives.[23] On 6 November the Committee of Eighteen adopted Mr. Riddell's proposal, somewhat expanded, as its Proposal No. 4A. The last paragraph of its resolution ran :

'If the replies received by the Committee to the present proposal and the information at its disposal warrant it, the Committee of Eighteen will propose to Governments a date for bringing into force the measures mentioned above'.[24]

Thus did the question of the 'oil sanction' enter history. The importance of Proposal 4A was not immediately appreciated in a Great Britain where an Election campaign was at its height (polling was due on 14 November). Indeed it is not clear that the Sanctions Committee itself, in its first discussions of this Proposal, fully grasped the importance of what it was doing. Nor was the alarm immediately sounded in Italy. By 19 November, however, a report that the Committee's Chairman was summoning an early meeting to consider the practicability of an oil sanction caused a reaction in the Italian press which showed that by then it was realized in Italy that this sanction, unlike those hitherto adopted, might cripple the Italian campaign. In 1935 West European Armies and Navies were already more petrol-propelled than not, their Air Forces of course wholly so. On 18 October the Italian Commander-in-Chief had reported to the Duce that he had only two months' supply of benzine for his Army.[25]

On 22 November it was officially announced that the Sanctions Committee was to meet on the 29th to discuss the implementation of Proposal 4A.

What was all the more alarming to Italy was the tag tied to that Proposal, the suggestion, invariably demonstrating that the proposers of any resolution 'mean business', that a date should be fixed for its implementation. What pressure (if any) Mussolini now put on Laval we do not know. Perhaps the latter would in any case have acted as he did, having regard to French national interests as he saw them. What we do know is that Laval proceeded to delay the next meeting of the Sanctions Committee. On 25 November he telephoned the Chairman to say that he was anxious himself to attend the next meeting but could not attend on the 29th because of Parliamentary engagements in Paris. (It must be remembered that since June he had been Prime Minister as well as Foreign Minister.)[26] He therefore requested a postponement and the Chairman agreed that the Committee should not meet on the 29th but also said that, on that date, the date of its next meeting would be fixed. Italian pressure was kept up, indeed stepped up, by an announcement on the 27th, in vague terms, of troop movements being made because of the threat of an oil sanction. On the 29th Laval, it seems, telephoned the Chairman again to ask that the date for the next meeting should not be earlier than 11 December. The Chairman is said to have consulted the British Government and, finding them acquiescent, agreed that the date should be 12 December.[27] At any rate it was announced at Geneva on 29 November that this would be the date of the next meeting and on the same day it was announced in Rome that there had been no movements of Italian troops towards the French frontiers.[28] Presumably this was Laval's payment for delaying the crucial meeting for nearly a fortnight.

Meanwhile, the Members of the League had been responding to Proposal 4A. By 12 December, when the Sanctions Committee of Eighteen did at last meet for its third session, ten Members had agreed to prohibit the export of oil to Italy. These ten were: Argentina, Czechoslovakia, Finland, India, Irak, the Netherlands, New Zealand, Rumania, Siam and the U.S.S.R. No reply had been received from either Britain or France, although the British Cabinet had agreed on the principle as early as 9 October.[29] But four of the ten (Irak, the Netherlands – including her East Indian Colonies – Rumania, and the U.S.S.R.) between them supplied 74.3 per cent of Italy's supplies of oil. The big question was plainly whether if, by League action, Italy lost virtually three-quarters of her oil supplies these losses would be substantially offset by increasing her imports from non-Members. There would be no technical difficulty in doing so; the question was political – would non-Members, especially the U.S.A., join in a League embargo? In 1934 Italy imported 6.4 per cent of her oil from the U.S.A. For the first nine months of 1935 the percentage was 6.3; in the last quarter it rose to 17.8.

On 30 October 1935 President Roosevelt had re-affirmed the American policy of neutrality but had gone on to say:

'However, in the course of the war, tempting trade opportunities may be offered to our people to supply materials which would prolong the war. I do not believe that the American people will wish for the abnormally increased profits that temporarily might be secured by greatly extending our trade in such materials; nor would they wish the struggles on the battlefield to be prolonged because of the profits accruing to a comparatively small number of American citizens'.[30]

On 15 November 1935 Mr Hull said:

'The American people is entitled to know that there are certain commodities, such as oil, copper, trucks, tractors, scrap iron and scrap steel, which are essential war materials although not actually "arms, ammunition, or implements of war" ... and that, according to recent Government trade reports, a considerably increased amount of these are being exported for war purposes. This class of trade is directly contrary to the policy of the Government as announced in official statements of the President and Secretary of State as also it is contrary to the general spirit of the recent Neutrality Act'.[31]

On 21 November Mr. Ickes, Secretary of the Interior and Federal Oil Administrator, called upon the American oil industry to suspend shipments to the Italians by its own voluntary act. On the 22nd Mr. Hull declared that an abnormal increase in the export of certain goods might force the Administration to conclude that these goods were essential war materials.[32]

It seems that in November 1935 the U.S. Administration was realizing that the increased American exports to Italy of war materials, especially oil, was not a trade to be morally exhorted out of existence and was moving to some action to render it ineffective or illegal.[33] At this juncture, however, an unfavourable impression was made upon American public opinion by the announcement of the postponement of the Sanctions Committee's meeting, planned for the 29th, to discuss the oil sanction. A still worse impression was made by the Hoare-Laval plan, accounts of which began to appear in the American press on 10 December.[34]

In mid-December 1935 the League's handling of the Abyssinian crisis could be seen to have had two phases; the first (from December 1934 to August 1935) in which the League had acted feebly, hesitantly, and slowly; the second (from September 1935 to mid-December) in which it had acted decisively, quickly and vigorously. In other words, the League's machinery had seemed to work badly up to the end of August, well from the beginning of September. The reasons for these appearances are to be found in the realities of Great Power politics. Two operations had, in fact, been proceeding simultaneously: the operation of the League's machinery, for the most part in public, and the operation of 'pre-League' diplomacy, for the most part in private – though the veil had been momentarily raised from the latter at Geneva on 2 November.[35] In mid-December the two operations became inextricably and publicly interlocked. The particular act which made it plain for all to see that two operations had been proceeding throughout and were now inextricably interlocked caused an explosion which illuminated, to say the least, the realities of the situation as a whole. A sheet of flame in a murky atmosphere has many disadvantages, but it does enable one to see a few things more clearly.

12

The Great Powers
(December 1934 to August 1935)

We have seen[1] how Massigli, by profession connoisseur of the bouquets of decomposing international situations, told Eden in mid-December 1934, that the Abyssinia one smelt of Manchuria. Laval was called in to the meeting at Geneva at which this comparison was made. Was it, however, in the front of his mind when, in the first week of January, he went to Rome for the meeting with Mussolini from which issued the agreement of 7 January 1935?[2] It would be pardonable if it were not; on Eden, by his own subsequent account, the full seriousness of the situation did not impinge till late February.[3] Certainly Laval, having made his anti-German agreements on 7 January, was not anxious to put them in the smallest degree at risk, when the League Council met on the 11th, by 'making difficulties' with Italy about Abyssinia. This substantially explains why the cracks were then papered over. Sir John Simon, in Geneva at this time, was impressed by Abyssinia's 'very conciliatory and constructive attitude'. His proposals for a settlement of the Wal-Wal dispute were, however, brushed aside by Mussolini on 14 January.[4] One British diplomat recalls Simon saying to him at this time: 'You realize, don't you, that the Italians intend to take Abyssinia?'[5]

On 29 January a Counsellor at the Italian Embassy in London (Vitetti) called at the Foreign Office for an informal conversation and, in the course of it, let it be known that Italian interest in the Horn of Africa was quickening and that agreement on its nature and course had been reached with France. This studied casualness in approaching Britain was in marked contrast with the methods by which the agreement with France had been arrived at. Maybe this was another instance of the technique of leaving a controversial question in Limbo for fear that a precise question might produce a wrong answer.[6] Mussolini, at this time, had no reason to anticipate British opposition to an Abyssinian adventure, but he had put himself in a position where he could say that he had given fair warning of his intentions in strict accord with both his treaty obligations and with his generally friendly relations with Britain. Sir John Simon, however, had been given a chance in return to warn that an Abyssinian adventure would severely damage those relations. In spite of what he had recently said to Mr. Thompson, he decided that, no precise question having been asked, no answer of any kind was needed.[7]

On 31 January Flandin, the French Premier, and Laval came to London in hopes of securing as firm an anti-German agreement there as that obtained at Rome the previous month. Over this they were disappointed. February was virtually a wasted month in terms of movement towards the solution of either the German or the Abyssinian problem. On 4 March a British White Paper on Defence, advocating a small measure of re-armament, was published (over the initials of the Prime Minister). Because of this Hitler caught a diplomatic cold the next day (surely a sign that the Paper was on the right lines) and deferred an impending visit to Berlin by Simon and Eden. Much British opinion was as hostile to this Paper as Hitler, though for opposite reasons.[8]

On 9 March Germany announced the existence of a German Air Force, her first open repudiation of her signature on the Treaty of Versailles. On 12 March France announced her intention to offset the decrease in the size of her Army, caused by the low French birth-rate during the First World War, by doubling (from one year to two) the period of military service. On the 16th Germany announced a second defiance of the 'Diktat' of Versailles, the re-introduction of conscription in Germany and a plan for an Army of some half-a-million men, a size greatly in excess of that of the French Army in Europe. Nonetheless, despite displeasure in Paris, Simon and Eden went to Berlin on 25 March in pursuit of a 'general settlement', to be told by Hitler that Germany had already attained parity in the air with Britain. Eden went on to Moscow, Warsaw, and Prague (the first British Minister to meet Stalin).

Before Simon and Eden started their journeys it had been agreed that, after them, an Anglo-French-Italian conference would meet at Stresa on 11 April to decide on a joint response to the German announcements of 9 and 16 March. On the last hop of his return journey Eden fell ill and was *hors-de-combat* till mid-May. Consequently a proposed British delegation at Stresa consisting of Baldwin, Simon, and Eden was replaced by one consisting of MacDonald (still Prime Minister) and Simon. A meeting between Baldwin, Laval, and Mussolini would have constituted a piquant combination of diverse personalities.[9] Ever self-confident, Neville Chamberlain wrote at the time: 'I believe the best person to go would be myself but that of course is impossible'.[10]

At this juncture it was plainly in the interests of all three Powers not to allow disagreement about Abyssinia to prevent, or mar, agreement at Stresa about Germany. As it had happened, the Abyssinian appeal to the League of 17 March,[11] arriving the day after the German announcement of 16 March, could not have been worse timed from the Abyssinian point of view. This could not have been foreseen in Addis Ababa, but understandably on 17 March the minds of European statesmen became concentrated on the news from Berlin. The German, not the Abyssinian, issue continued to be their first interest for many weeks. Italy made a clever contribution to keeping the latter in the background by announcing at Geneva, the day before the conference, her readiness to implement Article 5 of the Italo-Abyssinian Treaty of Friendship of 1928.[12] Laval no doubt remained as anxious as in January not even to raise the awkward issue of the Italo-Abyssinian dispute.

On 8 April 1935 the British Cabinet held a special meeting to discuss the impending conference. The minutes make no mention of Abyssinia. On the other hand, there is a mention of Memel, which, on British insistence, was discussed at Stresa.[13] Memel was an object of German irridentism,[14] but not so menacing an issue as Abyssinia nor one likely to be disruptive of what came to be called (in its short life) the 'Stresa front' of Britain, France and Italy against an expansionist Germany.

The paragraph which contains the mention of Memel is worth quoting because it illuminates the general lines of British foreign policy:

'It was pointed out that if France and Italy asked us to join them in a statement that we would not stand a breach of the peace anywhere, that meant in effect an undertaking that we should be prepared to take forcible action anywhere. . . . We ought not to agree to such a proposition unless we were prepared to take action anywhere, e.g. in the event of trouble in Memel. There was general agreement that we ought not to accept further commitments. . . .'[15]

So there was to be no 'war for Memel' and the tough anti-German line then being advocated by Italy was not to be followed: 'To adopt Signor Mussolini's point of view would be to throw German public opinion more behind Hitler than ever, and to drag us into escapades which we had no intention to follow'. For this reason to agree to break off conversations with Germany would be a profound mistake. On the other hand 'it was very desirable to show a firm front' for any anodyne communiqué from Stresa would encourage Germany and 'tend to throw many of the smaller weaker European nations on what they thought was going to be the stronger side. . . .' So far as France and Italy were concerned, we had 'to convince M. Flandin and Signor Mussolini that we had no intention of leaving them in the lurch. The idea of this was to get their confidence without isolating Germany at Stresa'. As to the immediately succeeding special Council meeting at Geneva, it was agreed:

> 'That pending the Stresa Conference it was impossible to foresee what the situation would be when the Council of the League of Nations met at Geneva, but that our general aim should be peace achieved by some system of collective security under the League of Nations, without acceptance of new commitments'.

Every minute tells a story. If those minutes had been revealed at the time they would surely have frightened our friends (France and Italy) more than our potential enemy (Germany). The imprecision of language (even such loose language as that about not intending to follow an escapade) would have revealed imprecision of thought; the bromide character of other phrases, e.g. 'peace achieved by some system of collective security under the League . . .' would have revealed, literally, thoughtlessness; some of the inconsistencies, e.g. gaining the confidence of France and Italy, without any fresh commitments and without isolating

116

Germany, would probably have seemed, what certainly they were not, deliberately tricky. As it was, Stresa gave Mussolini the opportunity to take the measure of the British Prime Minister and Foreign Secretary on the eve of his Abyssinian war. (He had met both before.)[16] If their words at the conference table corresponded with those written after the Cabinet of 8 April by its Secretary, Mussolini must have realized that he was dealing with irresolute men. But MacDonald returned to London full of confidence, reporting to the Cabinet:

'The main problem at Stresa had been to renew the confidence of the French and Italians in this country, which had been somewhat impaired. This had been successfully accomplished . . . .'[17]

On the railway platform at Stresa, just before leaving for home on the 14th, he was asked by a journalist: 'And did you not discuss Abyssinia with Mussolini?' 'My friend', he replied, 'your question is irrelevant'.[18]

But was it? Eden, from his sick-bed, had advised both MacDonald and Simon that the Abyssinian crisis should be discussed with Mussolini at Stresa. Drummond gave Vansittart the same advice.[19] It was accepted and the Foreign Secretary said he would take a Foreign Office expert on the subject (Mr. Geoffrey Thompson) with him. Mussolini gave an opening by remarking that the League had been effective in Europe (instancing the recent Saar settlement), but ineffective in Asia and South America. But the opportunity for speaking of the League's role in Africa was not seized.[20] Furthermore, when it came to drafting the conference's communiqué, and wording was proposed about the three Powers finding themselves in complete agreement in opposing 'any unilateral repudiation of treaties, which may endanger the peace', Mussolini asked for the addition of the words 'of Europe' and this was accepted in silence by the British and French Ministers. If so, MacDonald is almost as much to be blamed for his consenting silence at Stresa in April as Laval for his at Rome in January and Simon for his silence in London at the end of that month.[21] In any case, and whatever the reason, the fact remains that, at Stresa, Abyssinia was not on the agenda;[22] that there were no discussions about it, official or unofficial, between heads of delegations,[23] though there were informal discussions between members of the British and Italian delegations;[24] and, last, that there was no mention of Abyssinia in the conference communiqué. Another fact which remains is that when Stresa was debated in the House of Commons on 2 May Abyssinia was never mentioned. All in all, therefore, it is not surprising that after Stresa more than one effort had to be made to disabuse Mussolini of the idea that Britain was disinterested in his Abyssinian ambitions. On the other hand the Italian specialists Guarnaschelli and Vitteti (Counsellor in London) told Thompson that they saw no hope for a deal on Abyssinia and that they 'could not exclude the possibility of solving the Abyssinian question by force'.[25] So in this way Britain at Stresa received a clear warning of Italian intentions whilst giving in return no warning of any intention to resist them.

At the meeting of the League Council which immediately followed the Stresa Conference there was, as we have seen, no real discussion of the Abyssinian situation and any action was postponed until the next regular meeting, about a month later, on 20 May.[26] As that date approached, the fact that a major crisis was impending began to be appreciated by Britain. An early warning had come from Sir Sidney Barton, our Ambassador in Addis Ababa, in February: 'There is only one real issue and that is the independence of Ethiopia. . . .' He had added:

'Personally I can think of only one course likely to prevent perpetration of what may be widely regarded as an international crime and that would be for England and France to tell Italy that she cannot have Ethiopia.'[27]

But this was not done. On 26 February Eden advised 'a pretty strong hint . . . to the Italians that we should not view with indifference the dismemberment of Ethiopia . . .'; if such a hint were not given, dismemberment there would be.[28] The Foreign Secretary accepted this advice and a warning telegram was sent to Rome. (The Cabinet was advised of this telegram on 27 February).[29] Our Ambassador there, Sir Eric Drummond, put the main points of the telegram into a 'thoroughly friendly' memorandum. Even so, Mussolini, reading this memorandum in Drummond's presence, said with the utmost emphasis that 'until a *modus vivendi* was reached between the two countries, he would continue to send troops up to half a million if necessary'.[30] (That was just the number he did eventually send.) Mussolini had not taken the 'hint', in so far as there was one, and at Stresa, as we have just seen, there was not even the hint of a hint. Eden and Drummond's efforts, such as they had been, to some extent cancelling each other out, were of no effect. Indeed, Mussolini went on to ask Britain on 3 May, through Grandi, for the same free hand in Abyssinia that he had been given by France in January.[31] Part of Simon's answer was to point out the awkwardness which would be caused by Parliamentary Questions if Mussolini pursued his expansionist policy. There was no firm statement that Britain was opposed to it. Simon in due course told his colleagues that he had warned Grandi 'not only of the harmful effect Italy's becoming entangled in Abyssinia would exert on the European question, but also of the grave danger to Anglo-Italian relations of the very strong views undoubtedly held, and certain to be expressed by British public opinion, should Italy embark on an attack against Abyssinia.'[32]

Partly perhaps because of Mussolini's message via Grandi, on 8 May Simon 'made a full verbal report to the Cabinet as to the serious situation which had arisen between Italy and Abyssinia. . . .'[33] The circulation of a 'full appreciation' was called for and this was discussed at the next regular meeting, on the 15th. It may be noted that on 13 February the Cabinet 'took note' of a report by Simon that Italy had not sent Abyssinia an ultimatum as reported in the Press and on 27 February 'took note' of another report by Simon of the deterioration of the situation and, as we have just seen, of the warning telegram sent to Rome. With the meeting on 8 May, however, a new stage in the British handling of the crisis is reached; what had hitherto been a Foreign Office matter now becomes a Cabinet one.

The full, written 'appreciation', circulated before the meeting on 15 May,[34] is the able paper to be expected from the author and his staff. It opens with a résumé of the course of events since 5 December 1934 and proceeds to a firm forecast of their future course, in both military and political terms:

'We have the clearest indications from the Italian Government that they contemplate military operations on an extended scale

E

against Abyssinia as soon as climatic conditions permit. . . . It is quite certain that Italy no more intends to accept an adverse decision from the Council in this matter than Japan did in the case of Manchuria.'

One reads on, hoping to find the policy advised by the Foreign Secretary as the best in these circumstances, so clearly foreseen, only to meet the statement that His Majesty's Government is 'likely to be faced with an exceedingly difficult decision'. A lucid statement of the Government's difficulties follows:

'If they support against Italy a practical application of League principles, their action is bound greatly to compromise Anglo-Italian relations and perhaps even to break the close association at present existing between France, Italy, and the United Kingdom. Indeed, Italy's reaction in Signor Mussolini's present mood is incalculable; the possibility of Italy leaving the League must not be overlooked. In any event, the European situation will be most seriously affected, and it would, in fact, be hard to imagine a state of affairs which would be more welcome to Germany.'

'On the other hand, if the United Kingdom acquiesces in what would be a misuse of the League machinery by acting in a manner acceptable to Italy, but certainly unjust towards Abyssinia, His Majesty's Government will lay themselves open to grave public criticism. . . .'

One may note the same emphasis to the Cabinet, as to Grandi a few days previously, on the probable reaction of British public opinion to Italian aggression. There is no indication of the reaction to be expected from the Government itself.

It is as if a doctor, faced with the early stages of a most serious illness, is clear and unhesitating in diagnosis and prognosis, but silent as to treatment. It is fair also to comment that the foreseeable misuse of the League and injustice to Abyssinia, if acquiesced in, are judged in terms of their effect on British public opinion, not in terms of any adverse effect on British national interests. It is not, for example, considered whether 'misuse of the League' might damage those interests. Was this because it was not seen that such misuse would damage them or because the damage to them by using the League machinery aright (i.e. the damage to the 'Stresa front' and the consequent advantage to Germany) was easier to see?

Simon is not recorded as making on 15 May any reference to a forthright public speech of Mussolini's the previous day. (In this he denied, correctly, that there had been an Anglo-French *démarche* to Rome and said that Italy intended to feel thoroughly safe in Africa; that she would send there all the troops considered necessary for that purpose; and that no third Power could 'arrogate the intolerable claim to intervene').[35] On the other hand, Simon added to his paper that morning's news that the Italian members of the Italo-Abyssinian Conciliation Commission had at last been appointed. But the subjects of the conciliation procedure were still under dispute[36] and, if the question was again to be postponed from the May meeting of the Council until its next regular meeting in September, 'the rainy season in Ethiopia would be over and the Italians might be on the verge of hostilities, if they had not already begun'. The Chief of the Imperial General Staff had agreed that warfare was technically possible in the north, i.e. on the Eritrean frontier, in September, in the south, i.e. on the Somaliland frontier, even earlier.

It cannot therefore be said that the British Cabinet was taken by surprise by the outbreak of war in October. They had plenty of time, about five months in fact, to make up their minds what was best to do in such a circumstance; the future course of events had been clearly predicted. In Cabinet on 15 May, however, the Foreign Secretary's only positive counsel was not to delay a decision.

None the less, in the 'somewhat prolonged discussion' which ensued, no less than three suggestions were made for postponement at Geneva on the 20th. (One was on the ground 'of the accumulating evidence of the unpopularity in Italy of the anticipated Ethiopian expedition'. In such circumstances to base on such 'evidence' a case for inaction is scarcely a substitute for a positive policy.) In the end, however, the Cabinet decided against delay at Geneva 'which must result, not only in nothing being done before September to prevent hostilities, but which gives no opportunity for anything to be done'. Accordingly, Eden was to be given 'a wide discretion' (not a thing to be easily exercised by someone not himself a Cabinet Minister) 'as to the best course to be taken' at the Council Meeting 'in his endeavours to secure this aim'. (What aim, other than not to delay?) At the same time Drummond was to be recalled from Rome for consultations as 'an indication to Signor Mussolini of how seriously His Majesty's Government was concerned with the course of events'. Recalling an Ambassador for consultations is a move which customarily carries some weight in diplomacy but Mussolini had himself indirectly indicated, the previous day, that the move to which he would have attached weight was an Anglo-French *démarche*. His own move, of troops to Africa, spoke louder to the world than the British Ambassador's journey to London.

On 17 May the Cabinet met again, with Sir Eric Drummond present. Again it agreed on the sort of formula which has meaning only for politicians in search of one:

> 'It is therefore of the utmost importance that the course of procedure at the meeting of the Council should be such as shall satisfy the due discharge of the duty of the United Kingdom as a member of the Council without impairing in the least degree the friendly co-operation between the United Kingdom and Italy in all matters.'[37]

Drummond returned to Rome and Mussolini spoke to him on the 19th in words which, by contrast, made a meaningful and explicit point. If, in order 'to clarify the situation and to obtain security, it was necessary for him to resort to arms, in short to go to war, he would do so and he would send sufficient men to obtain his objective'. If the League seemed to support Abyssinia against Italy, he would have no choice but to leave it.[38]

On the same day Eden left for Geneva 'with reluctance and foreboding'.[39] The receipt of news the next morning of the interchange between Drummond and Mussolini can scarcely have brightened his mood. The proceedings in the Council have already been described.[40] With more difficulty than previously, a compromise was, superficially, arrived at. Outside the Council chamber, Eden concentrated on conversations with Laval, to increase Anglo-French co-operation, and with Aloisi, to make him grasp what was at stake. He had some success with both men and has given them credit for their contributions on this occasion:

'The temporary firmness of the first has done most to decide the issue'.[41] Aloisi began by remarking understandably, that 'we had swallowed *la couleuvre* [bitter pill] of Manchuria; why was Abyssinia creating such difficulties?'[42] He was, however, prepared to try and persuade Mussolini to accept some kind of settlement of the then outstanding issues. Laval had a difficult rôle to play, but Aloisi's was more difficult and required more courage.

On 18 June the Anglo-German Naval Agreement was signed and this event was as much to Abyssinia's detriment as the German rearmament measures of March. The latter led to a determination at Stresa that Britain, France and Italy should, at all costs, stand together against Germany. Among the costs was the abandonment of the legitimate interests of Abyssinia. Now the mood was changing and Britain was perceiving that to ignore those interests might be too high a price to pay for Italian friendship. But just when it was supremely important for Abyssinia (and not her only) that Britain and France should work together to restrain Mussolini, the Anglo-German Agreement struck at the heart of the Anglo-French relationship. (It did not help that the signing was done on the anniversary of Waterloo). There was something to be said for the Agreement on its merits as an Anglo-German affair, but nothing to be said for concluding it without any consultation with France, let alone her agreement. That brought a wave of Anglophobia to the surface of French politics and that too was to the detriment of Abyssinia. Moreover, Italy as well as France took umbrage at the Agreement and became the less likely to heed British warnings about Abyssinia and the more likely to believe that their motivation was mere self-interest.

In February the policy agreed between Britain and France in London had been that releases from the obligations of the Treaty of Versailles should only be conceded as part of a 'general settlement'. Now Britain had dishonoured that agreement.[43] There could not have been a worse diplomatic blunder; indeed, Britain may just have been stupidly springing a German diplomatic trap. Ribbentrop and Baldwin (not, it is true, co-operatively) applied great, almost bullying, pressure in driving the negotiations to success.[44] Baldwin was proud of the Agreement, describing it, in a speech in the country, as 'the first real and practical move in disarmament that has been accomplished since the War'.[45] Having regard to the Washington naval treaties of 1921, this was not an accurate statement of fact. An eminent German historian, Professor K. D. Bracher, calls the Agreement 'the first great act of appeasement'.[46]

On 19 June the 'Italo-Ethiopian dispute' was again before the British Cabinet, the new Foreign Secretary (Sir Samuel Hoare) raising it 'as a matter of immediate urgency'.[47] The situation, he said, had deteriorated very seriously; Mussolini's enthusiasm had not diminished; large Italian forces were on their way to the Red Sea; Italian public opinion appeared to have accepted the situation; French loyalty to the League was in doubt:

'There was every prospect therefore of being placed in a most inconvenient dilemma. Either we should have to make a futile protest, which would irritate M. Mussolini and perhaps drive him out of the League and into the arms of Germany, or we should make no protest and give the appearance of pusillanimity.'

The Foreign Secretary went on to propose, as a means of escape from this dilemma, an offer to Mussolini (based on an old Foreign Office plan) to cede to Abyssinia a corridor of British Somaliland (roughly 12 miles wide by 40 miles long) giving her a sea-coast of 18 miles, including the open anchorage of Zeila. In return for this cession of British territory to Abyssinia she would be expected to cede the Ogaden province to Italy.

This plan was endorsed by Vansittart and Drummond. The chances of Mussolini calling off his Abyssinian enterprise in return for a piece of desert, for that was what the plan amounted to from his point of view, seemed slim, but the Cabinet clutched at the straw offered them and Eden was authorized to go to Rome, via Paris, to make the offer to Mussolini, under cover of discussions with France and Italy about the recent Anglo-German Naval Agreement. Eden, a Minister with quite the wrong title for this particular chore, was not very happy about going.[48] The chances of a successful negotiation were spoilt by a leak (as later were those of the Report of the Committee of Five and of the Hoare-Laval plan).[49]

Mussolini received Eden on 23 June, and again on the 24th, and was as open with him as he had been with Drummond on 19 May. He, first of all, rejected the British offer 'not only as unsatisfactory but as positively dangerous'.[50] Eden's account of the meeting reads, on this point, as follows:

'It would give Abyssinia an outlet to the sea which would make her stronger, as it would give her a corridor through which she could import arms. . . . It would not enable Italy's two colonies to be connected and it would result in Abyssinia claiming a victory for herself. Abyssinia would point out that concessions had been made not to Italy, whom she detested, but out of friendship for England. His Majesty's Government would appear as a protector and benefactor of Abyssinia, in exchange for whose gift Abyssinia consented to make some territorial adjustments with Italy.'[51]

Mussolini went on to explain his Abyssinian objectives:

'If Abyssinia came to terms without war, he would be content with surrender of those parts of Abyssinia which had been conquered by her in the last fifty years and which were not inhabited by Abyssinians. In saying this, Signor Mussolini made a circular gesture which I took to mean that he regarded such territories as existing on all four sides of Abyssinia.[52] The central plateau could, he continued, remain under Abyssinian sovereignty, but only on condition that it was under Italian control. If, however, Abyssinia could not come to terms with Italy upon these lines, then, if Italy had to fight, her demands would be proportionately greater. Signor Mussolini made a sweep of his hand indicating that Italy would then have the whole country'.[53]

Eden stopped at Paris on his way home to tell Laval of the proposals he had put to Mussolini. He found that Laval already knew of them (and whom could he have got that information from?) and was as sore, or affected to be as sore, about the British offer, as about the Anglo-German Naval Agreement. *Perfide Albion* had already concluded one bilateral agreement, with Germany, behind France's back, and now she had just tried to conclude another, with Italy, again without taking France into her confidence in advance. Laval was particularly concerned that the development of Zeila might have reduced the dividends of the

Jibuti Railway. Alexis Léger, Permanent Head of the French
Foreign Office, was more concerned that a British breach of the
1906 Treaty had been contemplated.

Plainly Mussolini ('calm, relaxed, and reasonable' throughout)[54] was not to be put off by the offer of the Ogaden. The
complete failure of the Cabinet's opening move, Eden's mission,
had, however, the advantage of showing, all too clearly, the shape
of things to come and the hard choices that therefore had to be
made – or evaded.

The Foreign Secretary 'spelled out' to the Cabinet the consequences, as he saw them, on 3 July:[55]

'An invasion of Abyssinia would, therefore, raise the issues
envisaged by Article 16 of the Covenant, which involved collective, but not individual, commitments for signatories. If
these obligations were ignored or evaded, a heavy blow would
be struck at the whole of the Pacts and Agreements on which
the post-war system of Europe had been built up. It would
amount to an admission that the attempt to give the League
coercive powers was a mistake – an admission that would have
serious effects in increasing the existing confusion abroad, as
well as on public opinion at home.'[56]

From a 'preliminary discussion' there emerged 'various courses
open to the Cabinet. . .', but there was a chilly reminder 'that
previous investigations of economic sanctions had shown that
(since they involved blockade) they were almost bound to lead to
hostilities'. It was therefore agreed that, before the Cabinet's next
discussion, 'the appropriate sub-committee of the Committee of
Imperial Defence should consider and report on the application
of Article 16 of the Covenant to Italy, including the possible
closing of the Suez Canal'.

(The closure of the Canal would at this time have been illegal
under a Convention of 1888 signed by, among others, Britain and
France. Article 1 laid it down that the 'Canal shall always be free
and open in time of war as in time of peace to every vessel of
commerce or of war without distinction of flag'. Article 10, however, gave to the Sultan of Turkey a right, transferred to Britain
in 1919, to close the Canal for its own defence or if Egypt became

involved in war. Thus it would have been legal to close the Canal if Mussolini had made war on Egypt or Britain or both. Moreover, Article 4 in any case allowed the obstruction of 'the free navigation of the Canal', provided that acts with this object were committed outside 'a radius of three maritime miles' from its ports of access. In other words, while it would have been illegal simply to close the Canal it would have been perfectly legal to establish a blockade of the entrances to it.[57] Presumably it was this reading of the relevant law which caused the League of Nations Union and other people to advocate cutting Italian communications with East Africa rather than just closing the Canal. It is very important in this connection to notice that Baldwin, in a speech of 23 November 1934, had said : 'Never as an individual will I sanction the British Navy being used for an armed blockade of any country in the world until I know what the United States of America is going to do'. From this position he never budged.)

A week later the Foreign Secretary was telling the Cabinet that the 'position at the moment was so obscure' that he did not ask for any decisions. None the less there was again a 'discussion of a preliminary character' in which 'certain suggestions' were made, of which one was that, at the meeting of the League Council due on the 25th, 'we should not make any proposals. In any event it was urged that it should be made clear that no approach had been made to France for the application of sanctions and that none should be made'.[58]

This was really very extraordinary. It was the Foreign Office's view that Britain's most important international commitment was to the Covenant;[59] expressions of devotion to it came often from the mouths of Ministers. If Italy invaded Abyssinia the commitment to Article 16 would come into effect. France was the other leading League Power. It was imperatively and urgently necessary to know whether, in spite of her conciliatory policy towards Italy since January, she would in the circumstances so clearly envisaged and now seemingly so imminent, honour her obligations under Article 16. It did not need the conversations with leading Parliamentarians in late August[60] for it to be obvious in July that effective pressure on Italy would be difficult without French co-operation. By then the question of prime importance was the extent to which pressure should be put on France to place her obligations to the League before her understandable desire to retain her newly-gained friendship with Italy.

Between the regular weekly Cabinet meeting on 10 July and a special meeting on the Italo-Abyssinian dispute held on the 22nd, the Foreign Secretary seems to have done some thinking on these lines:

> 'The more he studied the question the more strongly he felt that the only card in our hands was the deterrent, by which he meant publicity and conversations with the French in order to get them to put pressure on Italy before the Geneva discussions.'[61]

These were now to open on the 31st. Even so, strong objections were made to the idea of a private, let alone a public, approach to the French. It was proposed that Eden should see Laval privately and tell him 'that the British Government were prepared in the last resort to fulfil their engagements under the Covenant and would eventually have to announce that this had been their attitude'. This was the kind of instruction he would have liked to have had.[62]

The minute continues, however,

> 'While it was suggested that this course would be consistent with the present trend of public opinion in this country (though not necessarily later on if it led to war) the comment was made that it would probably leak out at once and cause great irritation to Italy, and that in any event M. Laval would be under strong pressure to inform Italy and obtain the credit for having blocked our proposal for sanctions. This course, it was suggested, was not likely to be successful in stopping Italy from making war on Abyssinia, because it was extremely unlikely that France would co-operate in sanctions. . . .'

In the end the Cabinet fell back on the idea of a despatch to Sir George Clerk, British Ambassador in Paris, for him to hand to Laval. The dangers of a leakage must have been considered unavoidable.

On 24 July the Foreign Secretary told the Cabinet that he had followed up this idea:

'In this Despatch he proposed to deploy the whole case as to the dangers to European peace and security involved in an Italy-Abyssinian war, and to end on the note that the two Governments ought to agree a policy for averting war. His aim was to avoid crude questions being put by either side to the other as to whether they were prepared to carry out their obligations under the Covenant. The underlying assumption would be that both Powers realized their obligations and were therefore jointly interested to find a way out of the difficulty.'[63]

In the discussion following this statement 'the view was expressed, and met with a good deal of support, that we should be on our guard against proposals for a settlement which was not fair to Abyssinia, and that we should aim at a settlement acceptable to Abyssinia. . . .' On the other hand:

'There was general acceptance of the view that there were advantages, for the present, in playing for time in the hope of a weakening on Italy's part . . . though the prospects were not bright at the moment.'

So the July days drifted by in London, occupied by lengthy and indecisive discussions. In Italy, in Eritrea, and in Italian Somaliland there was a good deal of action. Eden was later to 'date our Abyssinian failure from these weeks. . . .'[64] He thought that even as late as July:

'An unmistakeable warning to Mussolini that we understood the choice we had now to make, between the League . . . on the one hand and his friendship on the other, that we knew what our decision must be and were determined to give effect to it, might have halted Mussolini even then, more especially if given privately.'[65]

Then it was August and time for British Ministers to take their holidays. Many of the preceding extracts can be charitably interpreted as evidence that those holidays were badly needed to freshen tired minds. It was, however, agreed in Cabinet on 31 July[66] that the Prime Minister would return from abroad for a full meeting of the Cabinet if a real emergency arose in connection with the dispute.

13

The Great Powers
(August to October 1935)

In August the pace of events quickened, their tone deteriorated, and their sinister undertones were strengthened. Not only did war in Abyssinia come to seem certain but the possibility of war between Britain (or Britain and France) and Italy (which had first impinged on the minds of British Ministers in July)[1] was increasingly canvassed. The meeting of the League Council (31 July – 3 August),[2] which in advance of the event they had discussed so much, came and went. Now the tri-partite conference between Britain, France, and Italy[3] had to be prepared for. The Prime Minister came up from Worcestershire and on 6 August there was a meeting at 10 Downing Street between Baldwin, Hoare, Eden, Vansittart, and Hankey.[4] It was agreed that Eden's aim in his 'preliminary conversations with the French Government ... should be to establish a programme for later discussion with the Italian representative'. He 'would, of course, be on his guard against giving the French Government any opportunity to suggest to Italy that we were pressing them to commit themselves to sanctions. Any detailed discussion of sanctions should be avoided, as this does not arise at present. ...'[5] No wonder that Eden wrote to a friend: 'I am simply dreading these conversations more than anything I have ever undertaken – vague instructions from home and a thieves' kitchen in Paris'.[6]

At the meeting on 6 August, Eden's instructions being settled, Baldwin asked for the Chiefs of Staff Sub-Committee of the Committee of Imperial Defence 'at once to examine the question of what the position would be if Italy took the bit between her teeth ... are there any steps that ought to be taken at once to provide against it?' Hoare said that the Foreign Office 'would have no objection to any relatively quiet steps being taken, such as, for example, raising the anti-aircraft defences of Malta to the approved scale. They would not even object if the movement of anti-aircraft guns become public'.[7]

Eden arrived in Paris on 13 August and had conversations with Laval and with the Abyssinian Minister (Tecle Hawariat). Aloisi arrived on the 15th. Eden and Laval asked him for a full statement of Italy's case aganst Abyssinia and a statement of the minimum terms on which Italy would agree to a settlement. The former was to come at Geneva on 4 September.[8] The latter Aloisi declined to supply in any detail. In these circumstances it was decided to draw up Anglo-French terms which could, with a good conscience, be simultaneously recommended to Abyssinia and Italy. These proposals foreshadowed those of the Committee of Five.[9] The economic development and administrative re-organization of Abyssinia were to be helped forward by Britain, France, and Italy collectively, without impairing her integrity or independence. The proposals did not exclude 'the possibility of territorial adjustment to which Italy and Ethiopia might agree'.[10] Mussolini, who had thought the meeting useless and indeed dangerous,[11] rejected these proposals out of hand on 18 August. That evening a communiqué announced the indefinite adjournment of the conference. De Bono received the news in a message from his master couched in the staccato style affected by many a dictator from Julius Caesar onwards:

> *'Conferenza niente concluso; C'è Ginevrà che concludera lo stesso. Concludi.'*[12]

On 19 August the Italo-Abyssinian Commission for Conciliation and Arbitration opened, also in Paris, what turned out to be its final session. Thereafter, as we have seen, the whole Wal-Wal affair petered out.[13] The break-down of the Three-Power Paris Conference, however, made it plain that Italo-Abyssinian war was imminent. 'Anthony', said Vansittart to Eden, 'you are faced with a first-class international crisis. We have got to reinforce the Mediterranean Fleet'.[14] The calling of an August meeting of the Cabinet and the return of the Prime Minister from his holiday abroad proclaimed to the whole world the British view that a first-class international crisis existed.

Baldwin was back in London on the 21st and that evening a meeting of Ministers was held at No. 10 to prepare for the

Cabinet the next day. In addition to the Prime Minister five other Ministers were present (MacDonald, Simon, Chamberlain, Hoare, and Eden) and four Civil Servants.

This meeting was probably more important than the succeeding Cabinet meeting (for the latter confirmed the decisions of the former) and the notes on it have for posterity the interest of indicating the views of individual Ministers.[15] Hence, no doubt, these minutes are indited in a way not, at that time at any rate, normal in respect of meetings of the full Cabinet: 'To be kept under lock and key . . . most secret'.

The subject was sanctions, the background the probability of war breaking out during the September meetings of League Council and Assembly. There was some discussion of the resolutions, interpretative of Article 16, carried by the 1921 Assembly.[16] The Ministers were advised that, according to Resolution 3:

'The unilateral action of the defaulting State cannot create a state of war: it merely entitles the other Members of the League to resort to acts of war with the Covenant-breaking State; but it is in accordance with the spirit of the Covenant that the League of Nations should attempt, at least at the outset, to avoid war, and to restore peace by economic pressure.'

Attention was also drawn to the fact that other Resolutions, notably Resolution 8, made it clear that not every sanction had to be imposed at once. Given this possibility there was great significance in Hoare's saying that he had learnt from the U.S. Chargé d'Affaires that the U.S. Government 'were taking the Abyssinian question very seriously, and their participation in the first stage of economic sanctions did not appear inconceivable'. There is less significance in Simon's saying that the Kellogg Pact had provisions not dissimilar from the first stage of economic sanctions inasmuch as that Pact had no such provisions whatsoever.

On the main question, what to do, the Foreign Secretary was definite, up to a point, the point of the procedure to be followed: 'the only safe line was to try out the regular League of Nations procedure'. His conversations with 'the leaders of non-Government parties'[17] had left him with the impression that there would be 'a wave of public opinion against the Government if it repudiated its obligations under Article 16 ... on the assumption that the French would go as far as we were prepared to do. ... Of course, if France found it impossible to proceed to extreme measures, there could be no question of "putting her in the dock". On the other hand, it would be desirable for us to make a statement at some stage in the September proceedings, to the effect that if all other Member States were ready to carry out their obligations, we were also ready'. This idea had been pressed on Eden by Lord Cecil, with all the weight of the League of Nations Union known to be behind him, earlier on the same day.[18] Here we see the genesis, at Cabinet level, of the key passage in Hoare's speech to the Assembly on 11 September.[19]

Eden 'hoped that in practice economic sanctions would not be begun until a Committee of the League Council had carefully worked out the methods of their application – that is, until it had ascertained definitely what attitude the non-Member States were going to adopt'. Hoare spoke again to point out that 'such an investigation by experts might very probably lead to a decision not to impose sanctions'. MacDonald was therefore 'clear that it was out of the question for the British Government to make any statement to the effect that Article 16 could not operate in the present crisis, before the Council Meeting on September 4th'. Hoare, following this, 'thought that we should have to agree a form of words very carefully with France before we said that the machinery of economic sanctions would not work. The French might agree that it would not work in the present crisis, but they would nevertheless want to keep it for use against Germany'. Chamberlain then applied his mind to the requisite 'form of words', remarking that 'if the final decision was against economic sanctions we should have to be most careful not to say "we were prepared to use them but France was not". The formula would have to be something to the effect that we and France had come jointly to the conclusion that they would not work'.

This record of the discussion between six powerful British Ministers on 21 August, when the Paris Conference had broken down and war was expected in the following month, is revealing. Is it too cynical to suggest, especially having regard to the previous references in Cabinet minutes to the state of public opinion,[20] that even in these circumstances these Ministers had it well in mind that they were members of a Government which must, ere long, face a General Election? Is not the impression given that, whether for this or other or additional reasons, their hearts were not in the business of upholding the sanctity of the Covenant of the League of Nations? At the start of their discussion they are advised by the Foreign Secretary that 'the only safe line' – not the right or the best line – is not to commit oneself fully to, but 'to try out the regular League of Nations procedure'. As the discussion, however, proceeds – and tapers off – the idea appears, again on the lips of the Foreign Secretary, that it may not, after all, be necessary to impose sanctions. At once the previous Prime Minister grasps at the idea that, instead of making a statement at Geneva in September that Britain was prepared to play her part in imposing sanctions, it would not be possible to say before 4 September that sanctions would be inapplicable in the present crisis. Then attention is turned to the form of words by which such a decision can be announced. And what of the Prime Minister's contribution to the discussion? He is reported to have asked one question and made one statement. He asked the Foreign Secretary whether he had any information regarding Germany's intentions and he 'called attention to M. Laval's genuine difficulties'. Certainly Hitler's intentions and Laval's difficulties were points of first-class importance and Baldwin did well to have them in mind. But, having asked about the one, and called attention to the other, what followed in the way of setting out a policy?

The night seems to have brought some better judgments than those seemingly prevailing at the end of the evening's meeting. At the emergency meeting on 22 August the Cabinet, 'who were most anxious if possible to avoid a war with Italy', agreed:

> 'That [H.M.G.] should keep in step with the policy of the French Government, and, more particularly in the matter of Sanctions, should avoid any commitment which France was not equally prepared to assume. . . .
>
> That [H.M.G.] should aim at following closely the procedure laid down in the Covenant (with the interpretations adopted by the Assembly in 1921) not in any quixotic spirit, and with due regard to the many difficulties . . .
>
> They should be careful to avoid trying to force nations to go

further than they were willing, and generally should make it clear that the question of Sanctions was one which the Members of the League had to examine in co-operation, and with a view to collective action. They should be on their guard against the possibility that other nations might not in practice fulfil their commitments'.[21]

It is impossible to cavil at the anxiety 'if possible to avoid war with Italy'. Nonetheless the conclusions of 22 August seem tepid and timorous. An international orchestra was about to assemble at Geneva. The British Government seemed anxious, not so much to pass the conductor's baton to somebody else, as to ensure that there should not be a conductor. The members of the orchestra were, leaderless, collectively to decide what tune to play, at what tempo, and with what volume. The British member was not to force any of these issues; in so far as he was to do anything positive he was to do his best to play the same tune as his French colleague.

All this was changed by Sir Samuel Hoare's speech to the Assembly. Did he deliberately decide to leap over and ahead of his colleagues or did he, as later implied,[22] find himself holding the conductor's baton unintentionally? In any event it was not, after all, to be his rôle to sit hidden in the middle of an orchestra waiting to see what collective activity would take place, half-hoping that none would.

From 11 September onwards the limelight beat upon Sir Samuel. It was in comparative darkness that he met Pierre Laval for the first time on the morning of the 10th. Eden was also present (as were Léger, Massigli, and Strang), but did little of the talking.

Laval set the ball rolling by reading a telegram from the French Ambassador in Rome according to which Mussolini had begged him 'to try to prevent, at Geneva, any talk of sanctions or expressions wounding to Italian susceptibilities, and above all to try to prevent an Anglo-Italian conflict. In the event of such a conflict, Signor Mussolini would have to denude the Brenner Pass, and this would give the Germans the chance they were waiting for'.[23]

'Monsieur Laval's conclusion' (we read) 'was that, as practical men, they would have now to see how far they could go in making a proposal to the Italian Government. It would be best to leave aside for the moment the moral issue. If negotiations failed, the moral basis for the attitude of the French and British Governments would remain'.

Hoare's opening statement (in the first of these three conversations) was that 'the consideration that was chiefly in his mind, the over-riding new factor in the situation, was the rearmament of Germany ... Throughout the whole Abyssinian conflict he had been thinking, not so much of an Italian dispute with a backward country, as of the reactions of the dispute on the European position, with Germany rearmed and under temptation to make a threat to European security some time during the next ten years'. If in this situation the system of collective security was 'gravely injured or destroyed' the movement for British isolation would grow.[24] The question whether a policy of collective security 'was possible did not very much matter. The public would insist on its being tried, even though it might be found to fail'. If he were to say that 'there was no collective force behind the League' and that it could only be 'an advisory body' that would remove a deterrent to Germany. The British Government did not wish to push the French Government 'into an impossible position', but there must be an investigation of possible sanctions. 'If it should come to a question of economic pressure under Article 16 ... His Majesty's Government did not at all take the view that it would be wise to begin with extreme measures'. He hoped that Britain and France could agree 'that anything that might be done would be done in as unprovocative a way as possible. ... The last thing he would say to Monsieur Laval would be to ask him whether it was still possible to make a further appeal to Signor Mussolini not to allow matters to go to extremes'.

Laval then said, not surprisingly, that 'Sir Samuel Hoare's moderation would facilitate his task ... France would be faithful to the League and to her friendship with Italy'. His concluding point (in this, first conversation) was that the French Ambassador in London (M. Corbin) would ask some precise questions about British policy in the event of further German breaches of Treaties, with special reference to the case of Austria. Hoare said he would send Laval a summary of his impending speech to the League assembly.

The second conversation took place the same evening.[25] Hoare said that his policy was 'moderation as regards the Abyssinian question, but resolution as regards the principles of the League'. Laval advocated a double policy in more precise and more familiar terms: 'If war broke out in October the Council would at once meet and would employ a double method in order to stop the war, namely, by exercising economic pressure and by conciliation'. But he asked Britain 'to appreciate the delicate position of the French Government and begged them not to force them to turn their backs on the agreement of January 1935'. He said that he 'was faithful to the Covenant in the measure in which His Majesty's Government would be moderate in their application of it'.

Hoare then suggested that probably Italian exports should be restricted, for the primary purpose of limiting Italian supplies of foreign exchange. Laval was at once strongly against this. He thought that a ban on the export to Italy of arms and materials for war industries would hit her so hard that no other sanctions would be needed: 'The prohibition of exports ought not to be applied before the second stage, i.e. at the stage when Signor Mussolini had refused conciliation'. The earlier application of this sanction 'would jeopardize the Rome agreements. . . . He was prepared to apply the Covenant, but would ask that it should be applied in a prudent way'. Stronger measures might save the principles of the Covenant, but if they brought Germany in to disturb Europe 'the cost of preserving the Covenant would be too high. Signor Mussolini ought to be made to feel economic pressure, but not to have the knife presented to his throat'. Hoare demurred to this to the extent of saying that 'the essential thing was not to take action which was likely to be ineffective and to make the League ridiculous'. Laval said that the 'problem was to reconcile fidelity to the Covenant with close agreement with Italy. . . . If the Abyssinian question were quickly settled, Signor Mussolini would collaborate in the better organization of collective security in Europe. At the same time it was desirable that world opinion should not be disillusioned as regards the League of Nations. . . . It was all a question of tact, the reconciliation of prudence with principles'.

'Sir Samuel Hoare did not disagree with what Monsieur Laval had said. He was confirmed in the opinion that with tact and the avoidance of provocation it could be possible to give the world a clear impression that the two Governments were acting together and that in such a situation they had no intention of abandoning the Covenant. If this could be done without threat it might be possible to influence Signor Mussolini. It was, at any rate, the only possible way of doing so during the coming weeks'.

Hoare made his speech to the Assembly the next morning. (We have already seen that he did not think it necessary to change it in any respect in the light of the previous day's talks with Laval.)[26] The third conversation with Laval took place on the afternoon of 11 September. Laval congratulated Hoare on his speech, adding however that he regretted that 'a speech of this kind had not been made earlier in years when France was more directly engaged'.[27] In his own speech on the 13th he would include some conciliatory words to Mussolini. Then followed a forceful recapitulation of previous points:

'International morals were one thing: the interests of a country were another. . . . He did not hide from Sir Samuel Hoare with what prudence he would approach the whole question of sanctions.'

This was succeeded by some 'back-pedalling':

'Perhaps it would be thought best, when war broke out, to rely upon concilation alone. All would depend on the attitude of Italy towards each of the other Governments at the time'.

Hoare responded to these cautions and misgivings by dwelling, as he had done at the start, on the German menace:

'If it were found in the present case either imprudent or impossible to do anything effective, the world at large – and Great Britain in particular – would almost certainly take the view that economic pressure could never be applied in the more difficult case of Germany. . . .'

Laval was quite undisturbed by this. He denied that it would be more difficult to put economic pressure on Germany than on Italy: 'It would certainly not be easier to apply it to Italy in the present circumstances'. Hoare seemingly had the last word. He repeated that League failure over Abyssinia would strengthen British isolationism. He believed that support of the League 'was the only deterrent likely to prevent Germany from embarking upon some aggressive act'.

On this note of muted disagreement ended the first Hoare-Laval meeting. Nothing specific had been agreed; the three conversations were plainly 'exploratory'. The two explorers appear to have spoken frankly to each other and to have had a smooth exchange of ideas. There had been a meeting of minds, but only on the level of generalities.

Had there been, overall, agreement or disagreement? The content of the conversations was first made public by Laval in a speech to the Chamber of Deputies on 28 December 1935. He claimed substantial agreement on a number of essentials:

> 'We found ourselves instantaneously in agreement upon ruling out military sanctions, not adopting any measure of naval blockade, never contemplating the closure of the Suez Canal – in a word, ruling out everything that might lead to war.'

The record does not show any of the three specific measures mentioned to have been even discussed. They may perhaps have been mentioned only to be instantly dismissed and not thought worth mentioning in the minutes. Laval's 'revelation', however, gives a fair impression of what was agreed (insofar as anything was), that is to say a most cautious approach, in the event of war, to the imposition of sanctions and certainly no rushing into any extreme measures. In a sense, therefore, the two men found themselves in step, but Laval was marching a fair distance behind Hoare. The latter was thinking seriously about sanctions, though admittedly only of mild ones (to begin with at any rate). The former required to be converted even to that case; all his hopes were still pinned on conciliation and wishful thinking about Mussolini, after a short war, being ready for that. It was lamentable that so soon before a war which both men expected for certain in the next month, and the possibility of which both had so long foreseen, so little exploring of each other's minds had previously been done.

Some serious disagreements were in effect uncovered. Hoare's pleas that the League should not be made to look ridiculous and for a show of diplomatic strength and, above all, of Anglo-French unity fell on deaf ears. Laval admitted that 'collaboration with England was more important for France than collaboration with Italy. But there was also the fact of the agreement with Italy'. In other words there was no corresponding fact of agreement with Great Britain. (He did use the word 'entente'.) Hoare's own summary, years later, is a fair one:

'The long talks, lasting many hours, eventually came to an end with a better understanding of our respective positions. Whilst, however, we seemed outwardly to have reached complete agreement, I never lost the feeling ... that, though our words sounded the same, the minds behind them were making reservations. Laval ... thought me irritatingly obstinate in my attitude towards Mussolini, and I had the uneasy feeling that he really wished to give the Duce a completely free hand.'[28]

Hoare's speech to the Assembly would have gladdened not only Laval, as he pointed out, but France herself if made earlier in a context concerning a vital French interest, which Abyssinia was not.[29] For the first time since Britain had killed the Geneva Protocol in 1925, she seemed to be taking the League seriously. What more natural than that this should make France 'hot for certainties' about the European danger spots not covered by the Locarno Treaties, especially Austria? Alas, French questions about these received only 'dusty answers'; M. Corbin was simply referred back to the text of the famous speech.

At a Cabinet meeting on 24 September Hoare received a hero's welcome:

'In the course of the discussion several tributes were paid to the Secretary of State for Foreign Affairs both for his speech to the League Assembly on September 11th and his general handling of the situation.'

At the close of the discussion the Prime Minister 'paid a warm tribute' to the Foreign Secretary's work 'and expressed the view that the Cabinet agreed generally on the policy he had proposed'.[30] A message from Eden, in Geneva, urging a 'tougher' line was not submitted to it.[31] A 'friendly message' had gone from Hoare to Mussolini on the 23rd.[32]

Hoare's advice to the Cabinet on 24 September (the day on which the Committee of Five announced the failure of its work)[33] was that 'we should continue to pursue the policy of fulfilling our Treaty obligations, which had been decided on 22 August, subject to the same conditions and precautions, seeking always to follow up any chance of a settlement; but that, if it came to the point where there was agreement at the League of Nations in favour of applying economic pressure and we were assured that States which were not members of the League would not undermine that, we should be prepared to play our part. . . .' in applying 'such mild sanctions' as 'would probably shorten the war. If the League confined itself to a moral condemnation of Italy, its futility would be exposed . . . if circumstances required it, collective security ought to be tried out as if it was not effective the sooner we knew of it the better'.[34]

Such was the Foreign Secretary's opening. A confused discussion followed. His ending was that the 'danger would be that if economic sanctions did not produce the needed result there would be a clamour for more drastic measures'.

The Cabinet met again on 2 October, the day before the Italian invasion of Abyssinia. Eden was back from Geneva and reported that 'the representatives of other nations were most reluctant to speak at all.[35] He would continue his efforts to induce them to do so. In the meantime he hoped his colleagues, in making speeches in the country, would continue to hammer on the theme that the Italo-Abyssinian dispute was not a British concern but a League of Nations affair and that the whole future of the League depended on how the question was handled . . . he was strongly impressed by the united and cordial support he had received at Geneva from the Dominions'.

The Cabinet agreed:

a) That Eden's influence should be used at Geneva 'to secure that the Council's Report on the Italo-Abyssinian dispute should contain a fair statement of the case without any concealment of the facts, but should not close the door to the possibility of territorial adjustment in the eventual settlement:

b) That military sanctions were out of the question, in view of the attitude of the French Government':

c) That the aim at Geneva should be the 'maximum of economic sanctions on which agreement could be secured'.

This last decision followed 'considerable discussion' about the 'relative advantages of imposing the strongest available economic sanctions and increasing them if they should prove ineffective'.[36]

On the 4th Baldwin spoke to the annual conference of the Conservative Party.[37] He spoke more of rearmament than of Abyssinia; he caused some annoyance by doing that again in the debate on the Foreign Office Vote on 18 June 1936, when the Abyssinian crisis was almost over.[38] (It seems true that, throughout the years 1934 to 1936, perhaps to his credit, his mind was more occupied with defence than foreign policy; certainly his main object during the first two of these three years, so far as public opinion was concerned, was to get a mandate for rearmament.) On this occasion he began, so far as League policy was concerned, by speaking against isolationism (then a popular doctrine with a large section of public opinion), went on to uphold 'true collective security', but ended by making it clear, with specific reference to Abyssinia, that 'His Majesty's Government have not, and have never had, any intention of taking isolated action in this dispute. . . .' Tom Jones summed the speech up: 'Denounced the isolationists, reconciled the Party to the League by supporting re-armament, and reconciled the pacifists to rearmament by supporting the Covenant. Spoke strongly in favour of Trade Unions. All with an eye to the election, on the date of which he was inscrutable.'[39] Election policy, and perhaps also its result, was foreshadowed; certainly the Party leader received a great ovation from the Party conference.

While Baldwin was speaking, Mussolini was acting. His Army had been invading Abyssinia since early on the morning of the 3rd. Baldwin, of course, knew this, but his only reference to the invasion was to say: 'Grave reports have reached the Council of the League within the last day or so regarding the movement of troops and aircraft within the boundaries of Abyssinia'.[40] When is an invasion not an invasion? When it is a 'movement of troops and aircraft' within somebody else's boundaries. Soviet newspapers of 1968, please copy.

14

The Great Powers
(October to December 1935)

On 9 October the Foreign Secretary told the Cabinet that 'at Geneva the course of events had been smoother than he had anticipated. . . . His communications with the American Ambassador had been particularly satisfactory'.[1] The Italian Ambassador had read him a long letter from Mussolini in the first part of which 'he had tried to indicate how little we understood the Italian position, and had suggested some kind of negotiations. . . .'

The Cabinet agreed that the Foreign Secretary 'should receive any Italian overtures for negotiations for a settlement outside the League of Nations very coolly at the present time . . . in any event he must receive detailed proposals before the possibility of entering into negotiations could be considered. . . .' The Cabinet also agreed 'that if oil-producing or supplying Member States, such as Roumania, were prepared to impose an embargo on oil, His Majesty's Government would be prepared to join in this and to consider further an embargo on exports of coal. . . .'[2]

On 23 October there was another Cabinet discussion of the possibility of a settlement of what was still, surprisingly, called the 'Italo-Ethiopian dispute'. In the course of this discussion Hoare said that 'any settlement must be within the framework of the League of Nations. . . .' He also told the Cabinet that he had sent a Foreign Office official 'who was an expert in Abyssinian affairs, to assist in Paris'.[3] This official was Mr. Maurice Peterson, who had been made head of a newly-created Abyssinian Department at the Foreign Office in August. His opposite number at the French Foreign Office was the Comte de St. Quentin, Head of the African Department.

On the same day (23 October) Baldwin announced the date of the General Election: 14 November. The British Constitution allows the reigning Prime Minister freedom (within a maximum period of five years) to choose this politically all-important date;[4] he cannot be blamed for a choice to suit the interests of the Government he heads; he is likely to think, sincerely, that they are also the interests of the nation. Baldwin chose well. He alleged a 'lull' in international affairs, but the atmosphere of an Election fought largely (a rare event) on international issues bred in Britain an atmosphere of international crisis. There was plenty of evidence that in times of crisis the British electorate tended to a Right turn. The ground had been further prepared by the Silver Jubilee (there was then an emotional identification of the Monarchy with the Right); by the replacement of Simon (identified with League's failure over the Manchurian crisis) by a new Foreign Secretary; by the immense success (at home and abroad), however unintended and unexpected, of Hoare's Assembly speech. The Labour Party was in obvious disarray, having just lost its Leaders in both Houses. (The new Leader of the Party, Attlee, was unknown and underrated).[5] Other factors, not of the Government's contriving, worked to its advantage. Unemployment was decreasing because world trade was improving.

The 'Peace Ballot' had plainly indicated that a sizeable proportion of the electorate backed economic, but not military, sanctions. This was now Government policy; 'All sanctions short of war' could have been a Conservative electoral slogan. The Conservative policy seemed to be one of rearmament and peace, the Labour policy one of disarmament and war.[6] The former option was by far the most attractive of the two. Chamberlain with his straight-forward and rebarbative mind had thought that the Election should be fought on Defence;[7] it was Baldwin, more far-seeing and more devious, who made the issue Peace.[8] This was the master-stroke, the old one of catching the Opposition bathing and putting on their clothes. It was not really surprising that the Labour party recovered so relatively little of the ground that it had lost in 1931. Its membership in the Commons went up from 52 to 154; the Government's majority came down from 427 to 247, but that is no trumpery majority.

The Government's Election manifesto proclaimed that the League of Nations would remain the keystone of its foreign policy and, for good measure, added that there would be no wavering in following the policy hitherto pursued. Not many voters could have known, or noticed, just how wavering it itself had been. Now a great mass of voters waited for the implementation of their votes. A Labour Member, David Grenfell, had asked in the old House of Commons on 22 October: 'Are we now preparing for the getaway which will satisfy Italy, which will be at the expense of Abyssinia?'[9] This was denied, but two days later the Election date was announced and the negotiations authorized which ended in the Hoare-Laval Pact. Ministers engaged in electioneering may well have been excusably unaware of the details of those negotiations;[10] the general public, for the most part, was excusably unaware even that they were going on. The Pact which eventually emerged from them was almost as much of a surprise to the former as to the latter.[11]

The new Parliament met on 3 December and the old Cabinet (there had been only one change since its formation in June)[12] held a special meeting the previous day to discuss the oil sanction. Hoare spoke first. He reminded the Cabinet that it had agreed to it on 9 October[13] and that the Committee of Eighteen had agreed to it on 15 November:[14]

> 'It might be said that all the Member States of the League except ourselves had expressed their willingness to support the oil sanction, and of the non-Member States the only one that counted was bringing pressure to bear on firms.'[15]

He had two recommendations:

1) On no account should we adopt a negative attitude to what we had already accepted on October 9th and November 29th, or give any appearance of refusing our part in genuine collective sanctions, provided that action was not going to be futile. Having taken the line that we have, and having fought the Election on it, incidentally, any other course of action would ... be disastrous and indefensible. Oil was obviously an effective sanction....[16]

2) We must press on with the peace negotiations as rapidly as possible, with a view to bringing the conflict to an end. Mr. Peterson, of the Foreign Office, was now in Paris engaged in conversations.[17] Not much progress had been made as yet.

He himself, however, had to go away for reasons of health for a short time, and he proposed on his journey to see M. Laval and to try and press on peace talks with him.'[18]

Thus was revealed to the Cabinet the Foreign Secretary's 'double policy'.[19] (He spoke openly of it to the House of Commons three days later.[20]) All that he was now in doubt about was whether the oil sanction 'ought to be brought in at once when the League Committee met, or whether, to give a better chance to the peace negotiations, the fixing of the date should be adjourned for a decision at a later meeting. On the whole he thought that, if the talks were going well, it would be wise to proceed with the embargo by two stages'.

Hoare's opening statement was followed by 'general discussion in the course of which the Prime Minister invited the opinion of every member of the Cabinet'. All 22 members were present and presumably each one spoke. Unfortunately we are only to a very small extent told who said what.

As might have been expected, given the responsible Minister's two recommendations, the ensuing 'general discussion' centred on the one point about which he had expressed himself as being in doubt, that of the date on which the oil sanction should be imposed. On this point, however, as we have just seen, he had in fact given a strong lead, in favour of imposition in two stages, 'if the talks were going well'.

In this connection we should remember that the question of a date for an oil sanction had been hanging fire since 6 November and that the necessary meeting of the Committee of Eighteen had already been postponed from 29 November to 12 December.[21] It was now 2 December and Eden told the Cabinet that his information was that the Committee's recommendations would be that the oil sanction should be imposed on the 21st. He 'urged strongly that if he was asked to do all he could to obtain a postponement in the date of sanctions he must be instructed on no account to break the common front.... If there were a good prospect of a result for the peace talks, it might be possible to obtain a postponement of the date, but if the prospects were not good he asked that he might not be given instructions to work for two stages'. But it is not clear whether or not the Minister for League of Nations Affairs carried the Cabinet with him about this:

'There was general agreement on the Secretary of State's proposal, if possible, to divide the application of the oil sanction into two stages, the principle being confirmed at the first, and the date left to be settled at the second stage if in the meantime no settlement had been reached.'

On this basis an oil sanction would have been imposed in fact in four stages, the second being the confirmation of the principle already agreed, the third the fixing of a date for its application, the fourth the actual application.

The fixing of the date for imposing an oil sanction at a second stage if, at the first stage, 'no settlement has been reached' is not the same as 'if the prospects were not good'. The Prime Minister 'was not willing to be committed at this moment to the 21st December as the date of the application of oil sanctions'.

One may judge that there was no drive for the imposition of an oil sanction at the earliest possible date. On the contrary much in the long, loosely worded, and rambling account of the 'general discussion' supports the view that there was no enthusiasm for it and considerable desire for delay. Certainly a Foreign Secretary, due to go away five days later for two or three weeks' holiday, was not going to give the matter much personal attention.

The efficacy of an oil sanction was not called in question. Doubts were not cast on the readiness of oil-producing Member States to apply one. The element of uncertainty about the American attitude was given as a possible, not a firm, reason for not going ahead. (The final decision on this point was 'further to test the attitude of the United States of America and the probability of effective action being taken in that country to stop the supply of oil to Italy. . . .') The negative attitudes were, to a small extent, concerned with the ill consequences of sanctions on the British economy ('That justified, not the wiping out of sanctions, but great caution, where British trade was concerned'), to a great extent with the future of the League. Thus, 'Another point made was that the position would be worse in the future if, having attempted sanctions, sanctions failed'. Again, one suggestion made in the course of the discussion was that, if the result of oil sanctions was to produce war, it would break the League of Nations, since no one would support a League which not only failed to stop the war but actually extended it'. 'If', said Baldwin, 'the claim that had been made that sanctions meant war proved by experience to be true, it would be a disaster of the first magnitude'.

One unusually crisp passage in the account of the 'general discussions' reads:

'The object of an oil sanction was to stop war. If the war could be stopped by making peace that would be better. That ought to be tried, therefore, if there were a reasonable prospect of success. The question at issue was whether an oil sanction would contribute towards a peaceful solution or make Signor Mussolini more intransigent.'

Much attention was given to his possible moves. Hoare had said at the start:

'Signor Mussolini was expecting the date of the oil sanction to be fixed at Geneva next week. If there were a postponement this would be such a relief to him that he was unlikely to take precipitate action in consequence of a mere confirmation of a principle already accepted.'

Baldwin said at the end: 'It had to be remembered that in dealing with Signor Mussolini we were not dealing with a normal kind of intellect'. In between, the First Lord of the Admiralty and the Secretary of State for Air weightily 'represented that our defence forces and defences in the Mediterranean were not in a proper condition for war, and from this point of view it was urged that an effort should be made to obtain peace, holding the threat of an oil sanction over Italy, and that the fixing of the date should not be decided until after a failure of peace discussions'.[22] *Per contra* the new Secretary of State for War boldly said: 'As regards the date, postponement for a few weeks, or a month, was not going to make much difference in our state of preparedness. . . .' Both First Lord and Air Secretary wanted 'binding arrangements with France'; the War Secretary said that 'the General Staff were somewhat doubtful as to the necessity for military conversations'.

On this important point the action to be taken was defined as 'An early continuation of the military conversations which had already begun between the Admiralty and the French Ministry of Marine, and which should now be extended to the Air Force and, if necessary, to the Army ... for ensuring full co-operation between the Naval, Military and Air authorities of the two countries. . . .'

At the end of the meeting 'The suggestion was made that a week was a very short time to establish whether the peace conversations were going well or not and to clear up the military point. It was hoped that the Foreign Secretary would take a generous view of the Italian attitude'. He 'agreed that the peace talks must be given the best possible chance'. He next said that he thought it best to open up the subject of further military conversations with France when he saw Laval on 7 December. It was then pointed out that this did not allow much time before the Committee of Eighteen met at Geneva on the 12th, 'before which time the Cabinet wished to be clear on the subject'. Hoare, however, maintained that 'the French Government was so preoccupied with their internal political troubles that it would be difficult to begin conversations in any event before 5 December.[23] On the whole, therefore, the Foreign Secretary's suggestion was accepted, on the understanding that he would press the matter forward as rapidly as possible'.

He was also charged with 'Pressing on by every useful means with discussions with the countries concerned, with a view, if possible, to a peaceful settlement. . . .' If the peace talks did not offer any reasonable prospect of a settlement or if the military conversations showed that France was not willing to co-operate effectively he was to bring 'the question' back for consideration by the Cabinet.

So far as the peace talks were concerned, the guidance of his colleagues apparently amounted only to the 'hope that he would take a generous view of the Italian attitude'. The minutes of this special Cabinet meeting taken as a whole confirm, however, the view that by this time Ministers had acquired very great confidence in the 'policy' the Foreign Secretary was pursuing. Looking back on its complete collapse which was so soon to follow, Lord Avon writes:

'The events of these days cannot be understood unless the reputation of Hoare is recalled as it stood with his colleagues at the time. Like all politicians, the Foreign Secretary had his detractors, but there was one conclusion in which most critics would have acquiesced, that he was cautious and shrewd. This belief strongly influenced members of the Government, including myself, and it explains, if it does not excuse, our conduct.'[24]

There were, however, palpable grounds for uneasiness. Three days after this Cabinet meeting and two days before his departure for Paris, Hoare spoke in the House of Commons of having 'consistently and steadily followed the double line that has time after time been approved by the League and by this House. On the one hand we have taken our full part in the collective action under the Covenant, and on the other hand we have continued our efforts for a peaceful settlement'. But there had been no double line in the sentiments of the speech to the League Assembly on 11 September: 'The League stands, and my country stands with it, for the collective maintenance of the Covenant in its entirety, and particularly for steady and collective resistance to all acts of unprovoked aggression'. The speaker had gone on to say, of the 'attitude of the British nation' at that time, that it showed 'no variable and unreliable sentiment, but a principle of international conduct to which they and their Government held with firm, enduring and universal persistence'. The British nation was now confidently expecting its Government to stick to the principle thus proclaimed on 11 September and ratified on 14 November; its faith in that Government was about to be severely tested – tested, one could say, almost to destruction.

15

The advice of Admirals

We have seen how in Cabinet the Foreign Secretary frequently referred to the state of public opinion.[1] But there was another sort of opinion to which His Majesty's Ministers, and especially the Prime Minister, had, perfectly properly, to pay most careful attention: the opinion of the men at the top of the Armed Forces about the probable outcome of a war with Italy. It would be an utterly irresponsible Government which went to war, or took action likely to lead to war, in defiance of professional opinion that the war was likely to be lost. The only exception to this would be a judgment that, in a given case, national suicide was to be preferred to national survival.

On 3 July (a critical day in the meetings of the Italo-Abyssinian Arbitration Commission at Scheveningen) Baldwin, through Hankey, asked the Chiefs of Staff for their views on the implications of Britain discharging her obligations under Article 16 of the Covenant.[2] On the 30th they reported that even economic sanctions 'would almost inevitably lead to war', as would 'any steps taken to interrupt Italy's communications with Abyssinia'.[3] At the Ministers' meeting on 6 August he asked for the Chiefs of Staff 'at once to examine the question of what the position would be if Italy took the bit between her teeth. . . .'[4]

One of the foundation-stones for British policy throughout the Abyssinian crisis was thus laid. Britain was to prepare herself against an attack by Italy arising out of the crisis, a so-called 'mad dog act'.[5] There was no conception, however, virtually no discussion even, of the possibility that it might be a British interest, whether as a Member of the League or in terms of national interests as defined in pre-League days or in both capacities, to take the initiative in cutting Italy's communications with Abyssinia, i.e. preventing the entry of Italian ships into the Suez

Canal.[6] More than once Baldwin said that there was to be no blockade.

A second foundation-stone was that all British preparations to meet an Italian attack were to be played down, not for security reasons, but because the policy was not to be that of deterring Italy from her Abyssinian war by a show of force. On the contrary pains were to be taken not to irritate Italy. On 22 August the Cabinet, at its special meeting on the crisis, 'were strongly opposed to the mobilization of reserves, either for the Navy or the Army, if this could be avoided, owing to the resounding effect it would have on public opinion both at home and abroad'.[7] The publicity for the arrival of the two battle cruisers at Gibraltar in September was not sought.

Thus did the Government refrain from some military preparations for a possibly imminent war, while refraining also from deliberate publicity for the military preparations which were made. It is now known that on 14 August Mussolini had received the opinion of his Chiefs of Staff that a war with Britain would be disastrous.[8] (To have ignored that advice would, by the definition stated at the start of this Chapter, have been utterly irresponsible.) It is also known, however, that as late as February 1936 no war orders had been sent to the Italian naval commander.[9] That may have been inefficiency; it may merely show that Mussolini never took the British 'threat' seriously.

The British Chiefs of Staff, however, took seriously the possibility of an Italian attack on the British forces in the Mediterranean. It was their duty to do so. It is therefore not surprising that in 1935 the British Chiefs of Staff stressed heavily the risks and dangers of war with Italy. It was, however, for the Cabinet itself in the last resort to weigh those risks and dangers alongside all the other factors to be put into the scales. Such measurements can never be scientific. In the last resort it is a matter of judgment and such judgments are the highest, and also the most difficult, function of the statesman, above all the statesman at the top. Winston Churchill confirms that point: 'The brunt of supreme decisions centre upon him. At the summit where all problems are reduced to Yea or Nay, where events transcend the faculties of man and where all is inscrutable, he has to give the answers. His is the function of the compass needle. War or no war? Quit or persevere?'.[10]

At the point just reached in the preceding chronological narrative, the special Cabinet meeting of 2 December on the oil sanction, the First Lord of the Admiralty and the Air Secretary had
been emphatic that 'our defence forces and defences in the
Mediterranean were not in a proper condition for war' and that
therefore 'an effort should be made to obtain peace, holding the
threat of the oil sanction over Italy, and that the fixing of the date
should not be decided until after a failure of peace discussions'.[11]
The minutes later record the view that:

> 'The Cabinet ought to give the greatest consideration to [their]
> grave observations and their warning of the possibility of
> serious losses, for if we proceeded with the oil sanction and it
> brought about a serious reverse, the public would not easily
> forgive the Government, especially when the serious warnings
> of the Defence Departments became known.'[12]

The First Lord of the Admiralty in 1935 was Sir Bolton Eyres-
Monsell, later Viscount Monsell. Before being given that office in
1931 he had been Chief Whip since 1923, when he was already
one of Baldwin's oldest political friends.[13] The First Lord's influence over the Prime Minister was therefore likely to be greater
than that normal in that relationship. On the other hand, the
First Lord, having once been Commander, R.N., was perhaps on
that account more likely to defer to the First Sea Lord than the
political head of the Admiralty normally would. In any event, the
First Sea Lord (and Chief of the Naval Staff) at the time of the
Abyssinian crisis, Sir Ernle, later Lord Chatfield, was an
altogether exceptional Naval Officer whose abilities few civilians,
or other Naval Officers, came near to matching. Chatfield has
described Monsell as 'a pleasant political chief' who gave him his
head.[14] Admiral Chatfield not only dominated the Board of
Admiralty but also the Chiefs of Staff Sub-Committee of the
Committee for Imperial Defence. Of this Sub-Committee he was
Chairman throughout his period of office as First Sea Lord from
1933 to 1938. (This office rotated between the Chiefs of Staff of
the three Services. In 1933 it just happened to be the Navy's
turn.) It is significant in this connection that his career culmin-
ated in his being Minister for the Co-ordination of Defence in the
War Cabinet formed in 1939 by Neville Chamberlain. In 1935

'Chatfield's views on strategic matters carried exceptional weight with the Government'.[15] This is what one would have expected, apart from the personal factors involved, inasmuch as the strategic matters concerned were primarily Naval. No one had more important advice to offer the Government on the 'military' aspects of the situation than the Chief of the Naval Staff.

Chatfield counselled a very high degree of political caution and was most anxious that Britain should not get involved in a 'League war' against Italy. This attitude did not derive from political but from strictly Naval considerations. In private, however, and speaking 'personally', he hoped that 'the "Geneva Pacifists" would fail to get unanimity' and that the League would break up, but this was because he did not 'want to go to extreme measures'.[16]

The Naval case for not wanting to go to 'extreme measures' may be summarized under five main heads:

1) *The danger from Germany*

After the Naval dispositions made in September 1935 the only naval forces readily available in Home waters were one six-inch cruiser, 17 destroyers, and nine submarines. Germany had three 'pocket battleships' which only the two battle cruisers (*Hood* and *Renown*), then stationed at Gibraltar, could take on.[17] War with Germany in these circumstances could have meant that British trade routes could be disrupted, British coasts bombarded, and no Expeditionary Force moved overseas. This nightmare came perilously near reality with the Rhineland crisis of 1936.[18] At that time it became quite clear that *either* no war with Germany could be contemplated *or* there would have to be a wholesale withdrawal of our Forces from the Mediterranean.

2) *The danger from Japan*

In these days of deliberate contraction of British interests 'east of Suez' it is hard to recapture the atmosphere of 1935 when there was a consensus, by and large, of British political opinion that deemed – rightly or wrongly – that we had important interests in the Far East, that these interests were in potential peril from Japan, and that we must stand ready forcibly to defend the Far Eastern interests of the British Empire against attack by the Japanese.[19] On the other hand, the danger from Japan was substantially overlooked by public opinion in general, even by those who had cried for sanctions against Japan only four years earlier. Perhaps this was because Japanese expansion in China had halted in 1933 and had rapidly been forgotten. Moreover, the pacificist British democracy was (and is?) reluctant to take an interest in Defence questions.

In 1935 the Japanese Navy was far more powerful than the German one. The Royal Navy could not take on the Japanese Navy if simultaneously heavily engaged with Italy in the Mediterranean; still less could Britain hope to beat both Japan and Italy if also at war with Germany. This nightmare became reality in 1941. By that time, however, Britain had two Great Powers as Allies. In 1935, though many Small Powers looked to Britain for a lead and were willing to do what they could to help, she could not count on the help of Russia, or to the fullest extent on the country whose help, in the particular circumstances, was most needed, France.

3) *The danger from the air*

The aerial danger to warships, whether at sea or in port, and the quality of the Italian Air Arm (*Regia Aeronautica*), were unknown quantities in 1935. It therefore behoved the Royal Navy to take the danger from the air seriously. The most important consequence of doing so was a decision (by the Cabinet), on 22 August, that on the 29th the Mediterranean Fleet should start to move from Malta (only 60 miles from airfields in Sicily) to Alexandria. This operation was completed by 24 September.

4) *Lack of help from France*

The move from Malta entailed a very serious diminution of the docking facilities which would be needed in the event of war. In these circumstances the 'only docks available would be those at Gibraltar, which could not take capital ships, and one at Alexandria, which could take nothing larger than a small cruiser. Repair facilities would be similarly limited. Damaged ships most probably would have to return to England for repairs, if they were able to do so, or remain out of action for an indefinite period. The availability of the French naval bases of Toulon and Bizerta would have solved this problem'.[20] For this reason, above all others, was the co-operation of France wanted in the event of an

Anglo-Italian war. In addition, 'Offensive French air operations (with the participation of an R.A.F. contingent) against suitable targets in northern Italy would divert to an important degree the air threat to Malta and to the Mediterranean Fleet when operating in the central area'. Moreover, 'Allied French naval forces in the western Mediterranean, along with the Gibraltar force, would constitute a threat to Italy's west coast that would prevent her withdrawing all her warships from that coast and concentrating them against the British Mediterranean Fleet'.[21]

On 15 October, however (after, that is to say, the start of the war in Abyssinia), Laval said that France fully subscribed to Article 16, Clause 3 ('The Members of the League will mutually support one another in resisting any special measures aimed at one of their Members by the Covenant-breaking State'), but added the reservation that he would not consider this Clause applicable if Italy alleged that the British Naval build-up in the Mediterranean went beyond the sanctions agreed at Geneva. The British Ambassador was therefore instructed to 'insist on a categorical and explicit withdrawal' of this reservation. Laval, under this pressure – and throughout the crisis he always yielded, or appeared to yield, to strong British pressure – gave on the 18th an assurance of military support and on the 30th a representative of the French Naval Staff (Admiral Decoux) met Chatfield in London and assured him that French naval bases, 'either in France or North Africa', would in the event of war, be made available to the Royal Navy for docking, repair, and, if need be, operational purposes.[22] It was also promised that France would mobilize when Britain did, but French unreadiness for war meant that actual entry into it might not follow mobilization for some weeks. In addition, there were Anglo-French Naval Staff talks which got off to a slow start; Army and Air Staff talks did not begin until 9 December. All three negotiations lingered on till mid-January, but little came of them. No detailed arrangements were worked out and what was agreed in principle was never officially approved by the French Government.[23] (It is only fair to remember that in January 1935 Britain had refused Anglo-French Staff talks outright.)[24] In these circumstances any British Government would have been bound to feel that French help, if war with Italy came, was not to be relied on.

On 13 December the three Chiefs of Staff summarized the

situation in a telegram to the three Commanders-in-Chief in the Mediterranean:

'It appears that our own forces will have to sustain the war for a not inconsiderable period. France and Greece, however, have promised full use of their ports, and Turkey is willing to co-operate with her limited air forces. The situation as regards the military co-operation of France is at the present time profoundly unsatisfactory....'[25]

It remained so for the duration of the crisis.

5) *British unreadiness for war*

By the end of September Britain had in the Mediterranean two battle cruisers, two aircraft carriers, and five battleships; Italy had no battle cruisers, one aircraft carrier, and two battleships. On the other hand, there were 17 Italian cruisers to the British 15 and 65 Italian destroyers to 54. Italy had far more submarines, 62 to 11. Chatfield was reasonably satisfied with the number of his vessels, but without mobilization the number of men was so limited as to put crews under great strain. There was also a shortage of ammunition, especially anti-aircraft ammunition, and many other supplies of all kinds. It was reckoned in mid-August that it would take two months to remedy these deficiencies,[26] and the next two months were taken good advantage of in this respect. The supply of anti-aircraft ammunition, however, continued to be a cause for concern, but laymen in London were more frightened by this deficiency than sailors on the spot. Lord Vansittart was later to reveal his opinion that the 'greatest among our many weaknesses was the fact, hidden, that we had only anti-aircraft ammunition enough to fire at full speed for less than half an hour.' This, however sounds much more serious than it in fact was, for it was technically difficult for any anti-aircraft gun to be fired continuously for as much as half an hour and highly improbable that any one aerial attack would last for more than a few minutes.[27]

By mid-October, therefore, Britain had, broadly speaking, the right ships in the right places with the right equipment. It must be appreciated, however, that the efficiency of a Fleet, kept in a state of constant readiness for action so far from home and with no 'fat' in terms of men and materials, was bound to be a gradually wasting asset. By Mid-November Chatfield was worried at the extent to which refit programmes and reliefs of personnel were over-due.[28] In other words, the point of maximum power for the British Naval Forces in the Mediterranean more or less coincided with the start of the war in Abyssinia. If British forces were at any time to be used to stop it, that would have been the technically best time to do so.

It must be emphasized that top Naval personnel were not reluctant to 'start anything' with Italy in 1935, or go beyond appropriate defensive precautions, because of any lack of confidence in a British victory if Italy 'started anything'. The very reverse was the case. Admiral of the Fleet, Lord Cunningham, who was then Rear-Admiral, Destroyer Flotillas, Mediterranean, has written that, to those in the Mediterranean Fleet at the time, it seemed a very simple task to stop Mussolini:

> 'The mere closing of the Suez Canal to his transports which were then streaming through with troops and stores would effectively have cut out his armies concentrating in Eritrea and elsewhere. It is true that such a drastic measure might have led to war with Italy, but the Mediterranean Fleet was in a state of high morale and efficiency, and had no fear whatever of the result of an encounter with the Italian Navy.'[29]

Chatfield himself asserted, early in the crisis, that 'the final outcome of a conflict with Italy cannot be a matter of doubt ...'[30] On 3 September, in a paper to the Defence Policy and Requirements Sub-Committee of the C.I.D., he dwelt on Italy's disadvantageous strategic position:

> 'With our forces based at Gibraltar and in Egypt, her main communications can be cut with comparatively little effort to ourselves, whereas to take any steps (excepting by submarine) to counter our action she would have to send her forces far from their bases where they would be brought to action. This strategical advantage is so great that it is unlikely that Italy could make any serious attempt with Naval forces to interfere with our control of the two exits to the Mediterranean except by the submarines, which could not prove decisive. Further,

Italy's object is the prosecution of her Abyssinian war, and the mere closing of the Canal to her by the presence of our Naval forces ... might be decisive within a reasonable period.'[31]

The Admiral 'on the spot', Sir William Fisher, C-in-C, Mediterranean Fleet, could not have been, in terms of warfare, more offensively-minded.[32] The policy he had advocated in August was to bring the Home Fleet as far forward as Malta, but (as we have seen) it was decided that, for the duration of the crisis, Malta should not be used as a base. Chatfield did not think this a serious disadvantage, writing to Fisher: 'Malta is a minor matter in the long run ... if Italy is mad enough to challenge us, it is at the ends of the Mediterranean she will be defeated and, knowing that her communications are cut, you yourself will have a freer hand in the Central Mediterranean....'[33]

Success in warfare, however, does not depend merely on the successful exploitation of strategic advantages, backed by adequate supplies and adequate man-power. Other factors, less easy to quantify, play an important part. One such is tradition, which includes stories of past success. To serve in a British Fleet is, from this point of view, in itself morale-raising. Not only its Admirals but its seamen held a low opinion of their potential opponents which at that time was probably justified. The 'high morale and efficiency', mentioned by Cunningham, were worth much in strictly practical terms.

So the British Navy was confident that it could win a single-handed war against Italy. But those on whom fell the duty of long-run thinking (whether Naval Officers or their political masters) had to think one war ahead. There was a good chance that there would be no trouble with Germany or Japan, or both together, if and while Britain was engaged in war with Italy. If so, it was a virtual certainty that that war would be won. It was, however, absolutely certain that it would not be won without losses, probably grave. And what then about the 'next war'? If it came soon after war with Italy it would be a victorious but weakened Royal Navy which would have to fight a German or Japanese Navy or both. Certainly the British losses could be made good, but that would take time, especially in respect of building new ships, and in any case also the quantum from which any expansion of the pre-war forces was to be made would be smaller.

This was the most sophisticated and also the weightiest argument against war with Italy in 1935. Putting it another way, although still a Great Power, Britain had over-stretched her resources; foreign policy had run ahead of defence policy; she really had not the resources to be simultaneously a Great Power in the Atlantic, the Mediterranean, and the Pacific. (This was appreciated at the time by many people as a short-run proposition; by few as a long-run one; by almost everybody by 1941). Chatfield told Baldwin's closest friend, J. C. C. Davidson: 'The cable of Imperial Defence is stretched bar taut. Italy is the gnat whose weight could snap it'.[34]

Professor Marder, whose researches have so brilliantly illuminated the subject-matter of this Chapter, opens his important article with the words: 'Ever since its unhappy dénouement, the Abyssinian crisis has been turned into a kind of morality play'.[35] In his next sentence he says: 'Without attempting an analysis of the pros and cons of the policy of appeasement . . . this essay will try to demonstrate that the orthodox judgment on British policy is far too simplistic, ignoring as it does powerful military considerations'. The demonstration, even allowing for the immediately preceding qualification, can be judged to be successful. Simple denunciations of British immorality, both contemporary and retrospective, have indeed ignored 'powerful military considerations'. In his penultimate paragraph Professor Marder writes: 'One cannot read the minutes of the Cabinet or of the Defence Policy and Requirements Sub-Committee without appreciating that military considerations, mainly naval factors, were very much in the minds of the decision-makers'.[36] That is abundantly true. It is right and proper that it was so and that that fact should be emphasized today. But a single set of factors, rightly in the minds of decision-makers, should not, however important, necessarily be decisive overall. In this particular case the military risks were sufficiently conjectural not to be in themselves decisive against war with Italy; a larger, political judgment was required. One comes back to Churchill's point:[37] in a supreme crisis in public affairs the man at the summit must do his best to weigh all the sets of factors (including powerful moral considerations) even if he cannot begin to be able to do so in a scientific fashion (the calculation of a risk is a contradiction in terms). 'His is the function of the compass needle'; he must reduce the complexities to 'Yea' or 'Nay' and point to one or the other. Was British support of the League, as the Abyssinian crisis approached its climax, to be wholesale, whole-hearted, and carried to its logical conclusion, despite the military risks? That was the question to which Baldwin, weighing all the factors, had to say 'Yea' or 'Nay'.

16

Hoare-Laval

In the first week of December 1935 each of four separate, though related, happenings were simultaneously moving towards a crisis: the discussion of a more determined effort, by means of an oil sanction, to coerce the Covenant-breaker; negotiations for Anglo-French military co-operation in face of possible 'mad-doggery' on his part; the Peterson-St. Quentin negotiations in Paris for an Anglo-French basis for possible peace terms between the two belligerents; and the state of health of the British Foreign Secretary.

Sir Samuel Hoare had not been physically fit when he had been talked into taking the Foreign Secretaryship in June:[1] in August he had had to take to his bed because of acute pain in one foot;[2] that trouble cleared up, but in late September he was telling Eden that he was far from well;[3] in November he was alarming his friends by 'black-outs'.[4] One account describes him as 'blue and mottled from fatigue and stress' on 5 December.[5] He was an enthusiastic, silver-medal skater and it was now arranged that he should leave London on Saturday, 7 December, for a skating holiday at Zuoz in Switzerland. At just this time Laval, seemingly no longer able to delay a Geneva discussion of the oil sanction and alarmed at Mussolini's possible reactions to it, invited himself to London to discuss the situation. It seemed easier all round for Hoare to stop off at Paris on his way to Switzerland. It was decided that Vansittart, who was already in Paris, partly by way of a holiday and partly for the purpose of countering an exceptionally violent anti-British campaign in the French Press, should join the Foreign Secretary for his meeting with Laval on the Saturday afternoon. Sir George Clerk, the Ambassador, and Mr. Peterson could also be present. It seemed unlikely that thus attended a new and inexperienced Foreign Secretary could make a bad mistake.

As we have just seen, it was agreed at the Cabinet meeting on 2 December that the opportunity of Hoare's meeting with Laval in Paris should be used to open up the subject of further military conversations with France. He was also to take the opportunity to discuss the possibility of a peaceful settlement of the 'Italo-Ethiopian dispute'. On the 3rd Peterson had asked for further instructions and was told that Hoare and Vansittart would take over the negotiations.[6] It would fall to Eden to state the British view on the oil sanction at Geneva on the 12th and the nature of that view would to a great extent depend on the outcome of the Paris conversations on the 7th.

Hoare's colleagues, however, did not expect those conversations to be more than exploratory. A Foreign Secretary would never normally undertake so important a negotiation as one for the ending of a war without detailed instructions. In this instance the only relevant instruction from the Cabinet was a 'hope that he would take a generous view of the Italian attitude'. (This phrase was to be echoed by Laval after the Hoare-Laval Pact had been drawn up.)[7] The Prime Minister said only: 'Have a good leave, and get your health back. By all means stop in Paris, and push Laval as far as you can, but on no account get this country into war'.[8] There was as friendly and informal a farewell interchange with the Minister for League of Nations Affairs. Lord Avon has described it:

'A short time before Hoare's departure, he and I stood talking at the top of the Foreign Office staircase. I warned him against Laval and added, more lightly, remembering our August negotiations: "Don't forget that in Paris, Van can be more French than the French". "Don't worry", came the confident reply, "I shall not commit you to anything. It wouldn't be fair on my way through to my holiday".'[9]

Hoare took some 'home work' with him, but it concerned possible negotiations with Germany, not the Abyssinian crisis.[10]

In retrospect, Lord Templewood blamed himself for not insisting on 'a special Cabinet, and a clear agreement as to how far I could go with Laval.... I did not then think it necessary, as I had no intention of committing the Government to any final plan'.[11] This seems disingenuous in the light of a letter he wrote to the King's Private Secretary (Lord Wigram), on 2 December:

> 'As my visit to M. Laval on Saturday may be very important, I am proposing to take Vansittart with me. If, as I hope, M. Laval and I agree upon a basis for a peace negotiation, Vansittart will stop on in Paris for a day or two in order to clinch the details. . . .'[12]

Moreover, on 5 December Hoare met the Dominion High Commissioners and told them that 'he was going to see M. Laval . . . and if it was possible to reach an agreement with him on joint proposals'.[13]

So the possibility of an agreement with Laval was in Hoare's mind before he left for Paris. Of course any such pact would only be provisional in the sense that it would have to be accepted by Abyssinia, Italy, the League, and (neither least nor last at this stage) the British Cabinet. It seems, however, possible that this normally so restrained a man may at this time have been overcome by a *folie de grandeur*; he may have hoped, relying on the exceptional confidence his colleagues had in him, to bring off a diplomatic success even more brilliant and sensational than that achieved, however unintentionally, at Geneva on 11 September. It seems possible also that his fatigue may have been the basis both of such a *folie* and of the impatience for which he later castigated himself. How anxious he must have been, after those strenuous years at the India Office, to have this new and appalling burden lifted, one way or another:

> 'As the weeks passed I became more and more impatient, and impatience is the unforgivable sin that all Foreign Secretaries must avoid. Perhaps it was the strain on my nerves during my four years at the India Office that had made them oversensitive. . . . Perhaps, also, the climbing of a very Everest of Parliamentary mountains had made me feel oversure of my ability to surmount new peaks. In any case, I rushed the attempt before I was ready for it. . . . Perhaps, too, I shrank from showing my weak hand to the world when I believed that I could still win with it, if I was left to play it myself. Had not

Sir Edward Grey kept his intentions to himself and away from colleagues who might have embarrassed him?'[14]

It was a sick man in a hurry, perhaps sick in mind as well as body, who arrived in Paris on the afternoon of Saturday 7 December.[15] It was perhaps in the same mood that at Zuoz on the morning of the 10th he hurried on to the skating rink, feeling that there was no turn or step he could not accomplish, had the worst black-out of the lot, fell and broke his nose on the thick ice.[16]

Hoare and Laval began their conversations at the Quai D'Orsay (the French Foreign Office) at 5.30 p.m. on the 7th. After some two-and-a-half hours' work Hoare agreed (contrary to his plan on leaving London) to continue it the next day.[17] The conversations were resumed at 10.15 a.m. on Sunday, the 8th, and continued, with a brief interval for lunch, till 6.30 p.m. Thereafter Hoare caught the 10.30 p.m. train to the Engadine, while Vansittart remained in Paris 'to discuss the details'. The two principals had been accompanied throughout by Vansittart, Clerk, and Peterson on the British side, Leger, St. Quentin and Massigli on the French.

On the Saturday evening an innocuous communiqué was issued. On the Sunday evening came another, liable to stir up a hornets' nest and seeming, moreover, to take for granted the Cabinet's agreement to proposals implied to be honourable. The crucial passages ran:

'... we have in the course of our long conversations today and yesterday sought the formulae which might serve as a basis for a friendly settlement of the Italo-Ethiopian dispute.

'There could be no question of publishing these formulae. The British Government has not yet been informed of them and once its agreement has been received it will be necessary to submit them to the consideration of the interested governments and to discussion by the League of Nations.

'We have worked together ... to reach as rapidly as possible a peaceful and honourable solution.'

Lord Halifax wrote to Eden a fortnight later: 'The more I think of it, the more clearly do I feel that Sam's communiqué was the *fons et origo* of all our troubles. And I think it's an amazing mistake for him to have made.'[18]

During the Sunday afternoon Hoare wired London asking for a Cabinet the next day.[19] While he travelled through the night to Switzerland, Peterson was returning to London by the overnight Dieppe-Newhaven service,[20] carrying with him a single copy of a four-page typescript in French, initialled by Hoare and Laval, and a short letter from the former saying it was essential that the Cabinet should take a prompt decision on the proposals set out in the first document. He also said that they were well within the framework of those put forward by the Committee of Five (in September) and were on the basis agreed in London.

Peterson did not bring with him a transcript of the second day's conversations. A transcript of the first day's conversations had, however, arrived at the Foreign Office on the Sunday morning, together with the text of the first communiqué. Eden, who was spending the week-end in London, studied these two documents and felt worried. His unease was increased by the telegram asking, without explanation, for a Cabinet on Monday. He called on Baldwin at No. 10 on Sunday evening to give him the little information he had about what had gone on in Paris and it was agreed that more information was needed. (The second communiqué had not then reached London.) Eden 'phoned the British Embassy in Paris. On asking for Hoare he was told that he was resting and unavailable. Vansittart was also unavailable because staying at the Ritz Hotel. A request for some indication of the course of events produced, after a short pause, the message that 'The Secretary of State and Sir Robert Vansittart are well satisfied with the day's work'. It was added that Hoare was about to leave for Switzerland and Peterson for London, 'with a full record of the conversations.'[21]

It seemed to Eden that Hoare's imminent departure for his Swiss holiday indicated an absence of any exceptional event. Baldwin agreed that they could only await Peterson's arrival the next morning. The two pieces of paper he brought with him to breakfast with Eden on Monday must have seemed to his host the equivalent of a ticking bomb.

Little or nothing is to be gained now by a detailed account of the Hoare-Laval conversations. They went smoothly. What matters is the 'Pact' which came from them, the reactions to it throughout the world, especially the reaction of British public opinion, and the results of those reactions. It must, however, at least be said that it is erroneous to envisage an innocent British fly being lured by a French spider into a Parisian parlour and eaten up for its benefit. Hoare, though an inexperienced Foreign Secretary engaged on his first important negotiation, was 'fly' enough to take on Laval on equal terms. Moreover, he had, if he chose to use them, strong cards to play against Laval. He subsequently made no complaint against Laval's conduct of the meeting, no suggestion that he had been unduly pressed, let alone tricked. His mind, after all, had been working on basically the same lines as his *confrère's*. It was easy for Hoare to go more than half-way to meet Laval's suggestions.[22]

Laval was genuinely concerned about the danger, as he saw it, of the oil sanction. He thought that Mussolini might react so violently to its imposition as to bring to an end the Franco-Italian Alliance, to the immense advantage of Hitler. Laval, therefore, was not prepared to agree to an oil sanction until after a determined attempt at a settlement. Hoare also was concerned about the German menace, anxious to retain Italian friendship, eager to arrange a settlement, reluctant to impose the oil sanction. This being so, the agreement initialled in Paris on 8 December 1935 was fairly described as a Hoare-Laval Pact as opposed to a Laval-Hoare one.

The two principal features of the Pact can be summarized under heads quoted from the text:

1. *'Exchange of territories'*
Abyssinia was to receive an outlet to the sea, with full sovereign rights, preferably by the Italian cession of a strip of Eritrea adjacent to French Somaliland, giving access to the sea, and including the port of Assab. In return, Abyssinia was to cede eastern Tigre to Italy and, further east, a portion of the Danakil country. Abyssinia was also to cede a substantial portion of Ogaden.[23]

2. *'Zone of Economic Expansion and Settlement'*
'The limits of this zone would be: on the east, the rectified frontier between Ethiopia and Italian Somaliland; on the north, the 8th parallel; on the west the 35th meridian; on the south the

frontier between Ethiopia and Kenya. Within this zone, which would form an integral part of Ethiopia, Italy would enjoy exclusive economic rights. . . .'[24]

To this zone would be applied the scheme of assistance which the Committee of Five had proposed for the whole of Abyssinia; in the administration of the scheme 'Italy would take a preponderating, but not an exclusive share'. In charge would be a 'principal adviser' to the Central Government 'who might be of Italian nationality . . .' There would, however, above this official be a 'Chief Adviser who would not be a subject of one of the Powers bordering on Ethiopia'.[25]

The proposals can be summarized still more briefly. Mussolini was not only to be allowed to retain the territory (which included the sacred soil of Adowa) he had already conquered, but also to acquire areas further east which he had not conquered and 'exclusive economic rights' in a vast area to the south. The only sacrifice he was to make in return was, possibly, the corridor to Assab. Even on this basis the heading 'Exchange of Territories' was an effrontery. It was added, however, that Abyssinia was to be allowed a choice between a corridor to Assab and a corridor to Zeila. The latter would be created by a British cession of territory. If, therefore, that preference was exercised, 'Exchange of Territories' would, as between Italy and Abyssinia, become a complete misnomer.[26]

Such was the essence of the pact agreed by the two Ministers on the evening of 8 December. The next morning full details of it appeared in two French newspapers. On the 10th this news ran round the world. Whether the original 'leak' was by Laval, or aimed at him, is a question which has been much discussed but is of little moment. What mattered was that the disclosure made nonsense of the proposed procedure of putting the plan in secret to the British Government in the first place and thereafter, if acceptable to them, as rapidly as possible, but still in secret, to Italy, Abyssinia, and the League, in that order.

The Hoare-Laval Pact, born on 8 December, was a weak infant. Slight shifts in the course of events just before the birth would have led to its being aborted or still-born. The premature announcement of its birth proved a death-blow to it. Its life was that of, almost literally, a nine days' wonder. It proved, however, stronger in death than in life.

The Pact had, in Halifax's phrase, a 'respectable parentage'.[27] The proposal for a port for Abyssinia (by a cession of British territory) had been put to Mussolini by Eden in June and went back longer than that. The Anglo-French proposals, agreed in Paris in August, had not excluded the possibility of territorial changes, neither had the Report of the Committee of Five in September, but December was not June, August or September; something of the utmost importance had happened in between, in October. In that month Italy had 'resorted to war in disregard of its obligations under Article 12 of the Covenant of the League of Nations'[28] Consequently the Pact was judged by millions a moral wrong in the light of that legal judgment. If the Pact had been put forward, and published, however short a time before the start of the war, it could and would have been discussed on its intrinsic merits. It could then have been argued that Mussolini was being offered less than he had asked for in June when, it will be remembered, his terms were the surrender of all the non-Amharic parts of Abyssinia. In those circumstances it could and no doubt would have been argued that the areas to be ceded to Italy were far greater than the area to be ceded to Abyssinia, counter-argued that that small area was more important in that it gave access to the sea; argued that the great Italian zone of economic interest in the south would inevitably pass under Italian sovereignty, counter-argued that it would become only a kind of mandate supervized by the League; argued that Italy had real problems of too many people and too few resources, counter-argued that these could and should be solved in other ways than at Abyssinia's expense; argued that her peoples were 'not yet able to stand by themselves under the strenuous conditions of the modern world', counter-argued that 'good government is no substitute for self-government'; argued that the plan as a whole was a menace to Abyssinian independence and integrity, counter-argued that they could be protected by the League; argued that the pact was far more in Italy's interests than Abyssinia's, counter-argued that that was a fair price to pay for the avoidance of war and the possibility of total Italian conquest; and so on, and so on.

As it was, all such argumentation in December seemed, to a vast number of people throughout the world, and especially to British public opinion, beside the point, which was that the victim of aggression was being asked to sacrifice some half of her territory to the aggressor. Mussolini was moreover to be offered far more territory than he had managed to conquer in two months' fighting. Not merely was crime to be allowed to pay, but the criminal was to be given a bonus for committing it. The ears of those whose eyes saw the situation in this way were more or less deaf to the contention that, failing such a settlement, however unjust, the aggressor might conquer all the rest. The answer to that was that he should, if possible, be prevented from so doing, but that in any event the Pact was plainly immoral. On this moral basis it was thought to have no merits whatsoever.

It seems extraordinary that a man like Lord Halifax missed this point completely, writing to Neville Chamberlain on 26 December: 'the whole affair was a thoroughly bad business. . . . I am still puzzled, though, by the condemnation meted out to proposals that were not, as you said all along, so frightfully different from those put forward by the Committee of 5. But . . . the Paris ones were too much like the off-stage arrangements of 19th century diplomacy. . . .'[29] His Lordship in 1935 was seemingly unduly preoccupied with Wilson's 1918 doctrine of 'Open covenants openly arrived at'. But this was not the issue. Sir Keith Feiling himself is on safer ground in saying that 'if the terms followed Article 19 of the Covenant in revising conditions that menaced the peace of the world, they had affronted Article 16 by giving a rich reward to aggression'.[30] But the terms were not arrived at, or presented as, an attempt to activate Article 19, but as a Realpolitik attempt to solve a problem of conflicting national interests. Moreover, Articles 10 and 12 rather than Article 16 were the ones to be affronted.

It must, therefore, be emphasized that the political events of 8–19 December (the crisis of the crisis) were enacted against this background of public opinion. The news which reached Britain from France on 9 December seemed to the overwhelming majority of the nation to report a complete betrayal of principles in which they believed, for which they had recently voted, and which had recently been reiterated by their leaders, not only at home, but also abroad and on their behalf. The shock was all the greater because it was sudden. The British people had little knowledge of the negotiations in Rome in June, in Paris in August, in Geneva in September. They had scarcely noticed Mr. Peterson's visits to Paris to talk with the Comte de St. Quentin. Even if information about the proposals discussed in all these negotiations had been available in the same measure as information was, from 9 December onwards, available about the Hoare-Laval proposals, it may be doubted whether such information would have been paid much attention. It would all have seemed too much a matter of technical intricacies. What had been understood and remembered were the issues of principle raised by the Peace Ballot, Hoare's pledge at Geneva of resistance to unprovoked aggression, the professions of pro-League policies by both Parties in the recent Election. Now the speech-maker of September had signed his speech away. This was no question of a negotiation by a Foreign Office official or a Second-in-Command; it was an act by the Foreign Secretary in person.

The crisis of conscience was most acute for Conservative Members of Parliament (especially new ones, like Mr Sandys).[31] They had to and did ask themselves whether, only three weeks previously, they had been elected Members because of promises now dishonoured. On 15 December Neville Chamberlain wrote to his sister: 'If we had to fight the election again, we should probably be beaten.'[32]

As early then as 9 December, many people in Britain had made up their minds that Sir Samuel Hoare was, morally, a fallen man. That afternoon, however, he was still in the train, blissfully unaware of the 'leak' to the Press, probably thinking of the congratulations of Vansittart and Clerk on his notable contribution to better Anglo-French relations and hoping for a still greater triumph, the end of the war.[33] On leaving the train he was quickly made aware of the storm now raging in London. He offered to return home, but Baldwin, kindly but unwisely, advised him to stay put. Nonetheless Hoare, after telephone conversations with the Foreign Office, decided to return.[34] There then supervened, however, the skating accident which has already been mentioned.[35] It resulted in two bad breaks in the nose; the medical advice was that the patient should stay in his room to avoid infection and should certainly not travel. Thus the Foreign Secretary, the key man in a sudden and major crisis, was unable personally to explain or defend the actions, principally his own, which had caused it. Not till the 16th did he make the return journey and on his return he was confined to his bed. He was visited there by some of his colleagues; his next public appearance was to be in the House of Commons on 19 December to make a resignation speech.

On the morning of the 9th, Eden – after seeing Peterson – was called on by Baldwin, who was in the Foreign Office for the purpose of opening a naval disarmament conference.[36] Eden explained the Pact to him on a map, saying that neither Abyssinia nor the League would accept it: 'Baldwin grunted and looked unhappy, and commented 'That lets us out, doesn't it?' but he agreed that the Cabinet must meet that evening. . . .'[37] In the afternoon Eden saw Baldwin again and secured his agreement to two points; first, that Haile Selassie should be told of the proposals in full at the same time as Mussolini and, second, that pressure from Laval to postpone the meeting of the Committee of Eighteen planned for the 12th should be resisted.

At 6 p.m. the special Cabinet requested by Hoare met to consider the Hoare-Laval Pact. It had remarkably little information before it, but it did know that these proposals were already known to the French public and would the next day be available the world over. In these circumstances amendments to the Pact could scarcely be negotiated in slow secrecy as had hitherto been envisaged. Eden explained the proposals and 'emphasized that the proposed exchange of territory in the north would be the hardest for the Emperor of Abyssinia to accept, but he would receive compensation in an outlet to the sea; and he pointed out the extent of the territory that it was proposed to include in the area for economic development, the whole of which, however, was non-Amharic. He also, 'while supporting the Foreign Secretary's proposals', warned the Cabinet that some features of them were likely to prove very distasteful to some League Members:

'He mentioned also that M. Laval, while stating that France would honour her obligations to the League . . . in the event of an Italian aggression as the result of further sanctions, had made it clear in the conversations that sanctions were unpopular to an important section of French public opinion. This, which had perhaps influenced the Foreign Secretary, raised doubts as to whether in the event, active French co-operation could be relied on, particularly if Signor Mussolini should accept the proposal but the Emperor of Abyssinia should refuse.'[38]

(Eden was later to write: 'I did not at the time plumb the full depths of Laval's scheme.... The consequences of giving Mussolini details of the plan at once, and only telling the Emperor that the proposals were in accordance with the principles of the Committee of Five and would be discussed at Geneva on the 12th, might be far-reaching. If the Duce were to accept and if the Emperor ... three days later, were to refuse, Laval would have a plausible pretext for calling off sanctions').[39]

'The proposals', we read in the minutes, 'were discussed by the Cabinet at some length ...', but not, it seems, to any great purpose. Some specific possible problems were set aside as 'for the future'. However, it is recorded that: 'Among criticisms of the actual proposals were that they were better for Italy than those of the Committee of Five, that it would be said that Italy's resort to force had gained her more than she could have gained otherwise....' Nonetheless there was 'general agreement' that 'the Emperor should be strongly pressed to accept them as a basis for discussion, or at least not reject them. The fact that the terms had leaked out in the Paris Press made this indispensable'. In the end and in short the 'Cabinet agreed to support the policy of the Secretary of State for Foreign Affairs....' It also agreed that Addis Ababa and Rome should be given the proposals simultaneously.

Lord Halifax, in his speech in the House of Lords on 19 December (the day after Hoare's resignation), a speech which has won much praise for frankness, especially in comparison with Baldwin's speech in the Commons the same day, justified the first of these two decisions in terms of personal loyalties. He spoke of the close 'bonds of trust that bind colleagues, and how essentially these bonds of friendship are the foundation of all that is best in the political life of a free nation. I am quite prepared to admit that we made ... the mistake of not appreciating the damage that, rightly or wrongly, these terms would be held by public opinion to inflict upon the cause that we were pledged to serve. Accordingly we share to the full the responsibility for the mistake that was made'.[40] This must have sounded a little hollow to Sir Samuel Hoare who had by then paid for his share of the responsibility by resigning his great office. Baldwin said on 17 December to Hoare 'We all stand together',[41] but by the 19th he had fallen and all the rest were still standing. 'It was quite clear', said Halifax on the 19th, 'that the Government could never refuse assent on that Friday night at the price of repudiating their Foreign Secretary, a colleague who was absent and who would have been unheard'. They did not, however, have to decide positively to support him; they could have summoned him home. A week later they did, in effect, repudiate him.

After the Cabinet meeting on the Monday evening Eden went across to the Foreign Office to telephone Vansittart. He did not think Laval would make difficulties about sending full information immediately to the Emperor. He was quickly undeceived for Vansittart 'phoned after dinner to say that he was under pressure for a shorter account of the proposals to go to Addis Ababa than to Rome. Eden insisted that the Cabinet's decision on this point was irrevocable. Shortly after midnight (i.e. very early on Tuesday, the 10th) Vansittart sent a message saying that, if Laval agreed to inform the Emperor immediately, he would expect the British Government to agree that the oil sanction should not be imposed. Eden said that he thought such a plan impracticable and that he could give no such assurance on his own responsibility.

At 2 a.m. Vansittart saw Laval again. He said that he did not wish to inform Abyssinia of the proposals because he had reason to believe that the Emperor would refuse in order to bring the oil sanction into play. In such circumstances he would find it impossible to persuade his colleagues, or French public opinion, to accept the new sanction.[42] Vansittart added to this report his own opinion that Laval's request should be accepted. If Italy accepted the proposals and Abyssinia rejected them the stick could not be applied to the accepting Government.[43]

In consequence of this message another special meeting of the Cabinet was held on the morning of the 10th. Eden had drafted an answer to the message, which was accepted, plus a draft by Neville Chamberlain for an additional concluding passage which was preferred to Eden's draft for this addendum. The telegram stated the principle that 'To submit terms for settlement to the aggressor and withhold them from the victim of aggression seems to us indefensible. It is not possible for His Majesty's Government to give the undertaking for which M. Laval asks that should Abyssinia refuse the terms there would be no question of enforcing the petrol sanction.... (That would be a matter for the

League as a whole and many factors as yet unknown would have to be taken into account.) For all these reasons an oil sanction in the immediate future seems very unlikely except in the contingency of Italy refusing the proposals. If Italy accepts and Abyssinia refuses, His Majesty's Government would neither propose nor support the imposition of further sanctions at once nor before it is clear that no chance remains of a possible settlement by agreement. But they could not pledge themselves to oppose further sanctions for all time or in new conditions which cannot now be foreseen'.[44]

That afternoon the new House of Commons was engaged in the debate, traditional at the start of a new Session, on an Address to the Throne in answer to the King's Speech. In this debate any subject may be raised. Public anger at the Hoare-Laval Pact was mounting rapidly and Mr. Pethick Lawrence, for the Labour Party, announced that its opposition to the Pact would be expressed by an amendment to the Address. It was then that Baldwin, in a couple of sentences, made a major blunder in an area where over the years he had built himself up as a grand master: management, indeed command, of the House of Commons:

'I have seldom spoken with greater regret, for my lips are not yet unsealed. Were these troubles over I would make a case – and I guarantee that not a man would go into the lobby against us.'[45]

Reasoned argument would have been more in place. The days when Baldwin could successfully appeal simply to confidence in himself personally had abruptly ended. The new House of Commons had 153 new Members. It was a much livelier one than its predecessor.

The Cabinet met again, for the third day running, on the 11th. Eden reported on the consultations with other countries about co-operation in the event of Italian aggression. Full co-operation had been offered by Greece and Turkey; the Yugoslav reply was less satisfactory, though the desired naval facilities had been agreed; consultations were going on with Czechoslovakia, Spain, and Roumania.

Eden next reported that the telegrams conveying the Hoare-

Laval proposals had gone to Abyssinia and Italy late the previous evening. The subject of discussion then became that of the line he was to follow at Geneva the next day (the 12th), especially on the crucial issue of the oil sanction. This discussion was lengthy and diffuse, revealing the same disarray as on the occasion of previous discussions of the same subject. The confusion of counsel expressed is astonishing: Mussolini could obtain enough oil to carry on his war unless and until the U.S.A. joined in an embargo; it was difficult for him to obtain enough oil because it was difficult to pay for it; the oil sanction should not be imposed unless it was certain to be effective; it was impossible to know whether it would be until it was tried; we should maintain existing sanctions but avoid an oil one; we should join with other Members of the League in imposing one if they wanted it, even at the risk of war, but this did not mean the fixing of a date; an oil sanction might precipitate a war and we had decided in no circumstances to be drawn into one unless certain of whole-hearted co-operation by France; that could not be relied upon, but when it came to the point Laval might co-operate in further sanctions; it was politically important not to give an impression of pusillanimity; the consequences of previous action had not been thought out.

It must be said that, in his opening statement, Eden had not given much of a lead on this particular question: '. . . our general attitude should be that we were ready to take any action that the members of the League were willing to take'.[46] The Prime Minister was more pointed: 'During the discussion he explained more than once that the question ought to be decided as a business proposition. . . . Until we knew what America was going to do we should hold our hand'. But he did not know, perhaps could not have known, that the best possible moment for securing American co-operation had been missed precisely because of the impact of the Hoare-Laval plan on American public opinion.[47]

The one point on which 'general agreement' is recorded is that at Geneva Eden 'must *not* say that we would in no circumstances agree to the imposition of an oil sanction at some future date. . . .' Later on in the minutes, however, a summing-up of the 'trend of the discussion' includes the statement: 'The important thing for him to secure was that during the coming week there should be no date fixed for oil sanctions'. This is immediately followed by a sentence doubtless inserted to show that Baldwin's point had been accepted: 'If circumstances should arise which brought the question once more to the front at Geneva, he should try and arrange for it to be dealt with as a business proposition and ask for an investigation of the practicability of rendering it efficacious, having in mind more especially the uncertainty of effective action by the U.S.A.'

Summing up the general issues, Eden showed his mind: 'If he had to choose between two risks, (1) an aggression by Italy, and (2) a collapse of the League, he would consider the former the lesser evil'. At once, however, 'the Cabinet were once more reminded of the fundamental principle that we were not to become involved in hostilities unless France was with us. We were, of course, prepared to take our part in collective action, but only on condition that that action was collective in every sense of the term, namely, both in its immediate application and in any consequences to which it might give rise'.

The secretarial summing-up of the trend of this part of the discussion reads:

'... in regard to the proposals made to Italy and Abyssinia, the Minister for League of Nations Affairs would have to use his discretion, according to the circumstances he encountered at Geneva, as to how far it was necessary for him to champion them, especially in detail.'

The retreat from the Hoare-Laval Pact had begun.

It was continued the next day (12 December) at Geneva when Eden, speaking to the Sanctions Committee and making full use of the discretion given to him by the Cabinet, made it clear that the League was welcome to reject or amend the Hoare-Laval 'suggestions'. British policy was still that any final settlement had to be acceptable to the League as well as 'to the two parties in conflict'. He suggested that the League Council should meet as soon as possible to hear 'a full statement of the proposals' and then decide what course it should follow 'in the light of the situation thus created'. But Eden had been anticipated by the Council's President who had already summoned it to meet in secret session on the 17th, nominally to discuss a quite different item of business.[48] One important decision was, however, taken by the Sanctions Committee on the 13th, viz. to postpone all further consideration of the oil sanction until the fate of the Hoare-Laval Pact was known. Only Mexico and Sweden objected to this, but not to the point of voting against it.[49]

The scene shifted back to London. Vansittart returned there on the 12th, Eden on the 14th, Hoare on the 16th. (It can hardly have seemed possible to him that he had only been away for eight days, so much had happened in them: the Paris talks, the skating accident, the massive and still mounting demonstration of public fury at the Pact which had seemed to him so statesmanlike.) At once preparations had to be made for the speech Eden would have to make to the League Council on the 18th. Something more precise and weighty would be needed on this occasion than what he had said to the Sanctions Committee on the 12th. On the 19th there was to be a debate in the House of Commons, and on that occasion the Foreign Secretary, forbidden by his doctor to go out meanwhile, would have his first chance to defend his proposals in public.

On the 16th nine Ministers met in the Prime Minister's room at the House of Commons to hold a preliminary discussion, prior to a Cabinet meeting the next day, of the lines of Eden's speech. In addition to Baldwin and Eden, the others present were: Chamberlain, Duff Cooper, Ramsay MacDonald, Monsell, Runciman, Simon, and Swinton. 'After considerable discussion' the key words were duly agreed which were uttered on the 18th with only two very minor changes.[50] (The formula was approved by the Cabinet the next day.)[51] The speech for the 19th which Hoare was now working on was to be the subject of even more considerable discussion and much more changed.

On the morning of the 17th Baldwin explained to the full Cabinet that the position had to be considered in relation both to the forthcoming meeting of the League Council and to the forthcoming debates in both Houses of Parliament. Eden had to leave for Geneva at 2 p.m. and wished to consult his colleagues and see Hoare before leaving; Chamberlain had already gone to see Hoare and would arrive at the meeting a little late. The Cabinet found itself, however, immediately involved in a prolonged discussion of one secondary muddle springing from the Paris conversations and in an unsuccessful attempt to straighten it out. This was the question of whether the proposed Abyssinian 'outlet to the sea with full sovereign rights' was nonetheless an outlet through which there would be no right to build a railway. It was this item in the Hoare-Laval Pact which had provoked the most stinging of all the attacks on it, the first leader in *The Times* of the previous day (16 December), written by the Editor in person, Geoffrey Dawson, under the title of 'A Corridor for Camels'.[52]

Eden explained that the original French draft of the Pact had contained a ban on the construction of a railway, but that Vansittart and Léger (on the former's insistence) had removed this proviso from the text because it had been inserted not in relation to the suggested corridor to Assab but in relation to the alternative corridor to Zeila. The construction of a railway through that corridor would be contrary to the 1906 Treaty. (Eden had had his nose well rubbed into this point by Laval and Léger in Paris on 26 June.)[53] It now transpired, however, that a telegram had been sent on the 10th to Sir Sidney Barton, on Eden's authority, reading in part:

'I add for your own information that the two Governments have agreed to obtain from the Abyssinian Government at the appropriate moment an undertaking not to construct from the port which it acquires any railway communicating with the interior. . . .'

There was no distinction in that between Assab and Zeila. At the Cabinet meeting it was 'pointed out, however, that this part of the telegram, which reproduced the terms of the agreement reached in Paris, was only for the personal information of the British Minister, that nothing had been said to the Emperor on this subject, and nothing had been arranged as to when "the appropriate moment" would arrive'.[54]

The idea that the Emperor should be asked to accept a string of proposals injurious to his interests, whilst hiding, even temporarily, the 'string' attached to the only proposal beneficial to him, seems less than straightforward. It is not surprising to read that 'embarrassment was felt that this aspect of the question had not been before the Cabinet' on the 9th when they agreed to support the Foreign Secretary's proposals.

Worse was to follow. Some Ministers proceeded to urge that the

Government's spokesmen in Parliament on the 19th should say that it had never been agreed that no railway should be built from the Abyssinian port. It then became clear that, before such an announcement could be authorized, 'it would be very important to check carefully as to whether in any telegram, document or minute that had been circulated the matter had in fact never been mentioned....' What had begun at Paris with confused discussion and faulty, because hasty, drafting was ending in London with less speed and considerable indignity.

At that stage of the discussion it became obvious that the point in question could not be decided in Hoare's absence. It is not difficult, however, to deduce that the discussion of this particular and secondary aspect of the Hoare-Laval Pact had shaken whatever measure of confidence remained in the Pact as a whole. 'It was suggested', ingenuously rather than ingeniously, 'that if the Cabinet were to decide virtually to drop the whole of the proposed basis of peace owing to the bad reception it had received, the particular difficulty of the port and the railway would be less acute'. That suggestion, however, was not carried further and it was agreed to leave it to Baldwin to clear up this particular issue with Hoare. In fact telegrams were sent the same day (17 December) to Sir Sidney Barton in Addis Ababa, cancelling the last paragraph of the telegram sent him on the 10th, and to Sir George Clerk 'instructing him to clear up the position with the French Government'.[55]

The discussion, however, had yet another important, and immediate, consequence, The Cabinet realized that they had not previously grasped a point in the Hoare-Laval Pact which raised 'a very serious political difficulty'. They were now being told that there was no bar to railway construction in the Assab corridor, only in the Zeila one. The question of railway-building being licit or illicit could only arise, therefore, if the Emperor preferred the latter to the former. If, however, he exercised that option he would inevitably draw attention to a larger disadvantage (to the British and French Governments rather than to his own): there would be no *exchange* of territory as between Abyssinia and Italy. (For the Zeila corridor he would not have to cede one square Abyssinian inch to Britain, but he would still have to yield to Italy large areas in Tigre and Ogaden, whilst receiving nothing whatsoever in exchange from Italy.) The Hoare-Laval Pact, in short, contained the possibility of the Emperor removing the largest fig-leaf, 'Exchange of Territory', concealing or attempting to conceal its naked nastiness. (Only two miniscule fig-leaves would remain, the description of two large cessions of territory to Italy as, in each case, 'Rectification of Frontiers'.)[56] This Emperor was being put in a position to illumine the fact of others having no clothes.

The Cabinet's confidence in the Hoare-Laval Pact having, no doubt, been further shaken, the discussion moved on to the subject originally put forward by the Prime Minister, the line to be taken by Eden at Geneva the next day and by Government spokesmen in both Houses of Parliament the day after, 'in view of the bad reception given to the Anglo-French proposals both at home and abroad'.[57] Eden read a telegram (of the 16th) from Barton 'stating that the Emperor and his advisers were bewildered at association of His Majesty's Government with the proposals. . . .' He then reported on a meeting between Grandi and Vansittart, the former asking 'a number of questions about the proposals, indicating that Signor Mussolini was not very enamoured with them'.[58] He next circulated the draft of the statement to be made at Geneva agreed on at the meeting of Ministers the previous evening. Chamberlain was able to report that the Foreign Secretary found nothing in the proposed statement 'that would embarrass him' except one minor point. The statement as finally agreed read:

'It must be emphasized that the Paris proposals which were put forward last week were not advanced as proposals to be insisted on against the disagreement of any of the three parties. They were advanced in order to ascertain what the views of the three parties might be upon them, and His Majesty's Government recommend them only for this purpose. If, therefore, it transpires that these proposals which are now before you do not satisfy the essential condition of agreement by the three parties, His Majesty's Government could not continue to recommend or support them. In their minds this particular attempt at reconciliation could not then be regarded as having achieved its object, and His Majesty's Government for their part would not wish to pursue it further.'

G

In other words, the Cabinet agreed (on 17 December) that the Anglo-French proposals were not to be pressed at Geneva. The Cabinet was, however, reminded that the Emperor had asked that the bases for terms of peace agreed on at Paris should be put to the League Assembly. After a very brief discussion it was agreed: 'That the Minister for League of Nations Affairs, while preferably not taking the lead in the matter, should endeavour to avoid a discussion at the Assembly'.[59]

The Parliamentary debates could not, however, be dodged. Indeed the only immediately outstanding question for His Majesty's Government now became that of the line to be taken in them. On this question there was an inconsequential and indecisive discussion in the Cabinet held on the morning of 17 December. Widely differing and mutually contradictory opinions were expressed.

The discussion began with Chamberlain giving what he was careful to call 'a general impression' of the speech Hoare proposed to make two days later. Its basic assumption would be that sanctions could not be carried further unless all the Members of the League were ready to face any possible military consequences; that there was no indication that any other country had prepared itself to do so; that the burden of any military consequences would, therefore, fall on Britain alone. Chamberlain said he had told Hoare that these were good arguments against more sanctions but 'somewhat vulnerable as a justification of the proposed basis of peace'.

Hoare had answered this by telling Chamberlain that, in the light of the military position in Abyssinia, there was no chance of better terms than the Paris ones. The public were thinking of terms which could only be obtained as a result of far greater pressure on Italy. In these circumstances he thought that the League of Nations 'ought to be faced up to the realities of the situation'. He 'did not dismiss the possibility that the Members of the League might be willing to make the military preparations necessary to support more decisive sanctions'.

Such, according to Chamberlain, was the current gospel according to Hoare. It seems reasonably clear that, in his mind, the process of making the League face up to the realities of the situation was not now to be by presenting it with bad peace terms but, more directly, by a presentation of the facts of the military situation, both as between Italy and Abyssinia and as between Italy and the League. However, this 'general line was criticized on the ground that it might be repudiated by France and other nations who would recall the undertakings they had given to support the United Kingdom if attacked'. It was also pointed out 'that there was no document which could be laid to show that any nation was unwilling to fulfil its responsibilities. What could be said was that militarily they were not in a position to act. That, however, was a more difficult point to make in public'.

It was then said, virtually accepting Hoare's reported line, that when the Pact had been agreed, Britain had, at Geneva, either to go forward or back. If the former, new risks of war were involved. Against them Britain had to be safeguarded by categorical assurances. The lack of such assurances justified the attempt to obtain peace.

A quite contrary suggestion followed, that 'it was not the danger of war but a growing conviction of the inevitable slowness of the operation of sanctions, even if backed by America, that necessitated peace'.

To both these lines Chamberlain's point was thought to apply, i.e. that while they might justify the avoidance of additional sanctions, they did not justify the Paris terms. Moreover, these lines 'would also give great reassurances to Signor Mussolini that effective sanctions would never be applied'.

At this point it was suggested that a better line would be one suggested by Chamberlain at an earlier meeting, 'of boldly defending, not so much the Paris proposals themselves, as the principles on which they had been based. To those conversant with the technical aspects, the Paris proposals were said to differ materially from those of the Committee of Five, although to the non-technical students, the difference was not so great'.

Chamberlain welcomed this, in language which reads a little obscurely:

'The Chancellor of the Exchequer said he himself had sug-gested to the Foreign Secretary that the best case might be to found himself on the Report of the Committee of Five which had been accepted by the Emperor of Abyssinia. It was true, as had been remarked in the discussion, that since then war had broken out and Italy had bombed hospitals and so forth, but a good deal could be said on both aspects. He agreed that it would not be sufficient to make only the point of the danger of the extension of the war to Europe, but he thought that combined with a defence of the proposals a good case might be made.'

It was next urged, 'from a similar point of view', that – Eden having made his statement at Geneva – 'the right line would be a bold defence of the proposals on the lines already suggested. In this connection it was recalled that from the first it had been assumed that Abyssinia must in some shape or form come under the direction of the League of Nations, and the proposals for an area of development in the non-Amharic territories of the South could be defended from that point of view. After that, a more realistic line might be taken, and it might be brought home to the Members of the League that a great nation could only be stopped in its aggression and punished if all the Members were actually prepared to play their part'.

On this note of a bold and realistic line further discussion was postponed till the next day, as Baldwin, Chamberlain, and Eden had to see Hoare and several members of the Cabinet had to make important speeches in Parliament.

What happened next is not altogether clear. Baldwin, Chamberlain and Eden went to see Hoare. Eden left fairly soon to catch his boat train. It was probably on this occasion that Baldwin, on leaving, said: 'We all stand together'.[60] Some time the same day (17th) Simon wrote to Eden saying that he 'was horrified at the idea that Hoare should defend us by saying, in effect, that the peace terms were necessary as an alternative to war. He did not believe it, and to say so would be to give Mussolini the biggest score of his life....'[61] On the 18th Eden pronounced to the League Council the formula agreed by the Cabinet the day before, the broadest of hints to the League that it was welcome to kill the Hoare-Laval Pact if it wished.

That morning the Cabinet met again. Only Eden and Hoare were absent, Chamberlain again acting as the latter's messenger. This Cabinet turned out to be the most important of all those in which the Abyssinian crisis was discussed. All the members present, with five exceptions, took part in the discussion. An unusually full record was made of it by Sir Maurice Hankey. (In a manner reminiscent of Pepys recording his amours in a foreign language as well as in code, he recorded the most significant remarks in his own hand rather than having them typed.) The names of all the speakers are given. Partly, no doubt, for that reason and partly also because of the contents of the discussion and its consequences, this record of it, of which there was then only one copy, was sealed and marked: 'Top Secret – to be opened personally by the Secretary of the Cabinet'. It was shown to the Prime Minister in January 1936; the next person to see it was the then Secretary, in June 1946. It is now open to the whole world.

The first words came from Baldwin, pointing out that 'the Foreign Secretary was probably feeling on trial, and must be allowed to make his speech in his own way. . . . He would have to point out that we had reached a position where it was essential to know what other nations would do in the event of war and how far M. Laval was prepared to go in the event of a sudden Italian attack'.[62]

Then it was Chamberlain's turn. He 'agreed that the Foreign Secretary probably felt himself to be on his trial, though, of course, the Cabinet were with him'. Hoare 'was prepared to make his defence in Parliament. He had not changed his mind as to the rightness of his action, although he was prepared to admit that, in view of public opinion, the Government could not adhere to his plan'. Chamberlain's own opinion was that Hoare, at Paris, had been 'greatly misled by his staff. . . .'

The Chancellor proceeded to report the outline of the Foreign Secretary's proposed speech. Chamberlain's résumé showed that the intended speech would fall into four parts:

1) The League had been simultaneously pursuing two policies, sanctions and negotiations:

'The sanctions adopted so far had worked rather better than had been expected, and this had led to a demand for stronger sanctions that would be still more effective. This had led to the proposed oil sanction, which brought us within the danger zone.'

If war came it might well be with this country single-handed. The result of such a war was not feared, but he 'had felt that, if there were a risk of a hostile act against us, he must assure himself of the attitude of other countries'. At Paris his 'impression had been that the war risk was so great that he ought to consider the possibility of a peaceful settlement'.

2) The proposed peace terms would be described. There was something to be said in their favour, e.g. their similarity to those proposed by the Committee of Five, the embodiment in them of certain principles accepted earlier by the Emperor, the favourable comparison with Mussolini's demands in June:

'He would be able to say that there were many of the proposals that he had not much liked, but that they were the best he could at the time get the French to agree to with a reasonable chance that Signor Mussolini would discuss them.'

3) The public must grasp that peace could either be negotiated or dictated. 'Force could only be exercised if either we were strong enough to exert it alone or had a definite and concrete arrangement with other Powers'. A negotiated peace would not be got 'at the present time ... without giving something to the aggressor'. The peace proposals were dead but they had been the best that could be got through negotiation.

'We had therefore to fall back on sanctions. This was very dangerous. The effect of sanctions was cumulative, and that was equally true of the existing relatively mild sanctions. As they approached the point of becoming effective there was always the danger of an act of aggression. The Foreign Secretary would probably speak with the utmost frankness as to the position M. Laval had taken up in the event of sanctions. Sanctions might mean war. We were not prepared to engage in war alone and had to look round and assure ourselves on the position. The actual situation was that no ship, no aeroplane or gun had been moved by any nation except ourselves. We alone had done all that we could. The future, therefore, lay in the hands of the League. Unless it was prepared to implement its action in putting on sanctions, success could not be expected. So the whole question must be cleared up.'

Cold water was at once poured. Sir Kingsley Wood 'was apprehensive of a speech on those lines'; Oliver Stanley 'feared the effect of such a speech would be disastrous', i.e. that the Government's future would be endangered. It was, however, with the next speech, that of Lord Swinton, that the course of the discussion was decisively turned.[63] His agreement with the proposed speech was 'on the assumption that it would be the Foreign Secretary's speech on his own behalf, but not on that of the Government'. They 'were bound to admit that they regarded the Paris proposals as dead. They would never have approved negotiations on those lines if they had been asked to do so before the Foreign Secretary went to Paris; nor could they ever agree in the Paris communiqué expressing satisfaction with the terms'.[64]

J. H. Thomas proceeded to point out the logical consequence of Swinton's suggestion of Hoare speaking for himself alone. He should resign. (It is with the sentence in which this decisive word first appears that Hankey first slips into holograph.) The Government would get a reduced majority the next day, but the whole episode had staggered and demoralized the country. If Hoare made his speech as Foreign Secretary he would be discredited at Geneva, mistrusted everywhere in Europe, and his policy would always be mistrusted; if he resigned, 'the whole thing would be dead'. Walter Eliot went even further than Thomas, doubting if the speech, even as that of a Private Member, should go so far: 'the Cabinet ought to demand consideration of whether it should be delivered from the front bench or on a back bench'.

Other Ministers who called, in turn, for Hoare's resignation, were Mr. Ormsby-Gore, Lord Eustace Percy, and Lord Halifax; MacDonald and Simon more than hinted at it (Ormsby-Gore hinted at the need for Vansittart's removal also.)[65] Only Lord Zetland felt that the Cabinet should not repudiate on the 18th the responsibility it had accepted on the 9th. No one said that Hoare should stay. The Prime Minister said he had not made up his mind: 'All he could say was that, though he was not rattled, it was a worse situation in the House of Commons than he had ever known'. Halifax commented that much more was at stake than the loss of the Foreign Secretary, 'namely, the whole moral position of the Government before the world'. But Halifax also saw the danger to the Prime Minister personally, whilst apparently retaining his own respect for him: 'If the Prime Minister were to lose his personal position, one of our national anchors would have dragged'. Baldwin then remarked that 'he would stand or fall by what he said on the morrow' and the Cabinet had to be content with that. It was, however, obvious that Hoare could not continue in office when such stringent criticisms of his great *coup* had been made by his colleagues.

Again Chamberlain went off to see Hoare and again we do not know exactly what happened. Essentially, however, he was asked for a recantation. He declined, however, to say that the Paris proposals had been bad and that he should not have agreed to them. In his resignation speech the next day he said, 'I cannot honestly recant'.[66] He also said that his resignation had been proffered without any prompting from anyone. He felt that he had not 'behind him the general approval of his fellow-country-men'; lacking that he could not 'carry weight and influence in the councils of the world. . . .'[67] Geoffrey Dawson had seen him the previous day (the 18th), some time before 6.00 p.m. when Baldwin was due to call. Hoare told Dawson he had resolved to resign and 'the news came out officially about 9.30.'[68]

The debate in the House of Commons on the 19th was on a motion moved by Attlee (his first major Parliamentary speech as Leader of the Opposition):

'That the terms put forward by His Majesty's Government as a basis for an Italo-Abyssinian settlement reward the declared aggressor at the expense of the victim, destroy collective security, and conflict with the expressed will of the Country and with the Covenant of the League of Nations, to the support of which the honour of this country is pledged; this House, therefore, demands that these terms be immediately repudiated.'

Little did Attlee know that in Cabinet the previous day, Simon, having read this out, commented: 'This was very nearly what the Cabinet felt'. But Attlee did not make the best use of the oppor-tunity offered him. His error was to say, however truly: 'There is the question of the honour of this country, and there is the question of the honour of the Prime Minister. If . . . the Prime Minister won an election on one policy and immediately after victory was prepared to carry out another, it has an extremely ugly look'. This attack on Baldwin personally united the Con-servatives behind him and brought to his support the one man,

Sir Austen Chamberlain, whose lead could have overthrown him.

Baldwin, in replying to Attlee, bowed to the storm and in a single 'throw-away' sentence announced the death of the Hoare-Laval Pact:

'I felt that these proposals went too far. I was not at all surprised at the expression of feeling in that direction. I was not expecting that deeper feeling that was manifest in many parts of the country on what I may call the grounds of conscience and of honour. The moment I am confronted with that, I know that something has happened that has appealed to the deepest feelings of our countrymen, that some note has been struck that brings back from them a response from the depths. . . . It is perfectly obvious now that the proposals are absolutely and completely dead. This Government is certainly going to make no attempt to resurrect them. If there arose a storm when I knew I was in the right, I would let it break on me, and I would either survive it or break. If I felt after examination of myself that there was in that storm something which showed me that I had done something that was not wise or right, then I would bow to it.'[69]

The real hero of the occasion, in so far as so Stygian an occasion could have a hero, was Hoare, whose resignation speech, an unusually long one (it took 49 minutes in the delivery) immediately preceded the debate proper. He started with some advantages. There was sympathy for him because of his personal misfortunes, both physical and political, and some unshaken sympathy for the policy he had pursued. His position too was easier than Baldwin's in that he had not scudded before the storm but had done the straight and simple thing in resigning. But Hoare, courageously, was not content to try and tap these sources of sympathy, but to gain converts by a positive defence of his actions in Paris. This line, to succeed, required an exceptionally able speech and one came, though, it must be said, closely read, more persuasive emotionally than intellectually. Undoubtedly, however, Hoare made in the House many converts to his cause. Outraged public opinion, however, remained outraged.[70]

The speech was well-organized. The first and longest part describes the events leading up to, and justifies, the Hoare-Laval Pact. We hear once again of 'the double task' of taking a full part in sanctions and 'trying to find a basis of settlement of this unfortunate dispute'.[71] Sir Samuel had been concentrating on the second task 'in view of the situation I saw inevitably developing before me in the immediate future'. In fact in both tasks a turning-point had, unexpectedly early, been reached: '... about a fort-night ago it was clear that a new situation was about to be created by the question of the oil embargo ... supposing an oil embargo were to be imposed and that the non-member States took an effective part in it, the oil embargo might have such an effect upon the hostilities as to force their termination ... the situation immediately became more dangerous from the point of view of Italian resistance'.[72] The Government could not disregard reports received 'from all sides' that Italy would regard an oil embargo as a military sanction. The nation had no fear of Italian threats; against an Italian attack 'we should retaliate with full success'. But 'an isolated attack of this kind launched upon one Power without it may be ... the full support of the other Powers would, it seemed to me, almost inevitably lead to the dissolution of the League'.

Hence, the Paris conversations in an 'atmosphere of threatened war ... in which the majority of member States – indeed, I would say the totality of the member States – appeared to be opposed to military action. It was a moment of great urgency. Within five days the question of the oil embargo was to come up at Geneva, and I did not feel myself justified in proposing any postponement of the embargo, unless it could be shown to the League that negotiations had actually started. It was a moment when it seemed to me that Anglo-French co-operation was essential if there was to be no breach at Geneva and if the sanctions when functioning were not to be destroyed'.

The proposals that emerged from the two days of strenuous discussion contained features which neither he nor Laval liked. But they seemed to provide 'the only basis upon which it was even remotely likely that we could start a peace discussion. It was certainly the minimum upon which the French Government were prepared to proceed. ... I felt that ... the dangers of the con-tinuance of the war were so serious that it was worth making an attempt, and that it was essential to maintain Anglo-French solidarity. It was in this spirit and this spirit alone that we agreed to the suggestions. That alone is the explanation and justification of the Paris communiqué'.[73]

The proposals were then listed under three heads – international supervision, territorial exchanges, and opportunities for Italian economic expansion and settlement – in that order. These three classes of proposals were then said to be 'the three principles of the Report of the Committee of Five'.[74] The House was reminded that Mussolini had rejected that Report, but that the Negus had accepted it 'in principle when the threat of war was hanging over him'. Moreover, he had shown his great desire for an outlet to the sea. By the Paris proposals he was offered one by a cession of part of Italian-occupied Tigre. The outlet to the sea could be to Zeila rather than Assab if both sides preferred that. The large area in the South to be set aside for Italian economic development and expansion was non-Amharic. It had only recently been conquered by Abyssinia, it was sparsely populated, had been in some parts devastated by slave trading, while slave ownership was 'prevalent over the whole area as indeed over the whole country'. But the sovereignty of this area was not to be transferred; Abyssinian administration was to continue 'under the guidance and control of the League Plan of Assistance'.[75] The proposals as a whole were 'immensely less favourable to Italy' than the demands made to Eden by Mussolini in June. Hoare had been thinking 'equally ... of the Abyssinian side of the controversy'. He had been terrified 'that we might lead Abyssinia on to think that the League could do more than it can do, that in the end we should find a terrible moment of disillusionment in which it might be that Abyssinia would be altogether destroyed as an independent State'.[76]

He wound up this first and longest part of his speech by saying that peace must eventually come by negotiation or by the surrender of one side. He himself believed that peace would come by negotiation and on the basis of the three principles he had stated. The present negotiations had failed and that made 'the position more difficult and dangerous than it had been before'.[77]

Turning to this new and 'much more dangerous phase' he began by repeating his point that no other State had taken any military precautions. It was essential to go beyond 'general protestations and ... have actual proof by actions from the member States that are concerned'. He proceeded to a passage ending with the best remembered phrase of the whole oration:

'We alone have taken these military precautions. There is a British Fleet in the Mediterranean, there are the British reinforcements in Egypt, in Malta and Aden. Not a ship, not a machine, not a man has been moved by any other member State.'[78]

The climax of the resignation speech was reached by emphasizing this theme; as he did so, he was confirming or gaining the support of scores of Members on the benches behind him.[79] He repeated that more was wanted than 'general protestations of loyalty to the League ...';[80] he repeated that 'we, the British Empire', were not afraid of an Italian attack; he repeated that without active co-operation from others collective security was impossible and the League would dissolve.

This report of this important speech can fittingly be concluded by the quotation in full of the eloquent passage that follows:

'If every member State will by action prove that it is determined to take its full part in resistance to an aggressive act, if an aggressive act is made, then it will be possible to have the kind of peace that we all of us desire. Let the House remember the conditions of modern warfare. Let them remember that the aggressor has a great advantage, that the aggressor has his forces mobilized and is ready to strike and that, in the conditions of modern warfare, he can strike with appalling speed. That makes it all the more necessary that all the member States should here and now make themselves ready, not for an event, improbable though it may be, that will take place in three, four or six months, but an event that may take place at any time. I say this, not with a view of creating panic, not with a view of suggesting that we are afraid of an Italian attack, but because I believe that unless these facts are faced, and are faced in the immediate future, either the League will break up, or a most unsatisfactory peace will result from the conflict that is now taking place. It is a choice between the full co-operation of all the member States and the kind of unsatisfactory compromise that was contemplated in the suggestions which M. Laval and I put up.'[81]

And so he moved to his final personal explanation which has already been quoted.[82] He had begun to feel fatigued and, as he sat down, felt a sudden shoot of pain in his broken nose which caused him instinctively to put a hand to it.[83] This movement made many onlookers think, wrongly, that he had burst into tears.[84] He left the House and, a day or two later, left the country to resume his holiday and regain his health. This he did quickly.[85] He was back in London at the end of February and back in the Cabinet early in June.[86]

But if it was obvious on 19 December 1935 that the Hoare-Laval plan was stone dead, it was equally obvious that the Prime Minister's reputation for integrity had been mortally injured. He had often spoken in favour of League principles; he had, a month previously, won a General Election largely by his support of them; he had allowed his Foreign Secretary to become the co-sponsor of a plan entirely contrary to those principles; he had, possibly by putting loyalty to a colleague above loyalty to a policy, accepted that plan; and when a storm of public opinion blew against it he had forced that colleague out of office because he refused to repudiate it and then repudiated it himself. On 10 December he was in possession of a case which he guaranteed to receive, if only revealed, the assent of the House nem. con.; on the 19th he was admitting that he had 'done something which was not wise or right'. The picture was not a pretty one; the contrast between the Foreign Secretary who had resigned rather than recant and the Prime Minister who stayed in office and recanted was glaring. Moreover, the new House of Commons, the one which was to overthrow Chamberlain in 1940, had made it plain that Baldwin was not its master.

It is not surprising that in the following summer Baldwin had a kind of nervous breakdown and had to take a three months' holiday. A severe blow had been struck to his self-confidence at its most sensitive point, his conviction of his understanding of the British people. He had retained enough of his command of the House to talk his way out of his immediate troubles there, much aided, of course, by the overriding sense, on his side of it, of the need to avoid the downfall of his Government; he had sufficiently recovered his touch by the end of the next year to handle the Abdication crisis (one with which he found himself far more at home than with the Abyssinian one) in his most masterly manner. However, there had been instilled into many minds the doubts of his honesty which grew into the odium (much of it unfair) of 1940 and later years.

In Paris Laval, doubling, so to speak, the roles of Baldwin and Hoare, had an easier Parliamentary passage than them, but none the less a difficult one. A hostile Parliamentary question was tabled on the 13th by Pierre Cot, a former Minister and a leading Radical Socialist who, like Eden, was conspicuously not a member of his Party's 'old gang'. On the next day a Party meeting discussed, but did not adopt, a draft motion hostile to Laval's foreign policy. On the 17th the Chamber of Deputies agreed to a debate but on the date, the 27th, of Laval's choosing, rather than the date, the 20th, asked for by Cot, supported by Blum.

On the 27th the debate was opened by Laval with a definition of the issue:

> 'The essential question that has to be asked is whether the policy that I have pursued is, or is not, in conformity with the interests of our country.'

He recognized that the 'most serious charge' brought against him was that he had 'set limits upon the means which might be placed by other countries at the disposal of France to safeguard her or to defend her against some future act of aggression'. In other words, the charge was that he had not backed up Britain over an issue of Italian aggression and so might lose her support over a future issue of German aggression. But, said Laval, 'I have not done less than my duty towards the cause of Franco-British co-operation'. As to the League, its action in the crisis had been, and might continue to be, 'impeded by difficulties without its being permissible to draw from this instance any valid conclusion against the general principle of collective security. . . .' Laval closed the debate by emphasizing that what was at stake was not the fate of a Government which had defended the Franc or was about to pass the Budget but 'the orientation of the whole foreign policy of France'.

There were two votes. The first was on a procedural point, i.e. which should be taken first, the pro-Government or the anti-Government motion. It was agreed to take the former by 296 votes to 276 and it was then carried by 304 votes to 261. It was decisive to these two results that in the first vote 37 Radical-Socialists voted on Laval's side as against 93 on the other; in the second vote 44 voted with him as against 63 against. In other words, as the question to be voted on moved from a procedural to a substantive point, both Laval's majority as a whole, and the Radical-Socialist element in it, increased.

This was on 28 December; within a month the Ministry fell. This was not on account of a parliamentary debate, but because the Executive Committee of the Radical-Socialist Party ordered its Ministers (headed by Herriot) out of the Government.[87] Laval immediately resigned, on 22 January 1936, without even going before Parliament, much as Lloyd George resigned in 1922 when the Conservative Party withdrew its support from his Coalition. The Radical-Socialist Executive Committee made its decision as a sequence to the publication on 10 January of the Front Populaire's programme. This was an all-out attack on all the Government's policies, including foreign policy.[88] Laval was succeeded as Prime Minister by Albert Sarraut, as Foreign Minister by Pierre-Etienne Flandin. (This second appointment was a way, common in the history of the Third Republic, of asserting 'continuity of foreign policy'. Flandin, it will be remembered had been the French Premier at the time of the Wal-Wal Incident and had remained so, with Laval as his Foreign Minister, until the end of May 1935.) The new Ministry was plainly a 'Caretaker's Government' pending the Elections due in May. In the final stages of the Abyssinian crisis, on which was superimposed the Rhineland one, the French Government was therefore a peculiarly weak one. Laval did not hold office again until becoming Marshal Pétain's Deputy Prime Minister on 23 June 1940.

We do not know whether there was ever a serious chance of Mussolini accepting the Hoare-Laval deal.[89] Adowa had already been avenged. Italian public opinion could easily have been swayed in favour of an advantageous compromise peace as opposed to an uncertain total victory. In terms of real and immediate benefits Mussolini had much to gain by accepting the former and abandoning the chances of the latter. Moreover, if he were to accept and the Negus to refuse, he would have much to gain in terms of seeming morality and the good opinion of other countries. How, too, could the League, in such circumstances, continue to enforce sanctions on an Italy which had accepted a peace plan put forward by Britain and France?

On 6 December (the day before Hoare's arrival in Paris) Mussolini had made an important speech to the Italian Chamber of Deputies, in which, referring to the Peterson-St. Quentin exchanges, he said:

'During these last hours there are symptoms of a slight improvement in the atmosphere and perhaps of some mitigation of certain contemplated steps; but it is my duty to put you on your guard against any premature and excessive optimism. Contacts between two experts do not signify negotiations, and not even necessarily the possibility of them; and even if negotiations do begin, there is no guarantee that they will arrive at results which will be either prompt or happy.'

This cautious welcome of the work being done by the two experts had been preceded by a piece of temperately reasoned argument:

'There cannot be an Italy which is strong in Europe, as Sir Samuel Hoare desired and as we want for our part, without a solution of the problem of the entire security of Italy's colonies in East Africa. Italy cannot be strong if she cannot find scope, in backward territories, for those capacities of hers for expansion, population, and civilization which Hoare himself has clearly recognized. . . .'

But then came a declamatory, defiant and minatory passage on sanctions, intended perhaps to raise morale at home and lower it abroad:

'It will suffice to declare and repeat, once for all, that the 265th day of the siege will find us still in possession of the same will, the same courage, the same determination as the first day of all. There is no siege that can bend us, and no coalition, however numerous, that can realize the illusory hope of making us abandon our objectives. . . . The suject on the agenda for the

12th December – I mean the embargo on oil – is calculated to prejudice the development of the situation gravely.'

Mussolini received the Hoare-Laval proposals on 10 December.[90] He remained silent on the subject until the 18th when, in effect, he rejected them, shortly before a meeting of the Fascist Grand Council. It is possible that this body had been summoned for that day to be told the exact opposite and that the Duce changed his mind, just in time, in order to avoid the discredit to himself of accepting a discredited plan. If so, his delay in making up his mind about it may have been, as just suggested, a serious error from his own point of view.

Looking at this point the other way round, Baldwin's failure to back Hoare may have been a serious blunder from the British Government's point of view. They would, if Mussolini had accepted the plan, have been able to set against the storm of public disapproval of it, substantial credit for ending the war. They would also have been able, quite certainly, to end their differences with France and, possibly, again secure Italy as a member of a coalition to contain Germany. Furthermore, the prestige of the League as an organ for conciliation, as opposed to coercion, could gradually have been still more built up. The biggest loser would of course have been Abyssinia, but as it turned out, as many foresaw, the death of the Hoare-Laval Pact carried the consequence of a total loss of Abyssinian independence to which no end could be foreseen.[91]

The most important reaction to the rejection of the plan was probably that of the German Government. According to Lipski, Polish Ambassador in Berlin, when he stayed with Goering in April he heard nothing but abuse of Mussolini.[92] In October, according to another witness, Goering said: 'I wouldn't like to be in the Duce's skin at this moment'.[93] On 18 December Lipski had a long meeting with Hitler and 'subsequently' told Hoare:

'I gained the impression that Hitler was alarmed over the fact that, in the event of a liquidation of the Abyssinian conflict by compromise between Great Britain and France on the one hand and Italy on the other, a united front of the Powers, strengthened by the recent Pact between Paris and Moscow, would reappear.'[94]

In other words, Hitler saw the situation in the same way as Hoare and Vansittart: agreement on the Hoare-Laval proposals would make possible the re-creation of the Stresa Front. Did Mussolini see that their rejection would make more probable an Italian alliance with Germany?

Amid all the excitement of the rapid pace and high drama of the events which occurred between Hoare's arrival in Paris on 7 December and the debates in both Houses of Parliament on 19 December one important fact tended to be overlooked: any decision about an oil sanction had again been deferred. To this extent the Hoare-Laval Pact, although killed, had produced a solid gain for both Laval and Mussolini. Three years later, on the eve of the Munich conference Mussolini said to Hitler:

> 'If the League of Nations had followed Eden's advice in the Abyssinian dispute and had extended economic sanctions to oil, I would have had to withdraw from Abyssinia within a week.'[95]

Part Three
Checkmate

'I swear by Almighty God that I will faithfully
try the several issues joined . . . and give a true verdict
according to the evidence".

(Part of oath sworn by members of British juries.)

17

The defeat of Abyssinia

So His Majesty's Government, having sat on a fence for many months, had a great fall, but the King's Government had to be carried on and the King's men could put it together again. Eden succeeded Hoare as Foreign Secretary; the office of Minister for League of Nations Affairs was abolished. That was appropriate for – not immediately perceived – the League was the real Humpty-Dumpty and it had had a fatal fall. Its bits and pieces could not, after the Hoare-Laval episode, be picked up by anyone. Eden's task was, in this respect, a hopeless one.

It will be recalled that he had left for Geneva on the afternoon of the 17th.[1] He had therefore missed the decisive Cabinet of the 18th, Hoare's consequent resignation, and the debates in Commons and Lords on the 19th. He left Geneva for London that evening, travelling in the company of Stanley Bruce. (Mr. Bruce, a former Australian Prime Minister was at this time High Commissioner in London and the Australian member of the League Council.) The two men discussed the post-Hoare situation and agreed that, for the next year or two, Austen Chamberlain would be the best possible Foreign Secretary. (Someone who passionately agreed with them was the British Ambassador in Vienna who later wrote of the situation at that time that 'more clearly than any other statesman did Sir Austen express policy in his own person'.)[2] At Calais the British Consul delivered a message from the Prime Minister: would Mr. Eden, on reaching London, please go straight and incommunicado to 10 Downing Street? There Baldwin rejected his advice to put Chamberlain in charge of the Foreign Office and explained that in any case he had told him the previous evening that he was too old for it. (From a man of 68 to a man of 72 this was not the most fortunate of remarks and Sir Austen took great exception to it, saying afterwards: 'He told me I was ga-ga'.[3] He was not assuaged by an offer on the 21st, which he declined, of Cabinet office without portfolio.) Halifax's name was then mentioned, but that idea was also rejected and silence supervened. Finally Baldwin said: 'It looks as if it will have to be you'.[4] It was almost as unfortunate a way of telling a young man that he was to be Foreign Secretary as his way of telling an old one that he was not.

Eden, speaking for Britain, had dealt the Hoare-Laval Pact a mortal blow at Geneva on the 18th; Baldwin, the next day, had announced its death.[5] 'Stone dead hath no fellow' and no comparable plan was subsequently tabled. Indeed Eden, in retrospect, considered that 'it was one of the exasperating consequences of the Paris proposals that they made any later and better balanced compromise more difficult.'[6] 'Conciliation' having failed to settle the 'dispute', one would have thought that every possible effort should have been made to thwart the aggressor by turning the sanctions screw tighter. Hoare on the 19th had declared against any postponement of the oil embargo, unless negotiations had actually started.[7] They had not. In fact, however, the months between the collapse of the Hoare-Laval plan in December 1935 and the Italian victory in May 1936, were used by Italy in intensive and successful military operations, by Abyssinia in solitary and stubborn resistance, and by everybody else directly concerned in desultory and futile discussions about the oil sanction.

At Geneva nothing stirred between the Council Meeting on 19 December 1935 and a meeting of the Committee of Thirteen on 20 January 1936 when the obvious was pointed out, i.e. that there was 'no opportunity of facilitating and hastening the settlement of the dispute through an agreement between the parties within the framework of the Covenant.'[8] The Sanctions Committee met on the 22nd and decided to set up a Committee of Experts 'to conduct a technical examination of ... the trade in and transport of petroleum, its derivatives, by-products and residues' and to make an early report on the effectiveness of an embargo on them. This Committee held its first meeting on 3 February and reported on 12 February. It did its work, in short, with the same expedition that had marked the work of the Sanctions Committee the previous October.[9] However, the next meeting of the Sanctions Committee was fixed for more than a fortnight later (for 2 March). This delay was probably due to a desire to see the outcome of the discussion then proceeding in the U.S.A. on the renewal of the Neutrality Act.[9]

The experts' two principal findings were:

1) An embargo on the export of oil to Italy could not become fully operational before a period of about twelve to fourteen weeks.
2) The oil-exporting States were, with the exception of the U.S.A., all members of the Co-Ordination Committee, i.e. of the League. If the U.S.A. limited its oil exports to Italy to the level normal before 1935 the embargo would be effective; if applied only by League States it would make Italian purchases of oil more difficult and more expensive.

We have seen that in the first nine months of 1935 the percentage of oil imported by Italy from the U.S.A. had risen from a 1934 figure of 6·5 to one of 17·8.[10] Hence it is easy to see why an embargo imposed in March 1936, and not becoming fully operational until, say, mid-June at the earliest, would not be effective. But all this was because a bus had been missed. The British Foreign Secretary's September speech had made a profound impression on American public opinion, and on opinion inside the Administration, in much the same way as it had done on the opinion of other Governments and peoples.[11] In consequence the League and the U.S.A. approached the Abyssinian crisis along independent but parallel lines.[12] The Co-Ordination Committee was clever enough, acting on hints from Washington, not to ask the U.S. to join in sanctions;[13] that would only have had a rebarbative effect on American opinion. It did, however, report its recommendations to non-Members of the League. Come November the U.S. Administration 'had committed itself to avoid thwarting the League's actions in restraining Italy, and had all but proclaimed publicly that if the League finally implemented Proposal 4A ... the United States would find a way to co-operate.'[14]

All this was changed by the Hoare-Laval Pact. It had been motivated largely by a desire to avoid an oil sanction; it killed American support for that.[15] As January and February wore on it became increasingly obvious that the two Great League Powers (Britain and France) had no real intention of imposing an oil sanction. Up to mid-December 1935 the League had seemed to be giving a lead and the question was the extent to which the U.S.A. might, indirectly, follow it. Then that position was reversed. After mid-December the League ceased to give a lead, though it almost certainly would have followed an American one. But while the U.S.A. was prepared to co-operate with a League living up to its own ideals it was scarcely enchanted by a League revealed as just another arena for the operation of Great Power politics.

The League's Committee of Oil Experts reported, as we have seen, on 12 February. On the same day the U.S. Senate's Foreign Relations Committee voted to renew the Neutrality Act of August 1935. Nonetheless Eden now asked Sir Ronald Lindsay, British Ambassador in Washington, whether there was any chance of the U.S limiting its oil exports to Italy. Lindsay's answer came on 22 February:

> 'If the League imposed an embargo regardless of the United States' attitude, I think there would be expressions of shame and heart-burnings in some volume and perhaps even pressure, but it would be ineffective even if it became apparent that the United States alone were furnishing supplies. Nevertheless, this course of action would do more than anything else to restore the League's prestige and to influence American opinion in favour of collective peace system.'[16]

Two days later (without benefit of the Ambassador's telegram) Mr. Attlee, speaking in the House of Commons, hit the nail on the head. He insisted that the American Government and people had been prepared to co-operate with the League in November: 'It may be much more difficult now, but I think it possible.' Even if the Hoare-Laval plan had shocked American opinion, was that 'any reason why the rest of the League should not put on oil sanctions?'[17]

The approach of a Geneva meeting (that of the Sanctions Committee on 2 March) which might decide to impose an oil sanction stimulated the same reactions in late February 1936 as had a similar situation in early December 1935. In Rome there was again much barking intended to convey that biting would follow; in Paris the new Government resolved to do the same as the old i.e. everything possible to prevent the additional sanction being imposed; in London a Cabinet meeting (on 26 February) at which Ministers – once again invited by the Prime Minister to express their views one by one, a sign of the importance of the occasion – tramped up and down the highways and byways of substantially the same old arguments to reach a flaccid conclusion:

'There was a general agreement that we should avoid taking a lead in this matter, and that the affair should be so conducted that the Committee of Eighteen in its corporate capacity should take it; also that there would be no question of applying an oil sanction unless the other oil-producing or exporting countries co-operated, though it would not be necessary to hold up the whole plan in consequence of non-co-operation by Venezuela.'[18]

The views of individual British Ministers on this occasion are not recorded, except in the case of the First Lord (Lord Monsell) who said that the position of the Fleet in the Mediterranean was becoming increasingly intolerable: 'The spirit and morale of the Fleet . . . was as high as he could wish, but he did not want to try them too highly. . . . We could not afford to overlook Japan.' His dissent from what was agreed by the Cabinet, 'on the ground that no sanction ought to be imposed which was not likely to be effective, a view which he understood had been held by many of his colleagues and by the Cabinet itself', was (an unusual procedure) formally minuted.

A second recorded dissent was that of the President of the Board of Trade (Walter Runciman). He, it may be guessed, was concerned at the possibility of permanent damage to Anglo-Italian trade. There are certain remarks in the minutes of this meeting which, though not attributed to him, one would suppose to have come from the holder of his office:

'Up to now the principal burden of sanctions had fallen upon this country. . . . The coal export trade from this country to Italy had completely disappeared, and by next week 30,000 miners would be unemployed. . . . We had to aim at such a position that whenever peace was signed between Italy and

Abyssinia we should be strong enough to recover our Italian trade and nothing should be done to jeopardize that.'[19]

Later in the meeting it was counter-observed that the proportion of trade affected was greater in the case of some smaller countries than in our own case (as much as one-third for Yugoslavia) and that our coal trade with Italy 'had been virtually dead before ever sanctions were imposed because Italy could not find means of making payments.'

'Other objections to an oil sanction' recorded, but not attributed to particular individuals, were 'the probable effect on the success of the Naval Conference which would be gravely jeopardized:[20] ... the risk of precipitating an extension of the war (which, however, was felt generally to have receded); or that Signor Mussolini might be encouraged to ally himself with Herr Hitler; or that he might withdraw from the League and the Locarno Treaty.' However, it was later stated that the risk of extending the war was probably negligible; the risk of an Italo-German alliance small 'owing to the contempt in which Herr Hitler is believed to hold Italy'; and the withdrawal of Italy from the League and the Locarno Treaty improbable. 'Politically', the summary of the arguments against an oil sanction concludes, 'it was urged that the Government should not yield to "Left-Wing" opinion. Gestures and symbols of this kind were dangerous and to adopt a non-effective sanction was to get the worst of both worlds.'

Against this array of arguments were set others, concerned with the position of the League and the state of public opinion at home and abroad. Recent telegrams from the Negus indicated his anxiety about the military situation:

'If these telegrams were published in a last effort to secure support from the League and nothing had been done, we should cut a poor figure. Even more importance was attached to the reaction of a negative attitude on the future of the League of Nations itself. The effect would be very bad in Germany, the United States and in this country. Any nation contemplating aggressive action would be encouraged and the disturbance to the world would be greater than ever. For eighteen countries to meet and decide to do nothing would from this point of view be most detrimental and discouraging, especially to countries applying sanctions. The whole principle of collective security would be put in question.'

The record then turns to the reaction which a negative attitude to the oil sanction 'would have on the political situation in this country'. Great importance, it is said, was attached to this, and a new point is made:

'The carrying out of the programmes of Defence Requirements depended very largely on industrial mobilization, and for this the co-operation and goodwill of labour was essential. The Trade Unionist section of the Labour Party stood firmly for collective security, and if the application of an oil sanction was shirked by the Government, the opposition to the Government's defensive programmes would have a moral basis which at present it lacked. In fact, the application of an oil sanction was advocated on the ground that it might even enable the co-operation of Trade Unionists to be secured.'

An old point is stated once again:

'Some members of the Government who had little confidence in the efficacy of the sanction supported it on the ground that it was impossible after all that had been said at the General Election and before and since not to try out a policy of economic sanctions. . . . Our own country and the whole world were entitled to know whether they could be made to work. To repudiate an oil sanction after the statements that had been made in the Debate on the Hoare-Laval peace proposals would be politically disastrous.'

Baldwin, in summing up, 'agreed in the general view that an oil sanction ought now to be imposed'. In that respect his view had changed because of changed political circumstances:

'Politically he thought his own position as Prime Minister would be much affected according to the decision taken. Although the question of prestige was of no account to himself personally, undoubtedly the prestige of the Prime Minister affected that of the Government. For the reasons that had been given a refusal to impose an oil sanction would have a disastrous effect both now and at the next General Election. During the late General Election the feeling of the country had been in favour of trying out the League system, though he himself had made it quite clear that he would never agree to anything in the nature of a blockade.[21] The losses involved in the oil sanction would be part of the price for expediting a settlement, but the whole of Europe was entitled to know whether collective economic sanctions would work so that every country could make up its mind as to how far it could cooperate in a collective system. . . . He also attached the utmost importance to the labour side of the question which was of vital importance to the Defence Requirements programmes. In that respect the totalitarian States had a great advantage over this country. Therefore, the co-operation of labour was absolutely vital if the programmes were to be carried out. With that co-operation this country in five years time would fear no-one.'

It is at first sight surprising that so powerful a speech by so powerful a man had so little effect. The pass at Geneva was sold within the week, the oil sanction hardly heard of again outside the history books, all that battle of words at 10 Downing Street on 26 February entirely wasted. True, the Abyssinian affair was about to be driven into second place on the agenda of the British Cabinet, and in the minds of those throughout the world concerned with international affairs, by the German breach of the Locarno Treaties. However, the effective final abandonment of the idea of an oil sanction came before that. We must note that the Prime Minister had failed to carry with him two of his colleagues; that even if they had not formally dissented (such dissents are very rare and often prelude resignations) the Cabinet was still, fundamentally, divided, its support of an oil sanction at best lukewarm and highly qualified. No Foreign Secretary, personally in favour of such a sanction, could in all the circumstances have felt that he was getting from his colleagues their wholehearted support.

Eden, in short, was in no position to resist Flandin if at Geneva he took the same line as Laval – which is exactly what he did. There was no question of his resisting a British lead for the

Cabinet had specified that there was to be none. When the Sanctions Committee met on 2 March Flandin proposed that, before it proceeded to the question of an oil sanction, the Committee of Thirteen should meet again the next day, to consider a final appeal to the belligerents to end the war. Eden, speaking second, accepted this, remarking that 'this procedure need not cause any undue delay'; he did add that the British Government, having studied the Report of the Committee of Experts, was in favour of the imposition of an oil embargo and prepared to join in its early application 'if the other principal supplying and transporting States who are members of the League of Nations are prepared to do so likewise';[22] he did not stipulate for a time limit to the proposed effort for conciliation by the Committee of Thirteen; he did not press for the immediate imposition of an oil sanction if that effort should fail. In fact what happened was just what some members of the Cabinet feared would happen, 18 countries met and decided to do nothing.[23] Making this decision the Sanctions Committee disappears from history.

The Committee of Thirteen, it will be remembered, had on 20 January seen 'no opportunity of facilitating and hastening the settlement of the dispute through an agreement between the parties within the framework of the Covenant'.[24] Nonetheless on 3 March it resolved to send 'to both belligerents an urgent appeal for the immediate opening of negotiations within the framework of the League of Nations and in the spirit of the Covenant with a view to the prompt cessation of hostilities and the definite restoration of peace'. The Committee also decided to meet again a week later, on 10 March, 'to hear the replies of the two Governments'.[25]

Arriving back in London on 5 March, Eden explained to the Cabinet that the situation he had found at Geneva was 'rather different from that envisaged by the Cabinet before his departure when they gave him his instructions. He had found M. Flandin very keen to make an attempt at conciliation between Italy and Abyssinia before taking a decision on oil sanctions. He, himself, did not feel very hopeful of the result, but he thought it best to acquiesce. At the same time it had become clear from his conversations with the representatives of other States that the League must say something about its intentions on the subject of sanctions, otherwise the world at large, and Italy in particular, would assume that the oil sanction was dropped. In these changed circumstances he had decided that it was unavoidable, notwithstanding the Cabinet's desire that he should try to avoid taking an initiative, to announce the policy of His Majesty's Government to support the application of an oil sanction if conciliation failed'.[26]

'M. Flandin,' Eden told the Cabinet, 'had appeared very depressed by communications he had received from Italy to the effect that, if an oil sanction were imposed, Italy would withdraw from the League of Nations, refuse to sign a Naval Treaty[27] and denounce the military treaty concluded between Marshal Badoglio and General Gamelin.[28] M. Flandin also feared that Italy would disinterest herself in the Locarno Treaty. He was surprised when he learned that we had not received a similar message'.

It was Professor Toynbee's judgment in October 1936 that: 'On the 2–3 March 1936, as on the 7–8 December 1935, the British Foreign Secretary was out-manoeuvred and overborne by a French antagonist in the guise of a colleague'.[29] That now seems an over-simple and over-patriotic point of view. A Foreign Minister, of whatever nationality, who firmly holds to a well thought out policy, however mistaken from his own point of view, will always have an advantage over another Foreign Minister who has no firm policy to present. The decisions of 8 December 1935 and 3 March 1936 are not to be presented as triumphs, obtained by guile, of French diplomacy over British. Hoare's mind was working along exactly the same lines as Laval's; he did not have to be out-manoeuvred to accept what he personally was already convinced to be needful. Eden may to some extent have been overborne by Flandin – but who can doubt that most of his colleagues were only too ready to acquiesce in another attempt at conciliation?

The Committee of Thirteen's initiative was overtaken, as we shall soon see, by a much more important event. However, it is probably convenient to trace at this point the history of that initiative. Both Abyssinia and Italy quite promptly accepted in general principle the appeals addressed to them. On 20 March, however, Abyssinia pointed out that the Italian reply contained no acceptance of the specific principle of working 'within the framework of the League of Nations and in the spirit of the

Covenant'. The Committee of Thirteen did not meet, as resolved, on 10 March but on 23 March (in London). After two hours in secret session it announced a request to its Chairman (the Spanish representative, De Madariaga), assisted by the Secretary-General, 'to get in touch with the two parties and to take such steps as may be called for in order that the Committee may be able, as soon as possible, to bring the two parties together within the framework of the League of Nations and in the spirit of the Covenant, to bring about a prompt cessation of hostilities and the final restoration of peace.'[30] Eden had already told the Cabinet, on the 19th, that he was in favour of a mediation of this kind.[31]

No one could have acted more quickly than Madariaga. His first communication to Rome was sent on the very day (23 March) on which he had been appointed mediator. Italy, however, resorted to the same diplomacy of delay it had used so skilfully and, for itself, so profitably in the early months of 1935.[32] It was not until 15 April that Aloisi arrived at Geneva, empowered to hold discussions with Madariaga. Meanwhile Abyssinia had stuck to its point that it would not negotiate without an Italian acceptance of the specific principle of negotiations within the framework of the League and in the spirit of the Covenant. On 1 April Wolde Mariam, on behalf of Abyssinia, reiterated this point, adding that the Italian acceptance in principle (on 8 March, of the Committee of Thirteen's appeal of the 3rd) was only a manoeuvre to prevent the imposition of an oil embargo 'voted five months ago'.

On 17 April Madariaga reported to the Committee of Thirteen the failure of the mission with which he had been charged on 23 March. The Committee decided to report to the Council (which, it is pertinent to remember, was only itself under another name). Its Report was discussed, in public, on 20 April and at 10 p.m. that evening the Council passed a resolution regretting that the war was 'continuing under conditions which had been declared to be contrary to the Covenant and which involved execution of the obligations laid upon members in such a case by the Covenant. . . .' and addressing to Italy a 'supreme appeal . . . to bring to the settlement of her dispute with Ethiopia that spirit which the League of Nations is entitled to expect from one of its original members and a permanent member of the Council. . . .'

This was the last step taken by the League to try to bring the war to an end. The 'supreme appeal' was instantly rejected; Aloisi voted against the resolution. The delegate from Ecuador disassociated his Government from the phrase in it plainly referring to sanctions, his Government having as early as 4 April announced its abandonment of them.[33] The ship was sinking; the first rat had left. As things had turned out, Flandin on 3 March had succeeded in postponing the oil sanction, not for one week, but for ever.

On the morning of Saturday, 7 March, Germany informed Belgium, Britain, France and Italy (the four other signatories of the Locarno Treaty) that German troops were marching into the de-militarized zone of the Rhineland. This was an area stretching from Germany's western frontier to a line drawn 50 kilometres east of the right bank of the Rhine. Its de-militarization had originally been prescribed by the Treaty of Versailles, but had subsequently been accepted by Germany as a part of the Locarno Treaty. Hitler himself had recently confirmed his acceptance of that Treaty and specifically his respect for the de-militarized zone (in his speech of 21 May 1935). His thin pretext for a flagrant breach of it was the ratification, on 27 February, of the Franco-Soviet Pact (signed on 2 May 1935) by the French Chamber of Deputies. No doubt he took this step when he did because he had become sure not only that the half-hearted Anglo-French League policy had broken up the Stresa Front, but also had so strained Anglo-French relations that the full provisions of the Covenant were no more likely to be applied to him than to Mussolini.[34]

The event of 7 March constituted, in two ways, an enormous menace to the peace of Europe. In the first place, it virtually destroyed all possibility of trust in Hitler's word. (Eden was to say, to the Cabinet on the 9th, that it 'struck a severe blow at that principle of the sanctity of treaties which underlies the whole structure of international relations'.[35] That was also, of course, one of the foremost issues in the Abyssinia affair.) In the second, it threatened a tremendous increase, at the expense of France, of Germany's military power. So long as the Rhineland was demilitarized Germany could scarcely risk another war with France because her industrial entrails lay wide open to attack by the French Army; as soon as it was effectively re-militarized Germany's western frontier would become as secure as France's eastern one. In other words, if Germany thereafter attacked one of

France's allies in Eastern or Central Europe, France could only help that Ally by a war which might well be fought, like the 1914–18 one, mainly on French soil.

This German coup had consequences for the settlement of the Abyssinian crisis even more deleterious than the German coup of March 1935.[36]

In the first place, it understandably diverted attention from the Abyssinian crisis to a European crisis to an even greater extent than the German move of the previous March. (We have already noted the postponement from 10 March to 23 March of an important meeting of the Committee of Thirteen and the final killing-off of the plan for an oil sanction which ensued from that postponement. We may also remark the subsequent diversion of attention from the Abyssinian to the Rhineland crisis in the Cabinet minutes at the time and, in due course, in almost every history of the period at the point at which the narrative reaches March 1936.) More than six weeks later, Eden, on his return from a series of meetings at Geneva, told the Cabinet, on 22 April, that apart 'from the representatives of Portugal, Denmark and Australia who shared our general view as to the importance of this matter from the point of view of the future of the League, hardly anyone had been thinking of Abyssinia and Africa at all. For the most part they had been dominated by thoughts of the reaction of these events on the European situation, according as their respective countries were mainly concerned with Germany or Italy ...'[37]

The Rhineland re-militarization, in the second place increased still further the divergence of British and French foreign policies. Rôles were substantially reversed. French public opinion had been mainly indifferent to Italian expansion in Africa; it did not disadvantage French interests there and was indirectly to the advantage of her interests in Europe. Now that her most vital interests in Europe were menaced by her deadliest and most powerful enemy a different song was sung; the case for upholding international obligations by international force (if finally needed) was plainly perceived. British public opinion, on the other hand, did not think that in this new crisis the same fundamental issues were at stake as in the old one. Over and over again the remark was passed, on the British side of the Channel, that the Germans had the right to do what they liked in their own 'back garden',

H

especially some 20 years after the end of the war.[38] Neither the moral nor the strategic implications for Britain of this particular breach of a particular Treaty were properly or widely perceived. The only British newspaper to grasp them was the *Daily Telegraph,* but even its first leader of 9 March did not urge resistance.[39]

The re-occupation started, as we have just seen, on Saturday, 7 March. Two days previously the British Cabinet had addressed itself to a question put by Flandin concerning the British attitude in such an eventuality, whether if Germany violated the zone and Italy took no action, Britain would claim to be absolved from any. Flandin also asked whether, if Italy denounced the Locarno Treaty, Britain would, in that event also, claim to be absolved from its obligations. The Foreign Secretary thought that the answer to both questions should be 'No'.

Eden thought that if Flandin was given satisfactory answers to these questions, and if the policy of conciliation was tried once again, he would agree to an oil sanction. However, 'it appeared to some members of the Cabinet that the French Government's object in putting these questions was not so much to secure our active co-operation which they themselves must know was not feasible in the present state of our public opinion and armaments, but rather to give them an excuse before French public opinion to avoid acquiescing in an oil embargo on Italy'. It was the Lord Chancellor (Lord Hailsham) who rebutted this, pointing out that 'M. Flandin had quite a good case for raising this question. We were asking him to agree to an oil sanction. He was apprehensive that in that event Italy might tear up the Treaty of Locarno. Before deciding on an oil sanction, therefore, he appeared to be justified in asking what our attitude would be in that event'.[40]

As the Rhineland crisis developed the consequential question relevant to the Abyssinian one rapidly became not that of extending but of discontinuing sanctions. On 11 March Eden (just back from a visit to Paris, accompanied – on his first diplomatic mission – by Halifax[41]) told the Cabinet that the Italian Ambassador to France 'had not departed from the Italian point of view that they would not undertake any obligations' – arising, that is to say, out of the German breach of the Locarno Treaty – 'while they themselves were exposed to sanctions. At one moment M. Flandin had suggested that this could easily be got over by withdrawing sanctions, but he himself had given no encouragement to that remark'.[42] On the 12th Eden told the Cabinet that the Italian Ambassador in London 'had indicated a strong desire to try and liquidate the position as regards sanctions on Italy'.[43] On the 19th, i.e. just before the meeting of the Committee of Thirteen deferred from the 10th, Eden sought the views of his colleagues on an anticipated move to discontinue sanctions in return for a truce between Italy and Abyssinia. There followed the first of many Cabinet canvasses of the possibility of ending sanctions. On this occasion the discussion was short and a decision easily reached against swapping sanctions for a truce or even 'preliminaries of peace'. The last word came apparently from Chamberlain who 'suggested that if sanctions were taken off before peace were in sight there would be political trouble in this country. The imposition of fresh sanctions, however, was a very different question.'[44]

The end of the Italo-Abyssinian War came in sight sooner than had been expected and not in the manner so long striven for by Britain and France. On 6 April the Foreign Secretary informed the Cabinet that the military situation of the Abyssinians was desperate. The only effective action which could now be taken to aid them was to close the Suez Canal. (Had not this been true throughout?) It was recognized that closure could involve war with Italy which the Prime Minister stated (and without contradiction) he was unwilling to envisage in the present state of Europe.[45] This was no change of position; his first object throughout the crisis had been to keep his country out of war.[46]

It was also recognized 'that the Government would be criticized on the ground that it had failed to use the machinery of the League of Nations to save Abyssinia. It was suggested that the reply should be that at no time had there been a reasonable prospect of applying methods that might achieve success unless we had been prepared for the risk of war with Italy. Oil sanctions were a possible exception, but we had expressed our willingness to agree to oil sanctions which had been postponed in the hope of a successful effort at conciliation.' There had been, it must be remembered, more than one postponement of this crucial sanction, more than one effort at conciliation. None of the postponements of the sanction had promoted the success of the conciliation.

The Cabinet then went on to a long discussion, as a separate item on its agenda, of the Italian use of poison gas. Evidence of its use was overwhelming; this was a breach of yet another international agreement, the Anti-Gas Convention of 1925; the Italian plea that the use of poison gas as a retaliation for atrocities was not forbidden by that Convention had no legal validity whatsoever; the failure to enforce the Convention had most sinister overtones in relation to the future of warfare anywhere. Eden was to speak in a foreign affairs debate that afternoon: 'It was suggested that to point out the ineffectiveness of the League to prevent a breach of a Convention of this kind would be a good way of introducing that part of the speech of the Secretary of State for Foreign Affairs'.[47] What a clarion cry that would have been! In fact Eden revealed to the Committee of Thirteen, on 9 April, that the records of the Suez Canal Company showed that Italy had shipped some 260 tons of poison gas through the Canal up to the end of February 1936.[48] The closure of the Canal, however, even to that traffic, was not contemplated by the leading League Power. The Committee of Thirteen, describing itself as 'interpreter of the emotion aroused in public opinion' by the charges and counter-charges about the methods of war being pursued by both belligerents, addressed to both 'a pressing appeal' for 'assurances susceptible of making this emotion disappear'.[49]

The Cabinet meeting in London on the 6th ended on a more mundane note. Abyssinia had made frequent and fruitless attempts to secure help under the terms of a League Convention for Financial Assistance to States Victims of Aggression, a detailed plan worked out in 1930, but not formally in force.[50] Now the Chancellor reported that she was trying to get Treasury help for a loan on the London market. For this his authority was needed. If that was given it would be officially stated in the customary way that the Government accepted no responsibility for repayment. Nonetheless any subscribers might well blame the Government for any losses. The Cabinet agreed that the Chancellor would not be justified in refusing to allow such a loan to be floated, but that it would be advantageous to postpone that operation for a week or two.[51]

In the next week or two new and larger questions began to appear in the Cabinet's discussions. What would be the consequences of Italian victory in Abyssinia on British interests in Egypt and the Sudan? What was now to be the future of the League? Could the sanctions front be maintained? Could sanctions ever be imposed again? (They never were, by the League.) Could collective security work in a Continent dominated by two Dictators? (No mention of the third.) Would Hitler press or cozen Mussolini into letting him have his way in Austria? These new questions were discussed against a familiar background of old ones : should the British armed presence in the Mediterranean be diminished; should the existing sanctions be raised, retained, or even (it was still asked) extended? There was no lack of questions to discuss, but a lack (predominant but not invariable in the conduct of human affairs) of answers to be implemented.

On 2 May the Negus left Addis Ababa on the Jibuti railway. He arrived at Jibuti the next day and was from there taken to Haifa on a British cruiser. After a fortnight's stay in Palestine he left for England, again on a British warship, and arrived in London on 3 June. (The next day Sir Samuel Hoare re-entered the Cabinet as First Lord of the Admiralty.) Italian forces entered Addis Ababa on 5 May and, although fighting continued in outlying regions, Mussolini was justified in equating the Negus's escape into exile and the Italian occupation of his capital with Italian victory in the war which had begun on 3 October 1935. On 9 May 1936 he proclaimed (from a balcony of the Palazzo Venezia), 'to the city and the world' one might say, the Italian annexation of Abyssinia and the succession of the King of Italy, as Emperor, to its vacant throne. This was Mussolini's 'finest hour', but the topmost point of the flight of Icarus was also the point at which he started on his downward fall to an ignominious death and irrevocable discredit.

18

The defeat of the League

The total, or well-nigh total, Italian victory in the war transformed the situation not only of Abyssinia but also of the League. Sanctions had failed of their professed purpose, to end the war by stopping the aggressor in his tracks. Now, so far from aggression being checked, its victim had been not merely defeated but crushed. Crispi's spiritual successor had wiped Abyssinia off the map;[1] the pacifist dictum of those times that 'war settles nothing' had, once again, been shown to be false. Moreover, on 5 May 1936, no one could see how the new settlement could be unsettled except by force. That meant, at that date, the deliberate starting of a new war, not fought by an Abyssinian Army on Abyssinian soil, but organized (at first at any rate) from outside Abyssinia. Moreover, as it had so recently been decided not to use sanctions to try to stop Germany re-militarizing the Rhineland, the lack of sense in continuing them against Italy, after their failure to stop her conquering Abyssinia, seemed all the more apparent.

It took a few weeks for the facts of this transformed situation to be fully appreciated by politicians and peoples. The League's Council met on 11 May and on the 12th adjourned its deliberations on 'the dispute between Italy and Ethiopia' until 15 June. It expressed the view, however, 'that in the meantime there is no cause for modifying the measures previously adopted in collaboration by the membership of the League'.[2] In fact the Council did not meet again until 26 June and cognisance of the Abyssinian situation was then transferred to the Assembly which resumed its sixteenth ordinary session (which had been suspended on 11 October 1935)[3] on 30 June.

From mid-May until the end of June, therefore, much debate went on in many countries about the attitude to be taken to the new Abyssinian situation. In no country was this debate more important than in Great Britain, the country which had found itself willy-nilly (willy on the whole by its people, nilly on balance by their Government) in the position of leader of the League in the supreme crisis of its history. In the end the country which had marched the others half-way up the hill (the grand old Duke of York had at any rate got his men to the top) marched them down again. In that way more honesty and dignity (though not much of that) were achieved in the ending of sanctions than could have been achieved in any other. The decision, however, was not easily or hastily arrived at. The Cabinet discussed the matter at length at three meetings (on 27 May, 29 May, and 10 June) before deciding, on 17 June, to shoulder its responsibilities in the simplest and most straightforward way possible by taking 'the initiative at the League of Nations in proposing the raising of sanctions against Italy'.[4] This was at any rate a refreshing, if ignominious, change from eschewing the initiative on various previous occasions when there had been great need for initiative of a positive kind.[5] This decision was to be announced in the House of Commons the next day (18 June) 'without previous consultation either with the French or the Italian or, indeed, any other foreign Government'. The Foreign Secretary was, however, to see the French Ambassador and the Ministers of Greece, Turkey and Yugoslavia before his speech in Parliament 'in order to communicate to them the general line which he proposed to take'.

Thus various ingenious ideas for bargains with Mussolini and/or sheltering behind French coat-tails in raising sanctions were abandoned and the danger of sanctions just petering out was avoided. The only real alternative was to retain them as, at this stage, a moral gesture. Eden put the matter bluntly to the House:

'The fact has to be faced that sanctions did not realize the purpose for which they were imposed. The Italian military campaign succeeded. The capital and most important parts of Abyssinia are in Italian military occupation; and, so far as I am aware, no Abyssinian Government survives in any part of the Emperor's territory. That is a situation which nothing but military action from without – from outside the country – can possibly reverse. Is there any country prepared to take such military action? Or is there any section of public opinion in this country prepared to take such military action?"[6]

One 'Yes' came five days later, in muted terms, from Arthur Henderson (later Lord Rowley), the son of his father in policy as well as in blood:

'I can only speak for myself but, for what it is worth, I can state my own position. I believe that any one who supports the collective peace system, as set out in the Covenant of the League of Nations, has to be prepared to face all the consequences naturally flowing from the enforcement of the Covenant against an aggressor nation'[7]

On the same day (23 June), and again in the House of Commons, the leader of the Liberal Party, Sir Archibald Sinclair, said that he had 'had double or treble the number of letters, post cards and telegrams during this crisis' than he had 'had at the crisis of the Hoare-Laval negotiations. . . .'[8] Certainly the issue of retaining or raising sanctions was one which deeply stirred British public opinion. To admit that sanctions had failed, that the Fascist dictator had won, that the League had lost, that nothing (short of a European war) could be done to reverse those events, were the bitterest possible pills for League-loving people to swallow. However, on this issue there was in existence (in modern parlance) a silent, or largely silent, pro-Government popular majority which had not been in existence the previous December. The difference is to be explained in terms of the extent to which public opinion felt itself obliged to accept the *fait accompli*.

In the war of words outside Parliament, as in the then secret discussions of the Cabinet, the decisive voice was that of Neville Chamberlain, the Conservative 'Crown Prince'. (It is a major part of the interest of this whole story that it is the Abyssinian crisis which marks his entry into the field of foreign policy. In the early stages of the crisis he had been a relatively strong and consistent 'sanctioneer'.[9] It was some months after the end of it that Sir Austen Chamberlain said to his half-brother: 'Neville, you must remember that you don't know anything about foreign affairs'.[10]) His most decisive intervention, and his first major public statement on foreign policy, was made on the evening of

10 June (after, that is to say, the third inconclusive meeting of the series of four Cabinet meetings mentioned above). On 2 May Chamberlain had written to his sister:

'... the Italian successes will encourage the French to urge that, now everything is finished, we ought to lift the sanctions, let bygones be bygones, and get Italy back to the Stresa front at once. That seems to me intolerable. ... I am sure the time has not yet come for the League to own itself beaten. All the same, it is beaten.'[11]

With his cast of mind, however, he thought out the logical consequences of that beating more quickly than many others and coolly resolved that his view should prevail. The customary consultation of the Foreign Secretary by another Minister about to make an important pronouncement on foreign policy was deliberately avoided.[12] Chamberlain was anxious to give his colleagues a push in the direction he favoured by mobilizing public opinion in support of his own ideas. The secret of his success that evening, as of so many oratorical successes, was that what he said, although it aroused intense opposition, effectively expressed what a great many people were thinking.

The occasion for Chamberlain's momentous public intervention in the controversy about sanctions was a dinner given in his honour by a Conservative Club. By design, or more probably by accident, the ground was perfectly prepared for him by the chairman, a former Conservative Chancellor, Sir Robert Horne, 'blurting out' his own opinion, that it would be a delight to see the end of sanctions : 'When there is a corpse in your midst it is better to bury it'.

It is fair to Chamberlain to precede the quotation which 'hit the headlines' the world over, and is usually quoted without any context at all, by quoting some of the remarks which led up to it. He said that 'the circumstances in which the dispute between Italy and Abyssinia began appeared to offer an opportunity for the exercise of the policy of collective security which could hardly be more favourable for its success. The aggression was patent and flagrant, and there was hardly any country to which it appeared that a policy of sanctions could be exercized with a greater chance of success than upon Italy. ... That policy has been tried out and it has failed to prevent war, failed to stop war, failed to save the victim of aggression'.

From this experience he had, he said, drawn one or two conclusions, but there were some people, he also said, who did not desire to draw any conclusions at all. He instanced the President of the League of Nations Union, Lord Cecil, who had 'issued a circular to its members in which he said that the issue hung in the balance and urged them to commence a campaign of pressure upon members of Parliament and members of the Government with the idea that if we were to pursue the policy of sanctions, and even to intensify it, it was still possible to preserve the independence of Abyssinia. That seems to me the very midsummer of madness.'[13]

It will be seen that Chamberlain, unlike his chairman, did not just blurt out his famous remark or say, *tout court*, that in his opinion sanctions should be raised. He deliberately challenged the great apostle of the League cause and the letter he had sent, on 27 May, to all the Branch Secretaries of the League of Nations Union,[14] reinforced by a personal letter published in *The Times* the very morning of the dinner. What Chamberlain strictly said was only that the preservation of sanctions would not preserve the independence of Abyssinia. From this, however, it could be, and was, inferred that he and his Cabinet colleagues had decided, perhaps at their meeting earlier that day, that sanctions should be ended. In fact, as we have seen, this decision was not taken until a week later.

It remained for the Assembly of the League of Nations to ratify it. The second speaker in the debate which began in the Assembly on 30 June was the Negus himself and two days later, while that debate was still proceeding, he submitted to the Secretary-General two resolutions. The first was to be a proclamation by the Assembly that it would not recognize any annexation obtained by force; the second a recommendation to member States that, for the purpose of affording Abyssinia the aid to which it was entitled under Article 16, they should guarantee an Abyssinian loan of £10,000,000. The next day (3 July), however, the Assembly instructed its General Committee to draft alternative resolutions and this task was, not without difficulty, completed on the 4th. The text finally agreed by the General Committee was two-fold. The first part called for proposals for the reform of the League.

To this was 'tacked'[15] an unambiguous recommendation that the Co-ordination Committee should 'bring to an end the measures taken by them in execution of Article 16 of the Covenant'. This resolution was carried on 4 July by 44 votes to 1 (that of Abyssinia herself) with 4 abstentions (Chile, Mexico, Panama, and South Africa). The President of the Assembly (M. van Zeeland, Prime Minister of Belgium) ruled that unanimity was not required because this vote was a 'view' rather than a 'decision'. He also ruled that the first Abyssinian resolution was not to be voted on because covered by that just passed. He allowed, however, a vote on the second Abyssinian resolution. Only the same single vote was cast for it, whilst there were 23 votes against it and 25 abstentions. (Only 10 months before the aggressor had received only three supporting votes;[16] now the victim of aggression was left, twice over, in a minority of one.) On 6 July the Co-ordination Committee decided that sanctions should end on the 15th.

19
Epilogue

Three days after the end of sanctions General Franco started his rebellion against the Spanish Government. In July of the next year (1937) war against China was resumed by Japan and this war was still going on when the European War started in September 1939. Germany, with the connivance of Italy, invaded and annexed Austria in March 1938; the process of dismembering Czecho-Slovakia was begun at Munich in September 1938 (by international agreement) and finished in March 1939 (without the slightest pretence of it). Franco entered Madrid a few days after Hitler entered Prague. In April 1939 Mussolini annexed Albania. In the three years and six weeks between the end of the Abyssinian crisis and the start of the European War a whole world was shattered by the hammer blows of Franco, Hitler, Mussolini, and Tojo: only in Spain and China were Fascism and foreign aggression stoutly resisted, as they had been in Abyssinia. Irresolute pressure on Mussolini had the effect, anticipated by many, of driving him into Hitler's camp. (The question whether resolute pressure would have had the same effect earlier on is a different one.[1]) The first public indication that this was happening came as early as July 1936, with an Italian refusal to take part in a meeting of the Locarno Powers other than Germany. Mussolini proclaimed a Rome-Berlin Axis on 1 November 1936,[2] and a year later joined the Anti-Comintern Pact concluded by Germany and Japan.

If instead of counting forward from the end of the Abyssinian crisis we count back three years from its beginning we come to the world of December 1931. Germany was then a member of the League; the Disarmament Conference was about to meet; Hitler was not Chancellor; Abyssinia was an independent State under the rule of a youthful and reforming Emperor. Sir Keith Feiling describes the period between Germany's leaving the League and Mussolini's decision to attack Abyssinia as 'the last expiring season of hope'.[3] The pace of the subsequent descent into Hell was appalling. The world of 1936–9 was in no sense unified by a League of Nations; much of it was divided into two armed and hostile camps; powerful States acted with no respect whatsoever for their pledged word. This indeed was 'international anarchy'.

In this period of sharp and steep international decline after 15 July 1936, the League played little or no part. True, the danger from Italy brought Britain and Egypt together and, a by-product of the Anglo-Egyptian Treaty signed on 26 July, the League gained that September its last new member. *Per contra* between May 1936 and September 1939 the League lost, one way and another, 11 members and, during World War II, another four.[4] When Germany seized Austria nothing was done at Geneva, nothing was even said. When Germany invaded Poland, when Britain and France then declared war on Germany, when Russia too invaded Poland, the League was not asked to take any action by Britain, France or Poland herself. When, however, in December 1939, Finland found herself the victim of Russian aggression, (legally justified only by a faked frontier incident and the transparent hypocrisy of saying that one Kuusinen, a Communist puppet was the head of the Finnish Government, with which Russia was not at war) the true Finnish Government decided that it had at any rate nothing to lose by an appeal to the League. Council and Assembly proceeded to expel the Russian aggressor, the only State to be expelled from the League.

Council and Assembly, however, did more than that; they proceeded to organize, through the Secretary-General, some material help for Finland, the supply not of war materials but of money, food, clothing, and medicines. This was more than the League had done for China in 1931 or Abyssinia in 1935. In the case of China sanctions were never contemplated, but members had been asked to help her: an appeal which, however, was never followed up. In the case of Abyssinia sanctions were applied but all positive help consistently refused. There is a certain justice in Finland, which had preached the case for positive aid to the victims of aggression as an essential part of the League's machinery, having been the first, albeit the last, country to receive any. It can too be said that the last act of the League's life – or its final death spasm? – was, however mixed the motives (mere anti-Communism being one), a credit to it.

The League was formally ended by a resolution of the last Assembly on 18 April 1946; the successor body, the United Nations, had come into being with the signing of its Charter at San Francisco on 26 June 1945. Hitler's Reich, which was to last 1,000 years, only lasted 12; Mussolini's Abyssinian Empire lasted only six. The conflicting interests of European countries in relation to European affairs, expressed by diplomatic activities, came near to killing Abyssinia; expressed by European Civil War (for such the first part of the last World War can now be seen to have been) they brought the seeming corpse alive again. Putting it another way, we did not hesitate in 1941 to do, for our national interests, what we had not hesitated not to do for those of the League in 1936. Allied military operations in East Africa led to the collapse of Italian rule. The Negus re-entered his capital on 5 May 1941, five years almost to the day since he left it and today (1973), aged 80 and in, effectively, the 57th year of his reign, is still enthroned there, the most senior of all Heads of State. A final reconciliation with Italy was marked by his State visit there in 1970. Only four years on the throne when the hurricane broke on him, without Allies, with negligible resources, with only a brave people behind him, he hardly put a foot wrong. His wisdom and his dignity in those immeasurably difficult days deserve to be long remembered.

To those who played the other principal parts in the drama of 1935–6 Fate was not so kind. (Are the Gods, after all, just?) Four came to violent ends. De Bono, who led the Italian Army across the Abyssinian frontier on 2 October 1935, was executed by Mussolini's order on 11 January 1944. Mussolini himself, attempting, as the Allied Armies approached and the net closed round him, to escape from Italy to Switzerland, was caught by partisans and shot, on 28 April 1945. His body was hung by the heels in the Piazzale Loreto in Milan. Hitler committed suicide two days later. Laval was brought to trial by the Government of General de Gaulle and executed on 15 October 1946. At their deaths, Mussolini and Laval were alike 62, Hitler only 56.

These things are ordered differently in Britain. Of the British public men principally concerned only Lord Avon is still alive. The others lived to a ripe old age and died peacefully (Simon at

81, Baldwin at 80, Hoare at 79, Vansittart at 76, MacDonald and Chamberlain at 71). In none of these cases, however, can their later years have been notably happy. MacDonald, Prime Minister at the start of the Abyssinian crisis and head of the British delegation at the Stresa Conference, so deplorably a non-event in relation to it, retired from public life along with Baldwin in May 1937, went on a sea voyage 'in search of that most elusive of all commodities, rest' and died at sea. A few days before his death Baldwin went out of his way to praise his contribution to the 'National Government' and it is to be hoped that those kind words reached him. The fact, however, remains that he died regarded as a traitor by most of those with whom he had shared his political life and regarded by the general public as a somewhat ridiculous figure, notable for the rambling quality of the utterances of his old age.

Baldwin, as we have seen, having recovered by the autumn of 1936 from a kind of nervous breakdown, presided with deftness over the abdication crisis, with aplomb over the coronation of George VI, and then retired from the office of Prime Minister, at a moment of his own choosing, on 27 May 1937. He was succeeded by Neville Chamberlain, who will live in history primarily for his part in securing the Munich Agreement, the pros and cons of which are still hotly debated and seem likely to remain so indefinitely. Overthrown by the House of Commons in May 1940, he resigned as Prime Minister but remained a member of the War Cabinet until his death, from cancer, in November. In his case the fact remains that in September 1939, as he himself said, his life's work fell in ruins about him.[5]

Simon, having been a very unpopular Foreign Secretary, did not recover his popularity as Home Secretary. Churchill made him Lord Chancellor and, as might have been expected, he was more successful in that office than in a more political one.

Hoare, after a sycophantic speech in the House of Commons on 12 March 1936,[6] received a letter from Baldwin, written the very next day, offering him the Admiralty 'between Easter and Whitsun'.[7] He rejoined the Cabinet in that capacity on 4 June and his first task was to wind up the special naval dispositions in the Mediterranean which could have been used to great effect to back his diplomacy of September 1935. His next office was as successor to Simon as Home Secretary in May 1937. In that capacity he devoted his energies to preparing a Criminal Justice Bill which was not passed because of the outbreak of war. Chamberlain made him a member of his War Cabinet, but Churchill made him Ambassador to Spain.

Vansittart, whose predominantly anti-German views (though even he had his appeasing moments) made him an ardent adjutant to Hoare on the occasion of the conclusion of the Hoare-Laval Pact (which, it has been said, might well have been called a Vansittart-Laval Pact). was 'kicked upstairs' by Chamberlain and Eden jointly. In January 1938 there was created for him the new and powerless post of Chief Diplomatic Adviser. The new Permanent Under-Secretary at the Foreign Office was Sir Alexander Cadogan, but the official Chamberlain really relied on for specialist aid in the field of foreign affairs was Sir Horace Wilson, hitherto Chief Industrial Adviser. Vansittart had this in common with Chamberlain, that he too died thinking that his life's work had been a failure.[8]

Eden, disagreeing with Chamberlain about policy towards Italy, resigned the Foreign Secretaryship in February 1938. Churchill restored him to that office in 1940. He held it for the third time from 1951 to 1955. From 1940 onwards Eden was Churchill's 'Crown Prince' and succeeded him as Prime Minister on 6 April 1955. On that occasion Attlee re-told in the House of Commons the story of Melbourne's secretary saying to him at a similar moment: 'Damn it all, such a position was never held by any Greek or Roman; and if it only lasts three months it will be worth while to have been Prime Minister of England.'[9] Ill-prepared for the conduct of home affairs, Eden was in one way fortunate in that the main preoccupation of his short-lived Premiership was a foreign affairs question, the Suez crisis. 'The judgment of history' is eternally and infinitely amendable, but at present it seems unfavourable to Eden's conduct of that crisis, seeing his equation of Nasser with Hitler or Mussolini, of African nationalism with European Fascism, as cases of mistaken identity. At the climax of the crisis Eden was struck down by illness and, on medical advice, had to resign on 9 January 1957. It was a cruel fate for a statesman, aged only 60, to have his career so suddenly and prematurely ended by a physical break-down.

In the dark but stirring days of the Battle of Britain the British

nation found itself in need of a scapegoat as well as a hero. The
hero was to hand in the person of Churchill; Baldwin was cast in
the role of scapegoat-in-chief, with Sir Horace Wilson as, so to
speak, a sub-scapegoat. If Chamberlain, who in his years as Prime
Minister had had more, and more bitter, enemies than Baldwin in
his, had lived longer he might well have found himself the light-
ning conductor for the storm of execration which befell his predecessor. The power and glory which had surrounded Baldwin as
late as 1937 were replaced by venomous revilings. There was
rough logic in this. It was thought, not without reason, that the
war itself might have been prevented by a different policy, that
the initial defeats might have been prevented by better preparation. Either way the accusing finger pointed at the man in charge
before the war. True justice, however, has still to be done to
Baldwin's complex personality and mixed record.

Like Chamberlain, he bore his misfortunes, personal and political, stoically and with his self-confidence basically unimpaired. In
October 1947 he was present at the unveiling of the memorial
statue to George V, opposite the Houses of Parliament. A cheer
was raised for him. Old and deaf, he asked: 'Are they booing
me?'[10] He died a few weeks later.

20

Inquest

For what went wrong, who was to blame? Certainly not the Negus. No doubt he made his mistakes before the crisis, but throughout it (ably advised) he threw himself on the mercy of the League. This was the best possible policy. That the villain of the whole piece was Mussolini needs no argument. And what a villain :[1] Mussolini went to war, not so much because he wanted the fruits of victory, but because he wanted war. There can be no worse crime. Other Fascist leaders aided and abetted his militarist and imperialist ambitions, nor was the Abyssinian war all that unpopular with the Italian people.[2] Italian Fascism, however, was very much of a one-man show and in any case any Dictator bears more responsibility for national policy than any democratic Prime Minister.[3] It is of course possible that, if Mussolini had never been born and Italian Fascism had never been, a second Crispi might have organized a war to revenge Adowa and, perhaps also, to conquer Abyssinia: possible but not very probable. Wicked as Mussolini was, however, one cannot but admire his display, in this instance, of qualities which the contemporary leaders of democracies were without, above all resolute pursuit of pre-determined aims. One must also spare him a word of praise for the quality of his utterances, public and private, throughout the crisis. They were full of 'punch'; the ex-journalist well remembered the tricks of his original trade.

The tragedy of the defeat of Abyssinia and the defeat of the League is, in obverse, the tragedy of the failure to defeat Italy and thereby win a decisive victory for the League. The real problem is that of the responsibility for that failure. It has often been pinned on one man, Pierre Laval. The notion is over-simple on the face of it. It is rare in such an episode for there to have been a single villain of the piece. Moreover, the case for Laval being that villain is usually presented over-simply: Laval looked like a villain; was eventually judged to be and executed as a villain; the villain of the 1940–5 French piece was therefore the villain of the 1935 Abyssinian one.

It is not for a historian of that crisis to pronounce on Laval's record as a whole.[4] In respect, however, of his foreign policy between October 1934 and January 1936, one can point out that it was in line with that of his predecessor (Barthou) and was followed by his successor (Flandin); that it was little criticized by the French people or their politicians at the time; that it was indeed upheld by sizeable Parliamentary votes as late as December 1935.[5] The methods by which Laval pursued his policy are indeed open to criticism; its principles can be defended as in accordance with French national interests according to a particular and plausible point of view. Hitler's Germany, it was held, was the potential enemy; Mussolini's Italy must therefore be made an ally. After January 1935, from Laval's point of view, Italy was the bird in the hand, Britain and the League were birds in the bush; they had been, ever since 1919. Therefore, the first object of policy was to keep in hand the single bird of double value; what the other two were up to in the bush was of secondary importance. Amery on 8 October 1935 spoke of 'the stubborn common sense of Monsieur Laval', which might 'save us, in spite of ourselves, from a European war'.[6] Baldwin in 1940 said that he was 'morally sure that Laval had been bought by Mussolini'.[7] If so, Mussolini wasted his money; Laval would have followed the line he did in the Abyssinian crisis without being bribed.

Certainly it can be argued that the French view of French national interests, in relation to the Abyssinian crisis, was misconceived. Granted the German danger, a British alliance would be of much more value to France than an Italian one.[8] But could it be obtained? It seemed strange to the French that the British should, in respect of the Italian menace to Abyssinia, suddenly take so seriously their obligations to the Covenant while still not taking seriously their obligations to the Covenant in relation to the German menace to Austria, to France herself, and to her Allies (Poland and the three countries of the Little Entente).[9] It seemed plain in Paris, and indeed it was the case, that Britain still hoped for a settlement with Germany, was shaky as to her readiness to discharge her obligations under the Covenant; was not prepared, in relation to Western Europe, to add to her commitments under the Covenant and the Locarno Treaties, except perhaps for a Western Air Pact; was certainly not more prepared in 1935 than in 1925 to undertake specific commitments for the defence of the integrity and independence of countries in Central and Eastern Europe. This policy was only reversed in April 1939. From November 1918 to September 1939 there was no alliance (though some books slip into the use of that term) between Britain and France.[10] It is impossible to condemn France outright for judging, in 1935, her agreements with Italy of more value to her security than the entente to which lip-service was still paid. Be it too remembered that, to France, Britain in June 1935 seemed to put her security first without a thought for that of France; and the ink was still wet on the Anglo-German Naval Agreement when Eden was sent to Rome to negotiate, behind France's back, an Anglo-Italian-Abyssinian deal which would have been to some extent at France's expense.

It was the favourite and most frequent plea of the British Government for its limited actions in defence of the Covenant and Abyssinia in 1935 that it was expected to take the lead and that Britain was the only country to take effective action. This was unfair. Of course she was expected to take the lead; she was in fact the leading League and European Power; to take the lead should have been regarded as an honour and a privilege as well as a responsibility and a burden; and, in so far as she gave a lead, she was followed. The League members were not backward in imposing and enforcing sanctions, some of them at a high economic price to themselves. (Economically sanctions pressed heavily not only on Britain, but also on the Latin-American States, Yugoslavia, Norway and Roumania; they also involved political sacrifice on the part of Bulgaria, hitherto an Italian protégé.) League members who seemed likely to become directly involved in hostilities (Greece, Yugoslavia, Turkey) were not backward in accepting, at some danger to themselves, the military proposals put to them. All that anybody was asked to do was, for the most part, done. What else did Britain expect anyone else to do? Was it for Czecho-Slovakia to send her Navy to the Mediterranean to block the entrance to the Suez Canal? It is shameful that having taken the lead on 11 September 1935 Britain avoided taking it again until 18 June 1936. Only then did Eden speak publicly of 'a responsibility not only for compliance but for guidance'.[11]

One suspects that this inaccurate and mean-spirited, frequent and public, criticism of 'others' for not playing their proper part in the common effort was a round-about way of saying, perhaps too politely, that France was not playing, and would not, play her part. The famous phrase in Hoare's resignation speech, about 'not a ship, not a machine . . . moved by any other state', referred (on the evidence of his autobiography) to France.[12] True, Britain did not receive from France as much technical co-operation in planning preparations against possible Italian attacks as she had hoped and asked for, but the basic requirements were met. Neville Chamberlain did not have publicly to say '. . . we had from the Powers that we asked, and from France in particular, the most complete and loyal assurances that they would come to our aid if attacked by Italy.'[13] It is also true, moreover, that when she gave France a real lead it was followed.[14] If she had applied pressure to make France choose between British and Italian Friendship there could have been little doubt of the French choice, provided Britain undertook to follow the same line about aggression in Europe as about the Horn of Africa.

The Dominions, though in varying degrees, were in favour of a League policy; neither those 'varying degrees' nor the fact that the U.S.A. was not a Member was a real obstacle to the pursuit of one. American public opinion was passionately pacificist and this emotion was increasingly expressing itself, albeit in the low form of wanting simply to keep out of war; hence, isolationism and neutrality legislation. On the other hand there might well have been a positive response to more positive League action. Part of the evidence for that is the negative reaction to the Hoare-Laval Pact. It seems certain that neither the American Government nor the American people would have wished to hinder stronger measures against the aggressor, not inconceivable that they might have indirectly joined in them, at any rate up to the time of the Hoare-Laval *débâcle*. Sir Samuel Hoare, in his resignation speech, did not say that the oil sanction would be ineffective because of American neutrality. The argument was rather that it would be so effective that Mussolini would treat it as an act of war. It is true that the renewal of the American Neutrality Act (of 31 August 1935) on 29 February 1936 put paid to the oil

235

sanction account in the sense of making it plain that the U.S.A. was not going to give the lead to the League in this matter.[15] By that time, however, it was already plain that the two Great League Powers had lost all heart for an oil sanction.

The buck stops not with Laval or France or the British Dominions or the U.S.A., but with Britain.

Are excuses to be made for British policy on the ground that it is in the nature of a crisis to cause mistakes of policy to be made by men working against time? The Abyssinian crisis is an exception to that rule.

As, month after month, the Italian transports passed through the Suez Canal, plenty of time, much more than is usually given to any Government in a situation of crisis, was given to the British Government to decide how best to resolve a dilemma which had, by the Spring of 1935, been starkly revealed. It is true, however, that enough time to decide policy is usually less than is needed to change opinion.

Did British policy fail because based on a false assumption that time, as well as limited sanctions, were on Abyssinia's side? It was not foreseen by the best expert opinion that Italy could win the war before the 1936 rains; it was thought that by the time of a second season's campaigning the sanctions applied in 1935 would be 'biting'.[16] It was at no time, however, argued in Cabinet that all Britain had to do was to wait for Abyssinian resistance and limited sanctions jointly to bring the Italian adventure to an end. The oil sanction was discussed seriously in Cabinet as a sanction much more potent than those at first imposed.

Neither was it argued that the certainty of some British losses in an Anglo-Italian war made the avoidance of such a war an absolute necessity. In other words, it was not argued that the risks involved in winning a war against Italy must on no account be run for fear of losing a subsequent war against Germany or Japan or the two together. If Mussolini had perpetrated a 'mad dog act' plainly we should have struck back. The question, however, is rather whether fear of Germany and Japan was a decisive argument against any British initiative which might have precipitated an Anglo-Italian war. This fear derived from reasoned calculations and this reasoning provided the most respectable case for avoiding any such initiative. It does not, however, appear to have been the decisive argument against a decisive British initiative. The case for inertia sprang from other considerations.

The Cabinet had really only two choices. On the one hand, it could decide, like France, that national interests were not importantly involved in the Italo-Abyssinian dispute; that Germany was the principal potential enemy; that therefore friendship with Italy must be retained even at the price of sacrificing Abyssinia to Italy and conclusively destroying the 'credibility' of the League as an instrument for checking aggression. This decision would have implied that that 'credibility' was not a British national interest.[17]

If this choice had been made Britain could have tried to effect a settlement on Hoare-Laval lines to the disadvantage as opposed to the destruction of Abyssinia, though once it was clear that force would not be employed to impose such a settlement Mussolini could not have been stopped from an attempt to conquer the whole of Abyssinia should he so have decided. But if this was the policy to be followed, Hoare should never have been allowed to speak as he did on 11 September. Tom Jones 'cottoned on' to this, not early, but earlier than most: 'If Sam Hoare was right in settling with Laval, he was wrong in orating loftily at Geneva.'[18]

Alternatively, the Government could have decided that this crisis was no mere 'African quarrel' and that what was at stake was not merely the future of Abyssinia but the future of the League of Nations. If the League was thought of as a genuinely worth-while institution for the preservation of international law and order, no better opportunity for a spectacular demonstration of its practical effectiveness was ever likely to offer itself. Mussolini's forces in East Africa were hostages to fortune. Their supply lines were very long and could be cut with peculiar ease. On the very day when the Hoare-Laval talks started in Paris, Chamberlain, no less, wrote in his diary: 'By putting his great army the other side of the Suez Canal, Mussolini has tied a noose round his own neck, and left the end hanging out for any one with a Navy to pull'.[19] From this he drew the moral that Mussolini would not dare to attack Britain, not that the British Navy should pull the noose tight. If, however, Mussolini's threats of war against Britain were all bluff, why not pull the noose? The risk was that Mussolini was not bluffing; the probability was that he was. If the noose was pulled and he went to war it was certain that he would have lost it. Then the League, with one signal triumph to its credit, might well have been effectively used later, if necessary, against Hitler.[20]

This second policy (on the whole favoured by wisdom after the event), was never contemplated. Chamberlain let this cat out of the bag during the Election campaign, saying at Stoke, perfectly correctly: 'We have never discussed military sanctions'.[21] The important question is 'Why not?'

The answer is to be found somewhere near the heart of Conservative thinking at that time. The simplest hypothesis is the best: deep down the League was not thought of as an institution which, fully used, could in practice enforce international law and order. National safety was thought of as dependent on national armaments, a select handful of alliances, the preservation of the Balance of Power. Baldwin, in his speech to his Party Conference on 4 October 1935, said: 'The whole perspective on the Continent has been altered in the past year or two by the re-arming of Germany. I cannot be blind to the fact that the presence of another great nation armed alters the perspective in Europe in the fulfilment of obligations under the League of Nations'. But he concluded only that 'some day the fulfilment of those obligations may mean that the nations who are fulfilling them may have to maintain by force of arms the Covenant of the League of Nations.' 'Some day' and against Germany, not 'now' and against Italy. It was not until late in 1936 that one Conservative, with pre-eminent intellectual powers, organized a campaign to proclaim the practical virtues of the Covenant. Churchill, however, had been largely indifferent to the Abyssinian crisis and his 'Arms and the Covenant' movement was put in the shade by the wretched triviality of the abdication crisis.[22]

The Conservative doctrine of 1935 had been substantially proclaimed by Bonar Law in 1922. At the time of the Chanak crisis he wrote a letter to the Press, published in *The Times* and *Daily Express* of 7 October, in which he said:

'We cannot alone act as the policemen of the world. The financial and social condition of this country makes that impossible. It seems to me, therefore, that our duty is to say plainly to our French Allies that the position in Constantinople and the

Straits is as essential a part of the Peace settlement as the arrangement with Germany, and that if they are not prepared to support us there, we should not be able to bear the burden alone, but shall have no alternative except to imitate the Government of the United States, and to restrict our attention to the safeguarding of the more immediate interests of the Empire.'[23]

The publication of such a letter from someone of Bonar Law's authority (he had been leader of the Conservative Party from 1911 to 1921 and had held Cabinet office from 1915 to 1921) is a sufficiently rare event to make it important. This letter, however, had even more importance than that deriving from its source. Lord Blake, one of the great historians of Conservatism, sees it as 'the death-knell of the Coalition', which indeed fell within a fortnight of its publication. It is of great importance to the understanding of later history to realize that the cause for which 'the only person who could stand forward as an alternative Prime Minister' challenged the Government of that day was the cause of limited intervention in foreign affairs, even when, perhaps especially when, confronted by a crisis of world importance, with its central issue that of Treaty observance.

And what of the man who as much as, if not more than any other, broke the Coalition, Bonar Law's protégé and successor, Stanley Baldwin? What was his attitude to the idea of Britain, through the League, attempting to police the world? As we have seen, when Prime Minister at the height of his powers between 1925 and 1929 he saw the League, as did his Foreign Secretary, as a forum, an instrument of conciliation, not coercion. He never really budged from that position and propounded the case for it explicitly and precisely. On 22 June 1931, at the Albert Hall, he said:

'Article 16 of the Covenant was drawn up in the full belief that America would be a member. It was ... our fear of what blockade would mean with America not a member of the League of Nations that cast doubt and threw difficulty in relation to one of the most important articles in the Covenant of the League.'

On 27 February 1932, visiting a sick friend (Tom Jones) he said, à propos of the Far Eastern crisis:

> 'I think I see the position quite clearly. With Russia and America out of the League sanctions are a mistake. I've always thought so. The very people like Bob Cecil who have made us disarm, and quite right too, are now urging us forward to take action. But where will action lead us to? ... If you enforce an economic boycott you'll have war declared by Japan and she will seize Singapore and Hongkong and we can't, as we are placed, stop her. You'll get nothing out of Washington but words, big words, but only words. That's what I told Van this morning. We can't be going along one road, outside the League, with America, and also at the same time profess loyalty to the League and its procedure.'[24]

On 23 November 1934, when the Peace Ballot was getting under way, Baldwin said, at Glasgow:

> 'It is curious that there is growing among the Labour Party support for what is called a collective peace system. A collective peace system, in my view, is perfectly impracticable in view of the fact today that the United States is not yet, to our unbounded regret, a member of the League of Nations and that in the last two or three years two Great Powers, Germany and Japan, have both retired from it. It is hardly worth considering when those be the facts. A collective peace system would never be undertaken without those countries. Of that I am certain, and, so long as I have any responsibility in a Government for deciding whether or not this country shall join in a collective peace system, I will say this: never as an individual will I sanction the British Navy being used for an armed blockade of any country until I know what the United States of America is going to do.'

On the other hand, when on 23 July 1935 he received (accompanied by Hoare, who had arranged the meeting, and Eden) a deputation from the National Declaration Committee led by Lord Cecil, he assured the deputation that the League of Nations remained the sheet-anchor of British policy.[25] (In the Government's election manifesto 'keystone' was the word used.) This was not to recant his opinion about the League's coercive potentialities, but scarcely to obtrude it.

On 19 October, at Worcester, he said that no isolated action against Italy would be taken by Britain. On 19 December he developed this point in the House of Commons in the debate following Hoare's resignation speech:

> 'I am as anxious as anyone on any bench in this House not only to preserve the League of Nations but to make it effective, not only now but in the future, and if by any chance – and I will only put it like that – this country had to take part in a unilateral war, even for a short time before others could come in, what I dread is the reaction in this country. I am not thinking of any campaign that might be organized against the Government for bringing the country to war, I am thinking of this: that men will say: "Well, if by adherence to the League of Nations we find ourselves standing alone to do what ought to be done by everybody, this is the last time we will allow a Government to commit itself with regard to collective security because, for all we know, the next time we have to employ this, the field may be nearer home than the Mediterranean." '[26]

On 20 June 1936, when the decision to discontinue sanctions had just been announced, he said (at Wishaw) that the Government was 'making every attempt ... to keep our people, certainly unless the whole of the League nations will come in with us, away from the perils and horrors of modern war in Europe.' It was on 2 July that he compared his attitude to Walpole's and spoke proudly of having kept his own people out of war.[27]

Baldwin was a pacificist. He was in favour of the League so long as it was stopping wars by settling disputes. He was against it if it showed signs of starting war. He was dead against trying, as he saw it, to do its work for it by starting a unilateral war. There was neither insincerity nor inconsistency in his utterances, public and private, on these subjects. But he did not go out of his way to challenge opinions more militant than his own. He waited for events to confirm their correctness. (Meanwhile, he not merely swam with, but took advantage of the tide of opinion revealed by the Peace Ballot and by Hoare's Assembly speech to pilot his

Party into the safe harbour of a renewed majority.) This inconsistency in Baldwin's case was between his thoughts and his
actions. Was there not, too, a certain insincerity in supporting
sanctions at all and secretiveness in not making plain the limita-
tions of the sanctions he did support? Churchill was to write that
it 'was not until several months after the election' that he 'began to
understand the principles upon which Sanctions were built.'[28]
And what it took him a long time to understand was never understood by the people. Is it too much to suggest that Laval's policy
(as explained, for example, to Hoare) was more honest than
Baldwin's?

In an experienced and sophisticated democracy such as that of
Britain a Prime Minister has to carry the nation with him in
major acts of policy, above all in making war. (It is to Chamberlain's credit that he carried the bulk of the nation with him in
1939, to Eden's discredit that he deeply divided it in 1956.) It
must be emphasized that either of the two Abyssinian policies
open to the Government in 1935 required, for its effective discharge, a major re-education of public opinion. If the policy was
to be the thorough application of collective security the people
had to be made to understand that that might entail the use of
force. The argument that stopping a war by force was simply to
extend it had to be refuted; the choice between enforcing law and
surrender to criminal violence had to be made clear.[29] It had also
to be explained that it was unlikely that one nation, especially one
in the grasp of Fascism, would desist from aggression just because
50 other nations asked it to; unlikely that it could be made to stop
by merely moral or even by economic pressure; probable therefore that military sanctions would be needed; certain, in the
nature of the case and of the particular circumstances, that they
would have to be mainly of British providing. In this case only
Britain could act as 'world's policeman'; only the British Navy
could be the League's 'secular arm'. And all this re-education
would, a special conviction of Baldwin's, need much time.[30]

From this task Baldwin shrank. He judged (rightly?) that the
minds of his fellow-countrymen, confronted by an immense international crisis, were full of illusions.[31] He further judged
(wrongly?) that the education so badly needed had best be left to
the events which would follow the imposition of sanctions rather
than any words of his or his colleagues.[32] He lastly judged it to be

his duty to save his fellow-countrymen from too harsh an education by events. He was therefore determined to prevent the crisis involving his country in war, except in its own self-defence. It followed that there could be no question of military sanctions and that economic sanctions should only be of such a character as not to provoke Mussolini into war.

The other policy, to go all out for a Realpolitik solution, would have needed, for presentation to the public, more courage and more time because, using Keynes' excellent word, more 'debamboozling' of more people would have been needed. All the same, there again, there were foundations on which a sympathetic body of opinion could have been built. The facts were that Abyssinia was an anarchic and backward country; that for that very reason Britain had opposed her entry into the League; that the League had its own special method for modernizing backward countries, the system of mandates. Perhaps even the great Government apostle of support for the League, Eden, could have reminded his fellow-countrymen of how, not long previously, he had come near to recommending the expulsion from the League of the only other African country to be a member of it, Liberia, and why.[33] It is just possible that on some such basis a head-on collision with the League of Nations Union, and the great body of opinion supporting its ideas, could have been avoided and a realistic policy of conciliation pursued. But if the policy was thought right the possibility of such a collision would have had to be squarely faced.[34]

It is important here to repeat the point that if the Government fell between two stools so also did the Opposition.[35] If the thought of the rulers was muddled, so also was that of the ruled. Of all those citizens who thought about the Abyssinian crisis at all, those who thought clearly and consistently about it throughout its duration, whether rightly or wrongly, were a tiny handful. For all practical purposes we were all guilty men.

None the less leaders are for leading, responsible Governments are for taking responsible decisions and accepting responsibility for them. If there was a tide with which too many people were lazily drifting, it was not for the Government to drift with it. If self-deceit was widespread, it was more the duty of the Prime Minister than anyone else to undeceive. That duty was neglected by Baldwin. He neglected it because he thought that the people could, from words, learn only one new thing at a time, and only slowly. Therefore he spoke to them with a considerable measure of frankness about the need for rearmament – which he thought the first priority – and without corresponding frankness about the inadequacy, as he saw it, of the League.[36] A third type of frankness, 'appalling frankness', he reserved for November 1936, one year after the Election. He then disclosed that he had not gone to the country in 1933 or 1934, asking for a mandate for rearmament, because that would at that time have lost him the Election. No doubt it was his sincere view that for him to lose an Election on such an issue was against the national interest. He was very far from believing that his political opponents, even in responsible office, even goaded by an active Opposition, might do as well, or better, for rearmament than he could. And he had reason for that: not until the Autumn of 1936 did the Labour Party show the smallest sign of talking rearmament seriously. Baldwin's problem of national leadership in 1935 must not be under-rated.[37]

In genuine democracies leaders always have such a problem when their thoughts are in advance of public opinion. Roosevelt and Baldwin had a similar problem of leadership simultaneously. It was the latter's mistake to try and solve it by finessing the people and in the fulness of time they found that unforgiveable. Churchill was right when he said that to the British people, tough and robust, one should always tell the truth.

Appendix

Principal Dates

	1855	Coronation of Emperor Theodore II
	1862	French occupy Obock on Red Sea
	1864	British Consul and other Europeans imprisoned at Magdala
	1868	Sir Robert Napier's rescuing expedition; Emperor Theodore commits suicide
	1869	Opening of Suez Canal Italian Shipping Company (Rubattino) buys port of Assab from local ruler
	1872	Coronation of John IV
	1876	Egyptian invasion from Massawa defeated
	1882	Italian Government buys Assab from Rubattino Company British intervention in Egypt
	1884	British occupy Berbera and Zeila
	1885	Italians occupy Massawa
	1886	Britain and Germany carve up the 'Empire' of Zanzibar
	1887	Italian defeat at Dogali
March	1889	Emperor John killed in battle against Mahdist Dervishes
2 May	1889	Treaty of Uccialli (Menelik-Antonelli)
June & August	1889	Italians occupy Keren and Asmara
November	1889	Coronation of Menelik II
1 January	1890	Italian possessions on Red Sea united as Colony of Eritrea
	1891	Anglo-Italian Agreement recognizes Abyssinia as Italian 'sphere of influence'
February	1893	Treaty of Uccialli denounced by Emperor Menelik
December	1893	Crispi becomes Italian Prime Minister for the second time
April	1894	Uganda becomes British Protectorate
November	1895	First Italo-Abyssinian War begins
1 March	1896	Italian defeat at Adowa
5 March	1896	Resignation of Crispi

Appendix

October	1896	Treaty of Addis Ababa (Treaty of Uccialli annulled and Italy recognizes Abyssinian independence)
	1898	British victory at Omdurman; 'Fashoda incident'
	1899	Creation of Anglo-Egyptian Sudan
	1904-5	Russo-Japanese war
	1906	Anglo-French-Italian Agreement on Abyssinia
	1907	Jibuti Railway begun
	1913	Death of Emperor Menelik (succeeded by grand-son Lij Yasu)
	1914	Start of World War I
26 April	1915	Treaty of London, between Britain, France and Italy
	1916	Lij Yasu deposed and succeeded by Empress Zauditu, Menelik's daughter; his great-nephew, Ras Tafari, becomes Regent
	1918	Allied victory in World War I
	1919	Peace Treaties signed
	1920	League Covenant comes into force
	1921	End of Anglo-Japanese alliance
October	1922	The Fascist 'March on Rome'
August	1923	The Corfu incident
September	1923	Abyssinia joins the League
	1924	Britain cedes Jubaland to Italy
	1925	Britain rejects Geneva Protocol
		Locarno Treaties signed
		Poison Gas Convention signed
		Anglo-Italian Exchange of Notes on Abyssinia
	1926	Germany joins the League
		Anti-Slavery Convention signed
	1927	Lord Cecil resigns from British Cabinet
2 August	1928	Italo-Ethiopian Treaty of Friendship and Arbitration
27 August	1928	Kellogg Pact signed
	1929	Start of the Great Depression
April	1930	Death of the Empress Zauditu
21 August	1930	Four Power Treaty on Arms for Abyssinia
11 Nov.	1930	Coronation of Ras Tafari as Emperor Haile Selassie I
24 August	1931	'National Government' formed in Britain
11 Sept.	1931	'Mukden incident' (start of Manchurian crisis)
2 February	1932	World Disarmament Conference opens; warfare breaks out in Shanghai between Japanese and Chinese
23 March	1932	British Cabinet drops 'No war for ten years' rule for Defence planning
September	1932	King of Italy visits Eritrea (accompanied by De Bono)
30 January	1933	Hitler becomes German Chancellor
4 March	1933	F. D. Roosevelt inaugurated as President of the U.S.A.
27 March	1933	Japan announces withdrawal from the League
3 May	1933	Tangku Truce

12 June	1933	World Monetary and Economic Conference meets (ends on 27 July)
4 October	1933	Anti-War resolution passed at Annual Conference of Labour Party
14 October	1933	Germany leaves League and Disarmament Conference
25 October	1933	East Fulham Bye-Election
16 Nov.	1933	U.S.A. recognises U.S.S.R.
26 January	1934	German-Polish Non-Aggression Pact
6 February	1934	'Fascist' rioting in Paris
17 Feb.	1934	Three-Power Declaration (Britain – France – Italy) on Austrian independence
29 May	1934	End of the Disarmament Conference
14–15 June	1934	First meeting of Hitler and Mussolini
30 June	1934	'Night of the long knives' in Germany
25 July	1934	Assassination of Dollfuss, Austrian Chancellor
17 Sept.	1934	U.S.S.R. joins the League
9 October	1934	Assassination of Barthou, French Foreign Minister
13 October	1934	Laval becomes French Foreign Minister
4 Nov.	1934	Abyssinian attack on Italian Consulate at Gondar
1 Dec.	1934	King of Italy returns to Rome from visit to Italian Somaliland
5 Dec.	1934	The Wal-Wal incident
8 Dec.	1934	Italy demands apology and compensation
9 Dec.	1934	Abyssinian counter-protest and invocation of Article 5 of 1928 Treaty
11 Dec.	1934	Italian Note formulates demands in detail
14 Dec.	1934	Abyssinia reports Wal-Wal incident to the League
3 January	1935	Abyssinia invokes Article 11 of the Covenant
7 January	1935	The Rome Agreements
10 January	1935	De Bono becomes High Commissioner in Eritrea
13 January	1935	Saar Plebiscite
16 January	1935	De Bono arrives at Massawa
31 January	1935	Maffey Committee appointed
		Flandin and Laval arrive in London for talks with British Ministers
3 February	1935	Communiqué on Anglo-French talks in London
5 February	1935	Start of Italian mobilization
4 March	1935	British White Paper on Rearmament
9 March	1935	Göring announces the existence of a German Air Force (Luftwaffe)
12 March	1935	French Cabinet decides to increase the period of military service from one year to two
16 March	1935	Hitler announces the re-introduction of conscription in Germany
17 March	1935	Abyssinia invokes Article 15 of the Covenant
25–26 Mar.	1935	Simon and Eden in Berlin (Eden goes on to Warsaw, Moscow and Prague)
11–14 April	1935	Stresa Conference

247

I

2 May	1935	Franco-Soviet Pact signed
5 May	1935	Czech-Soviet Pact signed
13 May	1935	Franco-Italian air agreement
21 May	1935	Hitler's Reichstag speech on foreign policy
7 June	1935	Baldwin becomes British Prime Minister (for the third time)
		Laval French Prime Minister (for the second time)
		Hoare replaces Simon as British Foreign Secretary
		Eden enters Cabinet as Minister for League of Nations Affairs
18 June	1935	Anglo-German Naval Agreement
		Maffey Committee reports
19 June	1935	Franco-Italian military agreement
24–25 June	1935	Eden's conversations with Mussolini in Rome
27 June	1935	Peace Ballot's results declared
8 August	1935	The Pope (Pius X) speaks on the Abyssinian crisis
15–18 Aug.	1935	Anglo-French-Italian conference in Paris; Italy rejects Anglo-French plan
24 August	1935	Emergency meeting of British Cabinet
29 August	1935	Mediterranean Fleet leaves Malta for Alexandria
31 August	1935	U.S. Neutrality Act
3 Sept.	1935	Report of the Commission for Conciliation and Arbitration on responsibility for the Wal-Wal incident
4 Sept.	1935	Italian memorandum on Abyssinian affairs presented to the League of Nations
6 Sept.	1935	League Council appoints Committee of Five
10 Sept.	1935	Hoare's first meeting with Laval
11 Sept.	1935	Hoare's speech to League Assembly
17 Sept.	1935	Powerful units of the Home Fleet (including two battle cruisers) arrive at Gibraltar
22 Sept.	1935	Italy rejects report of Committee of Five
23 Sept.	1935	Abyssinia accepts the report
25 Sept.	1935	Negus requests despatch of impartial observers to Abyssinian frontiers
26 Sept.	1935	League appoints Committee of Thirteen
29 Sept.	1935	Negus orders general mobilization
3 October	1935	Italy invades Abyssinia (without declaration of war)
5 October	1935	President Roosevelt puts embargo on export of arms to both belligerents
7 October	1935	League Council unanimously finds Italy to have broken the Covenant (Italy dissenting); Council's findings accepted by 50 out of 54 Member States represented in the Assembly (by the 11th)
10 October	1935	League Assembly appoints Co-Ordination Committee
11 October	1935	Co-Ordination Committee appoints Committee of Eighteen (Sanctions Committee)
12 October	1935	First meeting of Sanctions Committee

19 October	**1935**	Sanctions Committee adjourns (after proposing five sanctions)
30 October	**1935**	South Africa puts into force all five sanctions (first State to do so)
6 Nov.	**1935**	Sanctions Committee adopts Proposal for 'Oil Sanction'
14 Nov.	**1935**	British General Election
17 Nov.	**1935**	De Bono replaced by Badoglio as Commander-in-Chief of Italian Forces in East Africa
18 Nov.	**1935**	Sanctions (Proposals 2–4) come into force
29 Nov.	**1935**	Meeting of Sanctions Committee postponed, at Laval's request, until 12 December
7–8 Dec.	**1935**	Hoare visits Paris and agrees peace plan with Laval
9 Dec.	**1935**	British Cabinet accepts plan; its details appear in French press
10 Dec.	**1935**	Plan briefly discussed in House of Commons
13 Dec.	**1935**	Decision on Oil Sanction postponed
18 Dec.	**1935**	Hoare resigns: Mussolini rejects plan
19 Dec.	**1935**	Plan debated in House of Commons; Baldwin announces its death
22 Dec.	**1935**	Eden becomes Foreign Secretary
22 January	**1936**	Sanctions Committee appoints Experts Committee on Oil Sanction
		Resignation of Laval; succeeded as Premier by Sarraut and as Foreign Minister by Flandin
12 Feb.	**1936**	Report of Experts Committee on Oil Sanction
16 Feb.	**1936**	Popular Front victory in Spanish Elections
27 Feb.	**1936**	French Chamber ratifies Franco-Soviet Pact
29 Feb.	**1936**	U.S. Neutrality Act renewed
3 March	**1936**	Imposition of Oil Sanction again postponed
7 March	**1936**	German troops enter de-militarized zone of Rhineland
31 March	**1936**	Battle of Lake Ashangi (Negus decisively defeated)
4 April	**1936**	Ecuador abandons sanctions
20 April	**1936**	League Council makes 'supreme appeal' to Italy
2 May	**1936**	Negus leaves Addis Ababa
3 May	**1936**	Popular Front victory in French Elections
5 May	**1936**	Italian troops enter Addis Ababa
9 May	**1936**	Italy proclaims annexation of Abyssinia; King of Italy declared its Emperor
11 May	**1936**	League Council decides to continue sanctions for one month
3 June	**1936**	Haile Selassie arrives in London
4 June	**1936**	Hoare rejoins the British Cabinet; Leon Blum becomes French Premier; Yvon Delbos, Foreign Minister
7 June	**1936**	Ciano becomes Italian Foreign Minister
10 June	**1936**	Neville Chamberlain's 'midsummer madness' speech

17 June	1936	British Cabinet decides to recommend end of sanctions
20 June	1936	Roosevelt ends embargo on export of arms to Abyssinia and Italy
30 June	1936	Haile Selassie addresses League Assembly
4 July	1936	League Assembly votes for (44 to 1) the ending of sanctions, votes against (23 to 1) financial assistance to Abyssinia
11 July	1936	Austro-German Agreement
15 July	1936	Final end of all sanctions
18 July	1936	Start of Spanish Civil War Mediterranean Fleet leaves Alexandria
25 October	1936	Germany recognizes Italian annexation of Abyssinia
1 Nov.	1936	Mussolini proclaims Rome-Berlin Axis (at Milan)
26 Nov.	1936	Germany and Japan sign Anti-Comintern Pact
28 May	1937	Chamberlain becomes Prime Minister
7 July	1937	Lukouchiao incident (renewal of Sino-Japanese war)
6 Nov.	1937	Italy joins Anti-Comintern Pact
11 Dec.	1937	Italy announces withdrawal from the League
20 Feb.	1938	Eden resigns
11 March	1938	Germany invades Austria
30 Sept.	1938	Munich Agreements
8–14 Nov.	1938	Nazi Pogroms
17 Dec.	1938	Italy denounces Rome Agreements of 1935
15 March	1939	Germany seizes Bohemia and Moravia
28 March	1939	Madrid surrenders to Franco
31 March	1939	Anglo-French guarantee to Poland
13 April	1939	Anglo-French guarantee to Greece and Roumania
26 April	1939	Chamberlain announces introduction of conscription in Britain
28 April	1939	Germany denounces Anglo-German naval agreement Hitler denounces 1934 Treaty with Poland
3 May	1939	Litvinov replaced by Molotov
22 May	1939	German-Italian 'Pact of Steel'
23 August	1939	Soviet-Nazi Pact (Molotov-Ribbentrop)
1 Sept.	1939	Germany invades Poland
3 Sept.	1939	Britain and France declare war on Germany
17 Sept.	1939	U.S.S.R. invades Poland
14 Dec.	1939	U.S.S.R. expelled from League
6 June	1940	Italy declares war on Britain and France
5 May	1941	Negus re-enters Addis Ababa
25 July	1943	Mussolini dismissed
11 January	1944	De Bono executed
28 April	1945	Mussolini murdered
30 April	1945	Hitler commits suicide
26 June	1945	United Nations Charter signed
18 April	1946	Formal end of the League (by resolution of the last Assembly)

15 Oct.	**1946**	Laval executed
16 Dec.	**1966**	Sanctions against Rhodesia (Security Council Resolution 232)
23 July	**1972**	Haile Selassie's 80th birthday

Notes on Books

(All the books mentioned below have, unless otherwise indicated, been published in London. The date and place of publication, if not London, of every book not mentioned below but referred to in the text is given at the point where it is first referred to.)

Of books specifically on the Abyssinian crisis the best is still the Royal Institute of International Affairs' *Survey of International Affairs, 1935,* Volume II, (1936). This is sub-titled 'Abyssinia and Italy' and is mainly the work of Professor Arnold Toynbee. (There is a useful chapter by H. V. Hodson on 'The economic aspects of the Italo-Abyssinian conflict'.) Toynbee's contribution is partisan, but not really the worse for that. One could, however, wish that he had had the time to write more shortly. It is a pity that this book has been allowed to go out of print.

G. W. Baer's *The Coming of the Italian-Ethiopian War* (Harvard, 1967) tells the story of events, mainly the diplomatic events, from the Wal-Wal incident to the start of the war in great and scholarly detail. To anyone already interested in the subject it is fascinating; for others it may be stiff reading. One hopes that Professor Baer will carry his story on, particularly as much archival material, especially British material, has become available since he completed his work.

The latest history of the war itself is A. Del Boca's *The Ethiopian War, 1935-41* (Chicago and London, 1969). A. J. Barker's *The Civilising Mission* (1968), sub-titled 'The Italo-Ethopian War, 1935–6', is disappointing. The prime interest of Emilio de Bono's *Anno XIIII* (1937), from the point of view of my subject, is in its insights into Mussolini's mind.

The reader who wants to fit the Abyssinian crisis into the pattern of inter-war world history is recommended to G. M. Gathorne-Hardy's *Short History of International Affairs, 1920–1939* (4th edition, 1950), a straightforward, succinct and indeed elegant summary. A. J. P. Taylor's *Origins of the Second World War* (2nd edition, 1963) is admirably controversial. A more orthodox view of this subject is set out in Winston Churchill's *The Gathering Storm* (1948). This narrative is hung on an autobiographical thread, but the author is at pains to distinguish between his contemporary and his retrospective reflections.

The reader who wants to fit the Abyssinian crisis into the pattern of comparable previous crises is recommended to J. Barros' *The Corfu Incident of 1923: Mussolini and the League of Nations* (Princeton, 1965) and, for the history of the Manchurian crisis, to Christopher Thorne's

The Limits of Foreign Policy (1972). However, this has not altogether superseded R. Bassett's important pioneering study *Democracy and Foreign Policy* (1952), sub-titled 'A case history: the Sino-Japanese dispute, 1931–3'. The case history is of British public opinion (principally Press opinion) about, not British policy towards, that dispute. Professor Bassett's exemplary standards of scholarship make him an impressive destroyer of myths.

F. P. Walters' *History of the League of Nations* (1952) hovers a little uncertainly between objective fact and subjective opinion and perhaps a more severely factual and compact account is called for. Sir Alfred Zimmern's *The League of Nations and the Rule of Law* (2nd edition, 1939) is still the best critical commentary. For full detail about sanctions, see A. E. Highley's *The Actions of the States Members of the League in Application of Sanctions against Italy* (Geneva, 1938). The story of sanctions has been carried on in Margaret P. Doxey's *Economic Sanctions and International Enforcement* (1971).

Alan Moorehead's *The Blue Nile* (1962) is an exhilarating mixture of geography, travel, and the history of some of the first contacts of Western Europe with Egypt, the Sudan, and Abyssinia. An excellent short *History of Ethiopia* is that by A. H. M. Jones and Elizabeth Monroe (1935). No praise can be too high for Christopher Seton-Watson's *Italy from Liberalism to Fascism, 1870–1925* (1967). One can understand Mr Seton-Watson's distaste for continuing his narrative through the Fascist period, but the fact unfortunately remains of there not being a book of the same quality for the years from 1925 to 1943. That he has had, for the most part, to build his work on secondary sources, is understandable in the case of one covering so long a period. From Esmonde Robertson's study of Mussolini's foreign policy, based on primary sources, much light on the subject, including fresh light on the origins of the war against Abyssinia, may confidently be expected. F. W. Deakin is engaged on a study of Anglo-Italian relations in regard to Abyssinia between the two World Wars.

The best introduction to the French background is Sir Denis Brogan's *Development of Modern France, 1870–1937* (2nd edition, 1967). (The wine of French history, *mise en bouteille au Chateau Brogan,* never needs a bush.) Geoffrey Warner's *Pierre Laval* (1968) has all the hallmarks of excellence. F. D. Laurens' *France and the Italo-Ethiopian Crisis, 1935–6* (The Hague and Paris, 1967) is stronger on information, especially about the attitude of the French press, than on conclusions. The corresponding book on the American role, *The United States and the Italo-Ethiopian Crisis* by Brice Harris, Jr. (Stanford, 1964) asks all the right questions and is short, clear, and scholarly.

The British background is best provided by C. L. Mowat's *Britain Between The Wars, 1918–1940* (1955) but this can be usefully supplemented by W. N. Medlicott's *British Foreign Policy Since Versailles, 1919–1963* (2nd edition, 1968). A specialist study by the same author (the Creighton Lecture for 1968) is invaluable. This is his *Britain and Germany, the Search for Agreement, 1930–1937* (1969). In considering Anglo-Italian relations throughout the period it is essential to remember that, on the British side, they were conducted against a background of Anglo-German relations rightly judged far more important. In this booklet a specialist sets this story out in short compass and with much chapter and verse from the Foreign Office papers.

Daniel Waley's balanced study of British public opinion on the Abyssinian crisis, with a special emphasis on the contents of M.P.s' postbags, is nearing the point of production. Dame Adelaide Livingstone's official history of *The Peace Ballot* (June 1935) is inadequate but a 'must'. There is no history of the League of Nations Union, but biographies of Lord Cecil and Professor Murray are being written by, respectively, Professor R. N. Swift in New York and Professor F. West in Canberra. Highly stimulating insights into many of the antecedents of British public opinion about foreign affairs in 1935 are to be found in A. J. P. Taylor's 1956 Ford Lectures published as *The Trouble Makers: Dissent over Foreign Policy, 1792–1939* (1957).

In the second series of *Documents on British Foreign Policy, 1919–1939,* three volumes covering the Abyssinian crisis are in the pipe-line and may be hoped for in or after 1974. Meanwhile the recent '30 years rule' allows access, at the Public Record Office, to the relevant Cabinet and Foreign Office papers. The best secondary sources for British policy in the Abyssinian crisis are the biographies of those then in charge of our affairs. Two autobiographies must be mentioned first, Lord Templewood's *Nine Troubled Years* (1954) and the first volume of Lord Avon's memoirs, *Facing the Dictators* (1962). They are important sources, but must be used with caution (as indeed all autobiographical material other than unexpurgated diaries). Next must be mentioned three autobiographies which reveal much sharper minds. L. S. Amery's *The Unforgiving Years, 1929–1940* (1955) (the third volume of *My Political Life* is an important and interesting source for a point of view far from 'trendy' at the time.) Lord Vansittart's *The Mist Procession* (1958) is so bright as, at times, to be almost wearisome, but very stimulating. This is supplemented by Ian Colvin's *Vansittart in Office* (1965). Lord Eustace Percy was in Baldwin's Cabinet, though without portfolio, from June 1935, to March 1936. He therefore claimed in *Some Memories* (1958) to be able to describe the 'Abyssinian muddle' from 'a semi-detached point of view', and this he does in a Chapter bravely entitled 'Complicity in Disaster'. His book is particularly useful for insights into Baldwin's mind. Other such insights are to be found in Tom Jones' *A Diary with Letters, 1931–50* (1954) and in *Memoirs of a Conservative: J. C. C. Davidson's Memoirs and Papers, 1910–37,* edited by Robert Rhodes James (1969). A. L. Rowse's *All Souls and Appeasement: End of an Epoch* (1948) has the characteristic Rowsean sparkle and is specially interesting on Simon. His own *Retrospect* (1952), Lord Cecil's *A Great Experiment* (1941), and Lord Halifax's *Fulness of Days* (1957) add little or nothing. That is, alas, also true of the memoirs of some lesser luminaries of British diplomacy: Sir Maurice Peterson's *Both Sides of the Curtain* (1950), Sir Walford Selby's *Diplomatic Twilight 1930–40* (1953), Valentine Lawford's *Bound for Diplomacy* (1963), and Sir Geoffrey Thompson's *Front Line Diplomat* (1959).

There is no satisfactory biography of Baldwin. The latest and largest,

Notes on Books

Baldwin by Keith Middlemas and John Barnes (1969), is alarmingly full of errors, but does serve up a mass of material. On the other hand Sir Keith Feiling's *Life of Neville Chamberlain* (1946) is a model mixture of fact, style and thought. Little is added by Iain Macleod's *Chamberlain* (1961), but much fresh material will be used in a new life by Professor David Dilks and Alan Beattie. There is ample room for a new life of Austen Chamberlain; in particular, his post-1931 role as 'Elder Statesman' needs justice done to it. Professor Douglas Johnson is filling this gap. David Carlton is writing a life of Lord Avon.

The official life of Ramsay MacDonald by David Marquand is still looked forward to. Perhaps the best thing so far published on MacDonald is his son Malcolm's essay on his father in *Titans and Others* (1972). Attlee, a good Prime Minister but a poor leader of the Opposition, was not at his best when new to the job in the difficult days of 1935. An official biography is being written by Kenneth Harris and meanwhile Roy Jenkins' brilliant *Mr Attlee: An Interim Biography* (1948) is out of print. Neither Raymond Postgate on his father-in-law, *The Life of George Lansbury* (1951), nor Colin Cooke's *The Life of Stafford Cripps* (1958) convey the man.

On the military considerations involved for Britain in deciding policy on the Abyssinian crisis, hitherto altogether unduly neglected, pride of place must be given to a major research article by Professor Arthur Marder, C.B.E., in *The American Historical Review* for June 1970 (Vol. LXXV, No. 5). This is principally based on the Chatfield papers, but one way and another presents a tightly-knit mass of information, not (dare one say?) too well arranged and a little lacking in conclusions. All in all, however, this important article is invaluable and likely to hold its corner of the field for a long time.

Notes and References

1 Introduction (pp. 3–7)

1. Vansittart, 514–5. For Wal-Wal, see below, 23.
2. Cf. Macleod, 189.
3. Cecil, 275.
4. Karl Radek, the Russian journalist, said in 1932 that the League in practice 'can do nothing that England and France do not want to do.' (M. Beloff, *The Foreign Policy of Soviet Russia*, vol. I (1947), 84). At the time of the Council session of 4 September 1935 'almost every delegate had instructions to follow the British lead'. (Avon, 248). Cf. Baer, 87: 'the League followed without much question wherever the two great Western democracies led.' Cf. also A. L. Rowse, *All Souls and Appeasement*, 4: 'There *was* a hope, then, and it did matter what line we took; during that last decade this country exercised a leading influence in Europe and still held a position of leadership in the English speaking world.'
5. Colvin, 48.
6. FO 401/J 54768/1/1.
7. Cf. below, 233–6.
8. British policy means that of the London Government, which was not positively influenced by Dominion attitudes. (Cf. David Carlton, *Journal of Commonwealth and Imperial History*, Vol I, No 1, October 1972, 59–77). Cf. also below, 235.
9. Cf. below, 205.
10. *Origins*, 96. Cf. Cecil, 274: 'the League has never recovered from the blow then struck at it.'

2 Abyssinian Background (pp. 8–13)

1. *Hansard*, 19.12.35., c.2115.
2. Toynbee, 242.
3. Cf. below, 27.
4. Seton-Watson, 117.
5. Ib., 178.
6. But see Ib. 139, n.2.
7. Ib., 139.
8. Ib., 125 and 179.
9. Ib., 179–80.
10. Ib., 181.
11. The Italian defeat at Dogali (above p.28) had been less decisive and the same was true of the British defeat by, the Zulus at Isandhlwana in 1879. More comparable to Adowa was the Spanish defeat by Abd-el-Krim at Anual in 1921.

3 Abyssinia on the Eve (pp. 14–25)

1. A Foreign Office paper of 1918 contemplated an Amharic Abyssinia on the central plateau and the recently conquered

257

southern areas forming a new state or states, possibly colonial, possibly independent but certainly independent of Abyssinia (Percy, 166). Mussolini in June 1935 made the same distinction between Amharic and non-Amharic areas (see above, 125).

2. Cf. above, p. 9.
3. FO/401/J4768/1/1.
4. *Study of History*, Vol II, 365.
5. CAB 24/256/CP 161, para 19. Under the chairmanship of Sir John Maffey (later Lord Rugby) an Inter-Departmental Committee was set up in March 1935, to define the nature and extent of British interests in relation to Abyssinia. It reported on 18 June 1935, in the factual manner such terms of reference required. Its *statement* of British interests, amounting to one of almost total disinterest, was not a *statement* of British policy, but – a copy having been obtained by the Italian Secret Service – this may have been misunderstood by Mussolini (Cf. Avon, 241). In addition to the Chairman (the Permanent Under-Secretary at the Colonial Office) the Committee comprised two representatives from the Foreign Office, and one each from the Dominions Office, War Office, Admiralty and Air Ministry.
6. Ib., para. 20.
7. Toynbee, 178, n.2, and Baer, 6–7.
8. Cf. above, 9.
9. In a list of *British Commitments in their relative order of importance* submitted to the Foreign Secretary by the Foreign Office in April 1926, the Covenant came first and the 1906 Treaty seventh out of thirteen. (See

Documents on British Foreign Policy, 1919-1939, Series 1A, Vol. I, p. 880). Mr. D. C. Watt, Jove nodding, is surely wrong to say that Britain denounced this Treaty in 1923. (*Origins of the Second World War*, Ed., E. M. Robertson (1971), 240.)

10. Maffey Report, 9.
11. Ib., *loc cit.*
12. Cf. below.
13. Baer, 15–16
14. Cf. below, 23.
15. In what follows in regard to the course of events between 1925 and 1928 I have had important help from a thesis on *Anglo-Italian Relations, 1924-9* by Dr Peter Edwards, now of the Historical Section of the Australian Department of Foreign Affairs.
16. To say that the British move was 'triggered' by the Mosul negotiations (Baer, 16, n.48) is too strong.
17. Cf. below, p. 22.
18. Cf. below, p. 22.
19. Cf. below, p. 85*ff*.
20. Toynbee, 128.
21. Toynbee, 127, n.1.
22. Baer, 147, n.12.
23. Cf. above, p.19.
24. Zimmern, 436.
25. Cf. below, p.66–7.
26. See below, p.60–2.
27. Robertson, 226.
28. Walters, II, 626.
29. Cf. below, 93.
30. Cp 98(35), mem. by Foreign Secretary, para. 1.
31. De Bono, 13.
32. Ib., 2.
33. Ib., 5.
34. Ib., 7.
35. Ib., 11.
36. Ib., 13.
37. Toynbee, 27–8.

38. Ib., 142.
39. Ib., 145, n.2.
40. De Bono, 116.
41. Ib., 118.
42. Ib., *loc. cit.*
43. Ib., 119.
44. Ib., 162.
45. Ib., 182–3.
46. Ib., 196.
47. Ib., 219.
48. Ib., 220.
49. Ib., 233.
50. Italy was also one of the four non-American States to have adhered (on 14 March 1934) to the Rio de Janeiro Treaty of 10 October 1933, which embodied the principle of non-recognition of territorial changes effected by force (Toynbee, 506, n.2. *Survey of International Affairs,* 1933, 336–7).

4 Italian Antecedents (pp. 26–33)

1. See above, 13.
2. See below, 29.
3. Cf. G. Bassani, *A Prospect of Ferrara* (1956), English translation, 140.
4. Cf. above, 13.
5. Seton-Watson, 179.
6. Ib., 182.
7. Ib., 381. Cf. Peterson, 94.
8. 'The young soldiers when they sailed from Italy . . . sincerely believed that they were the champions of a proletarian nation crying out for living room and justice, or that they were the bearers of light and civilisation to a race ground down by a ferociously feudal "upper class".' (Del Boca, 26–7.)
9. Cf. above, p.27.
10. Cf. below, p.78.
11. De Bono, XIV.
12. Ib., XIII.

13. Cf. an Italian historian's opinion (F. Chabod, *A History of Italian Fascism,* 1963, 77–8): 'At first, when the Abyssinian question seemed to boil down to a simple matter of colonial expansion, the attitude of most people in Italy was one of indifference and even hostility. It was a great mistake on the part of the British to make popular a war which would otherwise have been anything but that. This was brought about by the threat of the British fleet in the Mediterranean in September 1935 – a threat which was in fact mere bluff . . . the British move played into Mussolini's hands at home in bringing about a change in public opinion, which lost sight of Abyssinia and believed that Italy herself was actually threatened by Britain.'
14. Toynbee, 102.
15. Cf. *loc. cit.*, 238
16. A. Cassels, *Fascist Italy* (1969), 60.
17. John Strachey, *Menace of Fascism* (1933) 90–7; cf. Cassels, 58.
18. Interview published in *Le Petit Journal* on 27 September, 1935.
19. Cf. Chabod, 76: 'The years between 1929 and 1934 were the time when the régime achieved the greatest general support.'
20. Cf. Ib., 77–8.
21. Laval quoted Mussolini as saying, in December: 'Ce n'est pas tant de l'Ethiopie que j'ai besoin que d'une guerre victorieuse et sans trop de pertes pour tenir ma jeunesse', (J. D. de Bayac, *Histoire du Front Populaire,* Paris, 1972, 139).
22. Cf. below, p.118–19.

23. Warner, 421, n.3.

5 British Approach (pp. 34–56)

1. Avon, 19.
2. Templewood, 90.
3. Ib., 109.
4. Ib., 108.
5. Cf. Vansittart, 522: 'His mind was keen, his intentions good, and he might have left a better record if he had not been so punched above and below the belt before he found his feet.' He thought he might have an influence over Mussolini because of an incident in World War I: all in the day's work, no doubt, but of which Hoare seems curiously proud. He was in 1916 working for Military Intelligence in Italy, heard of Mussolini as a 'powerful mob leader in Milan', and had him paid to have his Fasci forcibly break up pacifist meetings there'. (Templewood, 54.)
6. Cf. Vansittart, 530: 'His future was assured in his own camp; he stood well with the Labour Party. "They say I'm the right man on the wrong side," he said to me. He learned early and instinctively all the things that please in Britain, and those things were right but not real ...' Amery (154) speaks of Simon's 'realistic, cold-blooded attitude' to the Manchurian crisis and the contrast between him and his 'good-looking and eloquent young understudy, Anthony Eden, who cheerfully voiced all the popular catchwords ...'
7. Cf. below, p.50–5.
8. Avon, 216–219.
9. Templewood, 136

10. Churchill, 123
11. Feiling, 264–5.
12. Amery, 112 & 168.
13. Churchill made this point forcibly, with specific reference to the Abyssinian crisis, in a Commons debate on 6.5.36 (the day after the fall of Addis Ababa): 'I consider that the Prime Minister ought to have spoken in the Debate. After all, he is the man who has the power. He has had all the power, and you cannot have all the power without having the responsibility. He changes his Foreign Secretaries as he thinks fit; sometimes he has had two at once. He has changed them and taken every decision.' (*Hansard*, c.1842).
14. His most sympathetic biographers confirm this view, though relating the failure specifically to the Hoare-Laval episode. Thus A. W. Baldwin (*My father: the true story*, 1955, 289) says, of its 'tragedy and absurdity', that 'by general consent it was the Prime Minister who cut the sorriest figure'. Middlemas and Barnes (898) say: 'Of all Baldwin's defeats this was the most complete, and the most incontrovertible mistake'. His friend, Geoffrey Dawson, 'regarded Baldwin as more culpable than Hoare' (Liddell Hart, *Memoirs*, 1965, I, 288). Vansittart (543) takes a different view: 'Baldwin never got over an episode in which he was loaded with more than his share of a general responsibility.' Both parts of this statement are open to question.
15. Tom Jones wrote in his diary on 6.12.35, the day before Hoare went to Paris to see Laval: 'The

PM's new collection of speeches came out on Monday, and is having a good press and it will help to establish confidence in his, or what people think is his, typical Englishness' (Jones, 157). This was the collection entitled *The torch of freedom*.

16. Davidson, 173.
17. Rowse, 37. Cf. Tom Jones' diary for 7.1.36: '10.30 AM. Saw the PM just back from a fortnight's Xmas holiday at Astley. He showed no signs of the crisis through which he had passed, and when I went in was in fact reading an essay on the *Use of Words* read by an Eton master to the Ascham Society.' (Jones, 158.)
18. Middlemas & Barnes, 1046.
19. In his speech at Astley, Worcestershire on 20 May 1950, *In the balance: speeches 1949 and 1950 by Winston S. Churchill*, ed. Randolph S. Churchill (1951), 281.
20. Private information.
21. Cf. T. Jones, 57: 'The Americans have been the devils of the piece – turning away from the League, from the guarantee, collaring the gold'. (Baldwin talking to Jones, on holiday, 14.9.32.)
22. Middlemas & Barnes, 743. The first Labour leader to take the same decision, Dalton, did so, by his own account, in April 1935 (*The Fateful Years*, 63).
23. A. L. Rowse, a harsh critic of Baldwin's later political attitudes, speaks of 'this honest Election' (*A Cornishman at Oxford* 1965, 112).
24. Cf. below, 242.
25. Vansittart, 547.
26. Percy, 176.

27. Cf. Blake, 243.
28. Templewood, 137.
29. Cf. above, 258, n.9.
30. Nicolson, 529. Cf. Colvin, 150–1, for the full text of the letter.
31. Cf. below, 87–8.
32. Colvin, 46.
33. Vansittart, 522.
34. In the House of Commons on 11 March 1935 (*Hansard*, c. 40), he said: 'We believe in a League system in which the whole world should be ranged against an aggressor. If it is shown that someone is preparing to break the peace, let us bring the whole world opinion against him . . .' On 22 October 1935, he said, again in the Commons (*Hansard*, c. 42): 'We want effective sanctions, effectively applied. We support economic sanctions. We support the League system'. But he went on to decry the piling-up of armaments and the concept of 'national defence'. His attitude to re-armament remained complex and curious as late as 1937 (Jenkins, 184–7; cf. Dalton, 104).
35. And, for the matter of that, home policy too. See his *Practical Socialism for Britain* (1935).
36. Cf. A. J. P. Taylor, *English History*, 318. At Margate two resolutions were passed, the first supporting the League of Nations, the second declaring that the workers would meet 'any threat of war, so-called defensive or otherwise, by organizing general resistance, including the refusal to bear arms'.
37. Ib., 144.
38. Trevelyan, a pacifist in the first World War, was on 9 June

1936, 'clamouring for sanctions and if necessary war against Italy'. (Jones, 219.)

39. See Lord Citrine, *Men and Work* (1964), pp. 350–2 and Dalton, 66.

40. Dalton, 89–90.

41. Cf. Chatfield, *It might happen again*, 1947, 87–8: 'Collective Security inflicted on Chiefs of Staff impossible responsibilities. No one could tell them when, or against whom, they might have to fight ... At almost a moment's notice our oldest friend might become our bitterest enemy.'

42. *Hansard*, 24.2.36, c. 84.

43. See below, p. 244.

44. Foreign Secretary in 1914, he had written in 1925: 'Every country had been piling up armaments and perfecting preparations for war. The object in each case had been security. The effect had been precisely the contrary of what was intended and desired.' (*Twenty Five Years, 1892–1916*, People's Library Edition, III, 265.) *Per contra* Arthur Henderson towards the end of his life spoke of 'the failure to tackle security effectively before we started on disarmament' as lying at the root of the disarmament failures. (Norman Angell, *After all*, 1951, 252.)

45. *I Renounce War* (the story of the Peace Pledge Union), Sybil Morrison (Sheppard Press, 1962). The Peace Pledge Union began (as the Sheppard Peace Movement) with an appeal to *men* to renounce war. Women were appealed to by the Women's International League for Peace and Freedom.

46. The diversity of opinions about this remarkable man is striking. Madariaga (*Disarmament*, 1929, pp. 190–1) wrote of 'the perseverance, the singleness of purpose, the creative mind of this true world-citizen, always ready to try a new line of attack through the intellect for a problem on which his heart is firmly set'. *Per contra*, Lord Birkenhead, passing judgment privately on his Cabinet colleagues in 1929. described Cecil as 'useless', (Davidson, 202.)

47. He became a member of the Executive Committee early in 1932, but on 5 May 1936 told Murray he was resigning in protest against a resolution for an Albert Hall meeting on the 8th calling upon the Government 'to urge the maintenance of sanctions against Italy until she is ready to accept terms of peace approved by the Council of the League'. However, on the 7th Sir Austen, always the gentleman, agreed 'to drop out quietly', so as not to damage the Union's reputation. (I am grateful to Professor Daniel Waley for this information.)

48. In this connection attention should be drawn to the close liaison between the New Commonwealth Society and the LNU. Lord Davies, the former's founder, was a member of the latter's Executive Committee. Joint *ad hoc* committees were set up from time to time.

49. 'Years later Baldwin said that he owed his personal misfortunes to the Union' (G. M. Young, *Stanley Baldwin*, 1952, 129). Mr. Young sees 'the beginning of the mischief' as between Bald-

win and the Union, in Lord Cecil's resignation from the Cabinet in 1927 and Baldwin's not taking it sufficiently seriously.

50. See *Peace Year Book, 1934*, 122.
51. There has been much recent research about the extent to which pacifism was the issue at this famous by-election. The important point, however, is that Baldwin thought it was. In his 'appalling frankness' speech of 12.11.36 he said that the Government lost the seat 'by about 7000 votes on no issue but the pacifist' (*Hansard*, c. 1144). In fact the Labour majority was 4840. Vansittart's robust reaction to East Fulham, called into counsel by Baldwin, was to say 'You have a *caisse de jeu* to make any gambler's mouth water. You can lose a packet and still have a majority of 250'. (Colvin, 31.)
52. Information from Mr. Henry Durant, founder of Gallup Polls in Great Britain.
53. Livingstone, 7.
54. Ib., 5.
55. 'This Ballot ... was probably the most remarkable private poll ever held in this country. The most noteworthy aspect of it was not the great majority in favour of a collective peace system (when a private organisation conducts such an inquiry its opponents are more likely to throw away their papers than to cast a negative vote), but the fact that over twelve million people participated in the Ballot. It was an indirect form of lobbying on an unprecedented scale' (Jenkins, 154–5).
56. The day Mr. Eden returned to

London from Rome after his unsuccessful attempt to 'buy off' Mussolini (Avon, 236). Lord Cecil had been keeping Eden informed of the Ballot's returns for many months before its completion (Information from Professor Waley).

57. Livingstone, 10.
58. Ib., 29.
59. Cf. A. J. P. Taylor, *Beaverbrook*, (1972) 355: 'The isolation movement ... is not making the progress it should' (Beaverbrook to F. W. Doidge, 25.7.35).
60. 1950 Ed., 148–9.
61. Cf. below 12.
62. FO 371/19126 J3929.
63. Ib., J3931.
64. Ib., J3879.
65. Ib., J3896.
66. Cf. *Gathering Storm*, 154: 'I was never in favour of isolated action by Great Britain ...'
67. J3692.
68. *Gathering Storm*, 148 (Churchill's italics).

6 The French Position (pp. 57–63)

1. Cf. Alexander Werth, *The Destiny of France* (1937), 47 (Mr. Werth was the correspondent in France, first of the *Glasgow Herald* and then of the *Manchester Guardian*, from 1929 to 1940): 'The events of January and February, 1934, with the Stavisky scandal, the financier's mysterious death, the outcry in Paris, the nightly Royalist demonstrations outside the Chamber, the resignation of the Chautemps Government, the savage anti-Parliamentary campaign in the Press, the short-lived Daladier Cabinet, with its record of heavy blunders, culminating in the

bloody riots of February 6, followed, in turn, by its hurried resignation and the formation, on February 9, of the national Government of M. Doumergue, were the most dramatic events Paris had seen since the Commune of 1871.'

2. When later accused of Anglophobia Laval often said that as Prime Minister he helped to save the Pound in September, 1931. This story is accepted by Templewood (168): '. . . on his own responsibility he had sent to London three billion francs in gold from the Bank of France to steady the value of the pound'. But Warner (41, n.1) casts doubt on it and concludes that he may have *offered* 'some money and plenty of sympathy. . . .'

3. Baldwin became British Prime Minister for the third time, Laval French Prime Minister for the second, on the same day.

4. See below, 197.

5. Cf. Avon, 274; Werth, 100; Pierre Tissier, *I worked with Laval* (1942), 38.

6. Pierre Tissier, who was Maitre des Requêtes au Conseil d'Etat and, as such, at one time one of Laval's Principal Secretaries, has recorded his opinion that if Laval could 'see the 900 Members of Parliament separately one by one, he is quite capable of winning each one. And that, at bottom, is the method he has always employed. His political activity has always taken the shape of conversations in the lobbies and interviews in his office. The only danger of this method is that it entails innumerable contradictory promises. . . .' (Ib., 42).

7. Cf. Brogan, 694.
8. Ib., 695; Werth, 181 and 190.
9. See below, p.197.
10. Werth, 211.
11. Cf. Halifax: 'I have never been one of those . . . who thought that it was any part of the League . . . to try to stop a war in Africa by starting a war in Europe'. (Hansard, *Lords*, 19.12.35, c.277.)
12. Cf. above, 56.
13. Warner, 94.
14. Churchill, 158.
15. Eight separate agreements were signed on 7 January. Four were published with a communiqué. The four secret agreements, disappointingly uninteresting, are now available in paperback. (E. M. Robertson, *Origins of the Second World War*, 1971, 235–9.)
16. See below, p. 85.
17. Gathorne-Hardy, 394.
18. Avon, 224.
19. Robertson, 233.
20. See below, p.117–18.
21. Werth, 126.
22. Vansittart, 540.
23. See below, p.197.
24. Cf. De Bayac, 141: '*Les accusations du gros des conservateurs, relayées par les pacifistes de gauche, trouvent un écho favorable dans la majorité des Francais: elles troublent et génent considerablement les partisans de la fermeté.*'
25. An Italian Note of 17 December, 1938 declared the 1935 Agreement to be cancelled. Its effective, as opposed to legal, death was lingering and correspondingly hard to date, but certainly occurred more than two years before the Italian cancellation. The Franco-Italian air and military agreements were formally cancelled along with the

political ones.

26. Cf. Werth, 233–4: 'He seems in fact less the sinister Machiavellian conspirator of mythology, than silly and short-sighted; a clever man overreaching himself, striving to catch a favourable constellation of forces, without realising their essential incompatability. . . .' Lord Avon (251) expresses sympathy with Laval and describes his policy merely as 'not wise'. See also, below, p. 222–3.

7 The Other Great Powers (pp. 64–71)

1. See below, p. 214–16.
2. See below, p.156–7.
3. Quoted Zimmern, 161.
4. Ib., 220.
5. Ex-President Theodore Roosevelt described the League as an idea of those who 'want everyone to float to heaven on a sloppy sea of universal mush'. He wrote this to Rudyard Kipling in 1919 and Kipling showed the letter to his Baldwin cousin. (A. W. Baldwin, 82.)
6. Cf. below, 79.
7. See Harris, 24–5.
8. 'The United States, which had abolished the evils of drink by the eighteenth amendment, invited the world to abolish war by taking the pledge. The world, not quite daring to believe or doubt, obeyed.' (D. W. Brogan, *The French Nation*, 1814–1940, 267.)
9. Beloff, I, 42. The Holy Alliance, of 1815, concluded between Austria, Prussia and Russia, became an engine for the absolutist and repressive policies, internal and external, pursued by those three Governments.

10. Ib., I, 81. More cautious and more accurate language had been used in the *Soviet Encyclopaedia of State and Law* of 1925–6. In it the League of Nations is described as 'a group of nations interested in the preservation and utilisation of the post-war international status'. (Quoted, ib., 134, n.3).
11. Ib., *loc. cit.*
12. K. E. Mackenzie, *Comintern and World Revolution* (London & New York, 1964), 325.
13. Report to the C.P.S.U. of 26 June, 1930, quoted Beloff, I, 43. The U.S.S.R. was a signatory of the Kellogg Pact and a member of the Commission of Enquiry into Briand's plan for a European Union.
14. As early as May, 1933 Karl Radek, the eminent Russian journalist, wrote: 'The way to revision of the predatory Versailles Peace leads through a new world war. Discussion of revision is the smoke-screen behind which Imperialism prepares the most terrible and ruthless war that the human brain can conceive.' (Gathorne-Hardy, 375).
15. Beloff, 129, 1.
16. Cf. Avon, 98.
17. See below, 214–15.
18. Beloff, I, 128.
19. Ib., I, 200.

8 The League of Nations up to the Crisis (pp. 72–81)

1. Cf. Walters, 52.
2. Mr. Gathorne-Hardy (24) acutely points to the limited language of Article 19 in that it speaks of the re-consideration of 'treaties which have become inapplicable', a phrase which seems

to bar the re-consideration of treaties which, it could be argued, have not become but never have been 'applicable'. To this one must add that international conditions likely to lead to international war are by no means limited to conditions imposed by treaties.

3. Mr. Walters points out (pp. 638–9) one consequent disadvantage which most manifested itself throughout the Abyssinian crisis. No more than Abyssinia did the League possess 'anything that could be called a diplomatic service. The League as such was barred out, about as completely as the general public, from all access to the diplomatic scene and from all influence upon whatsoever discussions might be going on behind the traditional curtain of secrecy. Nor does it appear that individual Members of the League, even during the period of sanctions, ever used their diplomatic services in support of their joint policy. Only the Italians were working in this secret and influential field and to this fact must be attributed no small part of their extraordinary diplomatic success throughout the months of crisis.'

4. Cf. Zimmern, 253–6.
5. Cf. below, 283, n.4.
6. The war with Germany was ended by the Treaty of Versailles, signed on 28.6.19; with Austria by the Treaty of Saint Germain, signed on 10.9.19; with Bulgaria, by the Treaty of Neuilly, signed on 27.11.19; with Hungary, by the Treaty of Trianon, signed on 4.6.20. The League's Covenant forms Part I of all four Treaties.

7. Sir Austen Chamberlain (British Foreign Secretary, 1925–9) said: 'I became a convinced supporter of the League by attending its meetings and taking part in its deliberations . . .' (*Hansard*, 19.12.35, c.2040). Vansittart attended only a single League meeting, that of the Council in April 1935, following the Stresa Conference.
8. Cf. above, 30.
9. At the Stresa Conference in April, 1935, the British delegation insisted on a discussion of Hitler's designs on Memel while passing over in silence Mussolini's designs on Abyssinia (see below, 115). In the end, in response to a German ultimatum, Lithuania ceded the Memelland to Germany on 22 March 1939, Hitler in person arriving with the whole German battle fleet the next day.
10. Gathorne-Hardy, 99–100.
11. Cf. above, 18.
12. Cf. Gathorne-Hardy, 123.
13. Quoted E. H. Carr, *International relations since the Peace Treaties* (1937), 173.
14. See below, 100 & 132.
15. Walters, 568.
16. Ib., 569.
17. Cf. Avon, 91–2.
18. *Annual Register for 1935*, 162.
19. *The Times*, 5.1.35.

9 The League's Machinery in Operation Dec. 1934 – Aug. 1935 (pp. 85–92)

1. See above, 23.
2. Cf. above, 80–1.
3. Avon, 193.
4. Joseph Avenol, who succeeded Sir Eric Drummond as the League's second Secretary-General in June, 1933, having been

his second-in-command for some ten years. Avenol resigned in August 1940; the third, and last, Secretary-General was Sean Lester. Sir Eric Drummond (becoming Earl of Perth in 1937) was British Ambassador to Italy from 1933 to 1939: 'it was surely wrong to appoint the Secretary-General of the League of Nations to a national diplomat's post immediately after he had left an international organisation.' (Lord Gladwyn, *Memoirs* (1972), 49).

5. Walters, 630.
6. Avon, 198.
7. 'Both Governments undertake to submit to a procedure of conciliation and arbitration disputes which may arise between them and which it may not have been possible to settle by ordinary diplomatic methods, without having recourse to armed force. Notes shall be exchanged by common agreement between the two Governments regarding the manner of appointing arbitrators.'
8. Quoted, Toynbee, 146.
9. See below, 114.
10. There had also been a procedural point. This meeting of the Council was an extra-ordinary session called to consider the German breaches of her treaty obligations announced in March. A year previously the Council had decided that at such sessions the agenda should only contain the item(s) for which it had been called. It was also provided, however, that, when the agenda was formally adopted, the Secretary-General should communicate a list of other urgent questions (Avon,

202). But, of course, the Council could have got round this procedural point if it had wanted to – and as it did in order to discuss an Iraki question (see Toynbee, 149).
11. Ib., *loc.cit.*, n.1.
12. Ib., 155.
13. Ib., *loc.cit.*
14. Avon, 239.
15. For its proceedings, see below.
16. Toynbee, 169.

10 The League's Machinery in Operation: Aug.–Oct. 1935 (pp. 93-100)

1. Avon 253.
2. See below, p. 113.
3. Avon, 197.
4. Cf. below, p. 119.
5. See above, p. 73.
6. Cf. Walters, 644.
7. From now on one must be at pains not to become confused between the various *ad hoc* committees of the Council which were set up. The members of this one were Britain, France, Poland, Spain and Turkey. Its chairman was Señor de Madariaga of Spain. It held its first meeting on 7 September, its last on 24 September.
8. See above, 90.
9. At this time T.G. Masaryk was still alive. Benes succeeded him as President of Czechoslovakia on 18 December 1935.
10. Templewood, 163 & 165.
11. Ib., 166.
12. Avon, 261. Cf. below, 268, n.17.
13. Templewood, 166.
14. Middlemas & Barnes, 155.
15. Templewood, 166; Middlemas & Barnes, 855, n.
16. Templewood, 166.
17. 'On his arrival at Geneva, Hoare had shown Cranborne

and myself the draft of his speech. We were both considerably surprised by its strength, which surpassed anything that the tone of discussions with our colleagues had revealed up to the time when I left London a fortnight before. While we were pleased and impressed by much of the text, some of it seemed to Cranborne and myself to go too far, not in the context of the present dispute, but in the general affirmation of our intentions, which might exceed our powers and perhaps the obligations of the Covenant.... Hoare made one or two corrections to meet us, but he was not prepared to make any major changes, arguing that the speech had been approved by his senior colleagues. . . . Never for an instant was a hint dropped that the speech was intended to bluff Mussolini into surrender. We should both of us at once have expressed the strongest opposition to any such folly.' (Avon, 260–1)

18. See below, 136–41.
19. Templewood, 169.
20. Avon, 261.
21. Templewood, 169.
22. Avon, 262. Hymans had been a notably active member of the committee which drafted the Covenant. He was President of the first Assembly and thereafter played an important rôle in League affairs on at least three occasions.
23. Marder, 1333; confirmed by Naval Historical Branch, Ministry of Defence. Avon (262) gives the date as 'the day after Sir Samuel Hoare's speech' and adds: 'There could have been no more spectacular curtain to

his words.' Churchill (151) also makes the same mistake. At the time Admiral Sir William James, Deputy Chief of Naval Staff, took nearly an hour to convince Eden and Vansittart to accept a plan of Admiral Sir William Fisher's which involved sending *Hood* to the Mediterranean: 'They told me quite frankly that Mussolini was in an excited state and the strengthening of the Fleet at Alexandria by the mighty *Hood* might tip the balance over to war, which was the last thing they wanted.' (James, *The sky was always blue*, 1951, 184.)
24. Templewood, 170. In the House of Commons on 11 July he had said: "As things are, and as long as there is an effective League, we are ready to take our full share of collective responsibility. But when I say collective responsibility, I mean collective responsibility" (*Hansard*, c. 518).
25. Avon, 262.
26. Lord Cecil wrote, in retrospect (269): 'Altogether, it was understood to be an uncompromising statement that unless Italy abandoned her invasion of Abyssinia, Britain was prepared to co-operate with the other nations to make her do so . . .'
27. Churchill, 150–1.
28. Murray to Cecil, 12.9.35, Murray Papers (Bodleian Library, Oxford).
29. Templewood, 170–1.
30. Toynbee, 189. Having regard to the strained state of Anglo-Irish relations at the time, Mr. De Valera's speech was an act of special moral courage.
31. Cf. below, p. 232.
32. Toynbee, 196.

11 The League's Machinery in Operation: Oct.–Dec. 1935 (pp. 101–112)

1. Cf. below, p.105.
2. Toynbee, 207.
3. The American neutrality legislation of August 1935 (cf. above) had made it obligatory on the President, on the outbreak of war, to impose an embargo on the export to belligerents of war materials, on a list to be proclaimed by the President. In advance of League action such a list had been proclaimed by Roosevelt on 28 September. On Eden's proposal this American list was now made the basis for the League's list of arms to be denied to Italy alone. This was all the easier because the list was based on one contained in the Geneva Arms Traffic Convention of 1925. Professor Toynbee, however, comments that the American list 'was compiled on rather old-fashioned lines which took little account of the *de facto* extension in the range of commodities constituting arms and munitions under the technical conditions of modern warfare' (241, n.1). Amery (182) spoils his powerful argument by an error of fact about Proposal 1 which he describes as 'an embargo against the shipment of arms to either party, a ridiculous piece of pedantry which could only injure Abyssinia'.
4. Toynbee, 231.
5. Ib., 286.
6. The Peterson-St. Quentin discussions in Paris had already begun (cf. below, 145).
7. Toynbee, 85.
8. Ib., 97. The U.S.A., spontaneously carrying out an undeclared co-operation with the League, closed a possible loophole in sanctions by refusing to allow its capitulatory rights in Egypt to be used by U.S. citizens for the purpose of trade with the belligerents (Harris, 84–5).
9. Toynbee, 217, n.3.
10. Cf. above, 65.
11. Toynbee, 237.
12. Cf. Avon, 292.
13. On 7 January 1936 Tom Jones said to Stanley Baldwin: 'Did you know that Bob Cecil, Lytton, and Salter refused to attend the Chatham House banquet the other day, over which the Prince of Wales presided, and at which all the diplomats were present, because Grandi had been invited to the dinner.' Baldwin answered: 'They have an extraordinary mentality.' Perhaps his failure to understand their attitude is more extraordinary. Lords Cecil and Lytton and the then Professor Salter were taking the Covenant seriously. (Jones, 160.)
14. Walters, 533–4.
15. Cf. below, 159 & 234.
16. Quoted, Toynbee, 211.
17. Ib., 225.
18. Ib., 225.
19. Ib., *loc.cit.*
20. Ib., 226.
21. Lord Avon in his memoirs, perhaps over-modestly, does not dwell on this phase of his activities. Three times, however, he refers to lack of support from London:–
    1. 'Even allowing for the novelty and risks in trying to constrain a man like Mussolini, I was too often first given my head and then

curbed' (Avon, 279);

2. 'In conversation with Massigli and Coulondre of the French delegation, I insisted that a decision about refusing to receive Italian imports must be taken by the end of the week. ... a telephone message arrived from Hoare saying that we ought not to be the sole active influence and initiator at Geneva' (Ib., 281);

3. 'Hoare sent me a message, after a discussion with his colleagues the next day [16 October?] that their meeting had been held in an atmosphere of great perturbation. Even though he had pointed out that other countries besides Great Britain had been firm about sanctions, the feeling persisted that I had recently been too much in the lead. It showed itself, Hoare explained, in a unanimous desire that I should go as slowly as possible and take the initiative as little as possible. ... *The answer to this was, of course, that if a leading power does not lead it is not likely to see its policies succeed.*' (Ib., 282; my italics).

22. A General Election had taken place in Canada on 14 October. On the 19th Mr R. B. Bennett was still Prime Minister. Mackenzie King became Prime Minister (and Minister for External Affairs) on the 23rd. Because of the political upheaval at Ottawa Mr. Riddell may well have been without adequate instructions from the Canadian Government at this time.

23. Mr. Riddell's initiative, but not the proposal itself was subsequently disowned by his Government (N. Mansergh, *Survey of British Commonwealth Affairs, Problems of External Policy, 1931–9* (1952), 117).

24. Toynbee, 275.

25. De Bono, 275.

26. Lord Avon (293) speaks of Laval in late November exploiting a British desire for delay 'with a ministerial crisis' and (294) fixing another week's delay in December under the pretext of another ministerial crisis. It seems too that the U.S. Government thought the plea of business in Paris a mere pretext for delay at Geneva. (Harris, 104.) But Mr. Geoffrey Warner (112) is emphatic that Laval did not invent 'these domestic political difficulties in order to gain time. ... His government had been coming under increasingly heavy pressure and it was only by the most astute management of parliamentary time that it managed to survive at all'. On 6 December there was a most important debate in the Chamber on the 'Leagues' and Laval won a vote of confidence by 351 votes to 219. The story goes that he afterwards said: 'Let's go and eat a dozen oysters. Tomorrow I have to work for peace; I am meeting Sir Samuel Hoare.' (Warner, 115.)

27. Cf. Toynbee, 278.

28. Ib., 280.

29. See below, 145.

30. Quoted, Toynbee, 243.

31. Ib., 244; Avon, 292; Harris, 89.

32. 'The distinction between normal and abnormal exports, now the basis for the Administration's moral embargo, was derived

from Hull's efforts during the
First World War, when he was
in the House of Representatives,
to differentiate between peace-
time and wartime profits.'
(Harris, 89.)

33. Cf. ib., 92; 'The Administration
hoped that if the moral embargo
failed in limiting American trade
with belligerents to pre-war
quantities, and if it became evident that such trade ... was
causing the defeat of sanctions,
an outraged public opinion
would force recalcitrant compa-
nies to conform or would
demand more effective legislation.'
34. Ib., 111.
35. See above, 103.

**12 The Great Powers: Dec.
1934–Aug.1935 (pp.113–130)**
1. See above, 85.
2. Cf. above, 60–1.
3. Avon, 197–2.
4. Ib., 195.
5. Thompson, 195.
6. Cf. above, p. 62.
7. Baer, 88–94.
8 Cf. above, 47.
9. Baldwin had met Laval when
he was in London from 31
January to 3 February 1935. We
do not know what they thought
of each other; we do know what
Baldwin thought Laval should
eat: 'I gave him good English
food and plenty of it. I didn't
attempt to compete with French
cooking. We had salmon trout,
mixed grill, very mixed... plum
pudding and brandy sauce. But
for that luncheon we should
never have got the important
declaration of February 3.'
(Jones, 153.)
10. Macleod, 178.

11. See above, 87.
12. See above, 87.
13. Avon, 179.
14. Cf. above, 77.
15. 20 & 21 (35), 1.
16. In Rome on 18 March 1933
when he put before them his
over-ingenious idea of a Four-
Power Pact.
17. 24 (35), 1.
18. Werth, 138 (diary entry).
19. Avon, 179.
20. Cf. Vansittart, 520–1: 'Eric
Drummond had come up from
Rome and urged sensibly that
we should *begin* by warning the
Duce of our wrath, should he
attack Abyssinia... I felt that
by such a course we might never
sit down at all. We should not
save Abyssinia by immediate
quarrel, and should certainly
lose Austria if we broke up
abortively. I told Eric that I
thought a better plan might be
to land Mussolini first and
lecture him later...'
21. Cf. above, 113–14.
22. In the House of Commons on 23
October 1935, Eden said that
'in the light of the fact that the
conference had been called
solely to deal with the complexities of the European situation, there was no reason whatsoever why it should have been'.
He added that, after agreement
had been reached on the questions which were on the agenda
'it was hardly to be supposed
that one of the three Powers
which had just declared that
the object of their policy was the
collective maintenance of peace
within the framework of the
League of Nations would take
any action in any other continent
which would jeopardize that

framework'. (*Hansard*, 23.10.35, c's, 213–14.)
23. Eden, *Hansard*, 23.10.35, c.214.
24. Hoare, *Hansard*, 22.10.35, c.25.
25. Thompson, 97.
26. Cf. above, p. 88.
27. Quoted, Avon, 198.
28. Ib., 200.
29. 12 (35) 5.
30. Ib., *loc. cit.*
31. Avon, 202–4.
32. CP (98) 35, para. 10.
33. 26 (35) 9.
34. CP (98) 35.
35. On that day also (14 May) MacDonald passed on to Baldwin a letter written to him by Mussolini expressing the hope that 'the atmosphere of sincere and friendly collaboration that made our work so fruitful on the shores of Lake Maggiore will continue'. (Middlemas & Barnes, 832.)
36. Cf. above, p. 88.
37. 28 (35) 9, Annex to Conclusion, para. 2.
38. Avon, 210.
39. Ib., 206.
40. See above.
41. Avon, 214.
42. Ib., 208.
43. Messrs. Middlemas & Barnes write (828): 'Britain's easy answer – that to her the Franco-Soviet Pact was an equal betrayal of mutual trust – would scarcely be understood in France.' Indeed not, inasmuch as that Pact had been approved in London, was within the framework of the League system, and did not condone any breach of treaty obligations. The only element in common between the Anglo-German Naval Agreement and the Franco-Soviet Pact was that both were bi-

lateral.
44. Ib., 827.
45. A. W. Baldwin, 233.
46. *The German Dictatorship* (1971), 296. Hitler repudiated the 1935 Agreement on 28 April, 1939.
47. 33 (35) 4.
48. Avon, 221.
49. Cf. below, 170.
50. Avon, 222–3.
51. Ib., 222.
52. On the next day these territories were delineated on a map (Ib., 226).
53. Ib., 223.
54. Ib., 225.
55. Avon, 236. Eden told the House of Commons, on 1 July, of the proposals he had put to Mussolini in Rome, but did not disclose how they had been received. In the House there 'was no enthusiasm for our offer, and no strong criticism either. . . .'.
56. 35 (35) 2. On 'public opinion', cf. above. It should be noted that the final results of the 'Peace Ballot' had been declared on 27 June.
57. Cf. *Political and Strategic Interests of the United Kingdom*. (R.I.I.A., 1939, pp. 40–53.)
58. 36 (35) 6.
59. Cf. above.
60. Above.
61. 39 (35) 1.
62. Avon, 242.
63. 40 (35) 1. Laval received this despatch on 31 July and at once pointed out to Eden that it lacked practical proposals. The latter's instructions did not allow him to say that Britain was prepared, if necessary, to implement Article 16. 'The delay caused by not having discussed sanctions beforehand with Laval increased the confusion and

hesitation, once the decision had been taken to give effect to the Covenant. This was the kind of uncertainty in which Laval revelled. He could only be kept to a narrow path if there were no gutters in which to drag his feet.' (Avon, 246.)

64. Avon, 245.
65. Ib., 244.
66. 41(35)6.

13 The Great Powers: Aug.–Oct. 1935 (pp. 131–144)

1. At the meeting on 3 July, cf. above, 126. The point came up again at the special meeting on the 22nd, in the discussion about telling Laval that Britain would, in the last resort, fulfil her commitment to the Covenant: 'This course, it was suggested, was not likely to be successful in stoping Italy from making war on Abyssinia, because it was extremely unlikely that France would co-operate in sanctions. Even if France should be willing to co-operate, however – and there were signs that French public opinion in this matter was rather in advance of M. Laval – it might lead to war between the United Kingdom and France on one side and Italy on the other.' The truism was added (but a truism is every bit as true as a truth): 'Wars are easier to start than to stop . . .'
2. See above, 90–2.
3. See above, 91.
4. Sir Maurice Hankey (later Lord Hankey) was Secretary not only of the Cabinet but also of the Committee for Imperial Defence and so of its Defence Policy and Requirements, and Chiefs of Staffs, Sub-Committees.
5. The Conclusions of this meeting are to be found in the Cab 23/82 series.
6. Avon, 249.
7. Cf. below, 154.
8. See above, 94.
9. Cf. above, 100.
10. Eden, reporting to the Council on 4 September.
11. Avon, 239.
12. 'Conference settled nothing; Geneva will settle the same. Settle it.'
13. See above, 93.
14. Colvin, 84.
15. Cab. 23/82, 149–168.
16. Cf. above, p. 106.
17. Cf. above, p. 55–6.
18. Cf. above, p. 56.
19. Cf. above, p. 97.
20. Cf. above, p. 120, 126, 128.
21. 42(35)1.
22. Cf. above, p. 97, 99.
23. FO/401/J4768/1/1.
24. That this was a very real fear of Sir Samuel's is confirmed by his making the point the next day immediately after the central passage in his speech to the Assembly (quoted above, 97): 'There, then, is the British attitude towards the Covenant. I cannot believe that it will be changed so long as the League remains an effective body and the main bridge between the United Kingdom and the Continent remains intact.'
25. FO/401/J4769/1/1.
26. See above, p. 97.
27. FO/401/J4818/1/1.
28. Templewood, 169, 2.
29. Cf. Vansittart, 533: 'Those vivid words were what she had been wanting to hear for sixteen drab years of retreat, yet when we said them she was the first to flinch'

Cf. also Major-General A. C. Temperley, *The Whispering Gallery of Europe*, (1938), 329: 'France was confronted by a situation which she had never envisaged, namely that instead of receiving protection from a world that was rushing to her aid, she was to play a leading part in according it.'

30. 43(35)1.
31. Avon, 269.
32. Ib., *loc. cit*; Middlemas & Barnes, 858.
33. Cf. above, p.100.
34. The Cabinet on this occasion received advice 'that the minor sanctions suggested by the Secretary of State would only reduce the period during which Italy could conduct war in Abyssinia from 24 to 21 months'. . .
35. This seems unfair to the Mexican representative who spoke in the Council on 6 September (above, 95) and the representatives of 19 other States who supported the British position in the Assembly debate of 11–14 September (above, 99).
36. 44(35)1.
37. Middlemas and Barnes (859) give this date wrongly as the 3rd; So does Toynbee (76); Amery (174) gives it as the 5th.
38. *Hansard*, 18.6.36, c.1236.
39. Jones, 155.
40. *Times*, 5.10.35.

14 The Great Powers: 3 Oct.– 12 Dec. 1935 (pp. 145–152)

1. 45(35)1.
2. 45(35)6.
3. 48(35)2.
4. This legal freedom is bounded by political considerations deriving from such matters as the Parliamentary time-table, the undesirability of Elections being held during the summer holidays or over Christmas, and so on. The net effect of these restrictions is that the dates most usually chosen are ones in the late Autumn or in the Winter. The only exception to this 'rule' in respect of the ten preceding Elections since the start of the century was that of 1929, held by Baldwin in May, which he lost.
5. Cf. above, 45. When he was re-elected Leader after the Election, defeating Greenwood and Morrison, Dalton wrote in his diary (26.11.35): 'A wretched, disheartening result. And a little mouse shall lead them.' (Dalton, 82.)
6. Chamberlain's pithy putting of this point in an Election speech was overlooked: 'Our policy is defence without defiance; their policy is defiance without defence.' (Macleod, 184.)
7. Feiling, 266.
8. Amery in a speech in his constituency (Sparkbrook, Birmingham) said on 8 October, 1935: 'I am not prepared to send a single Birmingham lad to his death for the sake of Abyssinia'. (Amery, 425). He later wrote: 'From the electioneering point of view nothing could have been more adroit than the Government's tactics. My Sparkbrook voters were grateful to me for my part in insisting that there should be no war; Neville Chamberlain's next door were, apparently, no less appreciative of his high moral stand for the Covenant' (ib., 180–1). Cf. Lord Birkenhead's *Halifax*

(1965), 346: 'the attitude of the British Government, although as fundamentally dishonest as that of the Opposition, was from an electioneering point of view extremely adroit.'

9. *Hansard*, 22.10.35, c.136. The Labour Candidate for Camborne, Mr. H. R. G. (now Professor) Greaves, wrote in his Election Address: 'When the Election is safely over they will, if you return them to power, desert the League, betray the Abyssinians, and do a deal with Mussolini.'

10. Cf. Templewood, 176.

11. Cf. Percy, 173–4: 'the British electorate – and, indeed, I think, British Ministers themselves – had no idea of the extent to which, behind the public façade of "resistance to aggression", the statesmen and diplomatists at Geneva had been concerned, from the beginning, to find means of conciliation with Italy, or of the lengths to which they had already gone, before the Hoare-Laval conversations...' In this connection it must be borne in mind (a) that Cabinet Ministers, other than the Prime Minister, would not normally seek to influence the course of foreign policy, and (b) that, right up to the end of his term of office as Foreign Secretary, they had a special confidence in Hoare. (Cf. below, 151–2).

12. On 22 November 1935, Lord Halifax replaced Lord Londonderry as Lord Privy Seal and was himself succeeded as Secretary of State for War by Duff Cooper.

13. Cf. above, 145.

14. Cf. above, 108. The correct date seems to be 6 November

15. Cf. above, 110–11.

16. Indeed the Cabinet was told, later at this meeting, that Sir John Cadman, Chairman of the Anglo-Iranian Oil Company, confirmed this opinion.

17. The Peterson-St. Quentin conversations (see above) had been resumed on 21 November.

18. 50(35)2. 'A short time' meant 'two or three weeks' (Templewood, 177).

19. At three separate places in his memoirs (160, 167 and 177) Lord Templewood uses this term, defined as 'negotiation with Italy and loyalty to the League...' He was no stranger to a 'double policy'. In November, 1911, when there was a contest for the leadership of the Conservative Party between Austen Chamberlain and Walter Long, he pledged his support in advance to both. 'But,' Lord Blake urbanely comments, 'with the best will in the world one cannot always get these things right. He did not think it worth while to write to Bonar Law' – in whose favour both candidates retired. (*The Conservative Party from Peel to Churchill* 1970, 194.)

20. See below, p.152.

21. Cf. above, p.108.

22. See also the next Chapter, *passim*.

23. The crisis about the Fascist Leagues (above, p. 270, n.6) was at its height.

24. Avon, 302.

15 The Advice of Admirals (pp. 153–163)

1. See above, 126.

2. Cf. above, 89.

3. Marder, 1327–8.

4. Cf. above, 131.
5. The term had obviously gained political currency as early as 1 July 1934, when Neville Chamberlain, in a letter to his sister, spoke of British bombers based in Belgium as a possible deterrent to German 'maddogging'. (Feiling, 253.)
6. Admiral Sir William Fisher ('the tall Agrippa'), C-in-C, Mediterranean Fleet since 1932, 'saw no need to wait for the outbreak of a war provoked by Italy. He was confident that, if told to, he could stop Italian ships carrying troops and war material, through the Canal and put an end to Italian aggression in Abyssinia. He was prepared to deal with the Italians even if he had to go it alone'. (Marder, 1340.)
7. 42(35)3. Naval mobilisation would have taken seven days (CP 166 (35), para. 6(b)).
8. Baer, 253–4.
9. Ib., 352, n. 5.
10. *The World Crisis*, Vol. IV (1927), 224. Churchill is making a plea in mitigation for Nicholas II. I have changed the tense to present the point as a general and enduring one.
11. Cf. above, p. 150.
12. 50(35)2.
13. Middlemas and Barnes, 177.
14. Chatfield, *The Navy and Defence* (1942), 247.
15. Marder, 1337.
16. Ib., 1342 (Chatfield to Fisher, 25.8.35).
17. Ib., 1346.
18. Cf. below, 214.
19. In April 1934, Sir Warren Fisher, Permanent Under-Secretary at the Treasury and, as such, Head of the Civil Service, and a member of the Defence Requirements Committee, argued that, as we could not fight both Germany and Japan, we should come to terms with the latter. He went on to 'suggest that the first and, indeed, cardinal, requirement for this end is the disentanglement of ourselves from the United States of America'. (Medlicott, *Search*, 10, n. 1.) Neville Chamberlain wrote in his diary on 6 June 1934, of 'the proposition that we cannot provide simultaneously for hostilities with Japan and Germany, and that the latter is the problem to which we must now address ourselves'. In the Autumn he was on this account recommending a Japanese Pact. (Feiling, 253–4.)
20. Marder, 1346.
21. Ib., *loc. cit.*
22. Ib., 1347.
23. Ib., 1351.
24. Medlicott, *Search*, 13.
25. COS minutes, 159th meeting.
26. Marder, 1328.
27. Vansittart, 523. For this technical information I am indebted to Vice-Admiral Sir Peter Gretton.
28. Marder, 1345.
29. Cunningham, *A Sailor's Odyssey*, (1951) 173.
30. Quoted, Marder, 1338.
31. Quoted, ib., 1337.
32. Cf. Cunningham, 173–4.
33. Marder, 1331 (Chatfield to Fisher, 25.6.35).
34. Middlemas & Barnes, 876.
35. Marder, 1327.
36. Ib., 1355.
37. Cf. above, p. 154.

16 Hoare-Laval (pp. 164–200)
1. Cf. above.

2. Cf. above.
3. Avon, 269. Just after his Geneva speech his tone about the Abyssinian crisis had been robust; a little later it became rather weak. This deterioration is possibly explicable in terms of physical health.
4. Ib., 295.
5. Middlemas & Barnes, 882.
6. In retrospect Peterson thought Hoare's visit to have been 'in the nature of a diversion' and from the point of view of his own interests ill-advised; '. . . the result ultimately reached could have been achieved by myself if my instructions had been amplified by authorisation for further concessions'. The Cabinet could have deliberated on an agreement so reached without being rushed. (Peterson, 119). Vansittart (538) concurs.
7. Avon, 304.
8. Templewood, 178. The King had repeatedly pressed the same point on his Foreign Secretary. (Ib., 159–60.)
9. Avon, 298.
10. Medlicott, *Search*, 20.
11. Templewood, 178.
12. Quoted, Middlemas and Barnes, 881. As this letter was answered by Lord Wigram on the same day it seems possible that it was written before the Cabinet meeting. If so, Sir Samuel failed to make clear to his colleagues what he himself had in mind as the object of his 'stop-off' at Paris.
13. PRO, D114/66 (Dr. David Carlton kindly drew my attention to this).
14. Templewood, 191–2.
15. Perhaps Vansittart was also in

an exalted mood. Oliver Harvey was Head of Chancery in the Paris Embassy at the time and three years later recorded that 'Van, far from restraining S.H., was in a wild state of excitement and wanted to give everthing away – it was my first eye-opener as to Van's bad judgement and weakness as a negotiator . . .' (*Diplomatic Diaries*, 1970, 137–8). Vansittart himself wrote in his autobiography (543): 'I have always found difficulty in being tepid; it is easier to be passionate or indifferent'. He also writes (559) that at Paris he advised an unpopular compromise because Hoare said that neither Government nor nation had any intention of fighting.
16. Templewood, 184.
17. Miss Elizabeth Monroe (Fellow of St. Antony's College, Oxford) lived in Sir Samuel's constituency (Chelsea) at this time. She remembers receiving in December 1935 her copy of a circular letter to all his constituents which included the remark: 'Even at the inconvenience of leaving Lady Maud and the luggage, I decided to remain in Paris for an extra day for further talks with Monsieur Laval.'
18. Avon, 303. For Halifax's view on the Hoare-Laval pact, cf. also below, 172.
19. Ib., 299.
20. The train ferry service via Dunkirk and Dover was not inaugurated until 1936. At this time statesmen and diplomats still normally travelled on the surface and not by air.
21. Avon, 299.

22. Toynbee (281) speaks of Laval 'with consummate diplomatic skill' drawing Hoare 'into an even closer partnership in a game which the British Secretary of State seems never fully to have understood...' Again, (292–8) his account of the Paris meeting ends with 'the Frenchman's first two shots' being 'enough to make the British statesman strike his flag'. This part of Toynbee's narrative has not stood the test of time.

The broad pattern of events being, as we shall see (below, 210–11) repeated later, Toynbee writes (339): 'On the 2nd–3rd March, 1936, as on the 7th–8th December, 1935, the British Foreign Secretary was out-manoeuvred and overborne by a French antagonist in the guise of a colleague. Monsieur Flandin's victory over Mr. Eden was less sensational than Monsieur Laval's over Sir Samuel Hoare; but the consequences of this second diplomatic battle were perhaps not less important.'

23. The second and third cessions were both described as 'Rectifications of frontiers'. The first was not so described.

24. In the immediately preceding Peterson-St. Quentin negotiations in Paris, the former wished to draw the western boundary of such a zone at the 40th meridian, the latter at the 38th. The difference was now, it seems, settled by a 'compromise'. (Cf. Peterson, 118.) As between him and St. Quentin: 'The main points in dispute were the extent of the Abyssinian homelands to be sacrificed and the restrictions, if any, to be placed upon the Abyssinian acquisition and development of a port.... The French urged the cession to Italy of the whole of the Tigre province, west and east. My instructions only extended to Eastern Tigre.'

25. Abyssinia, in the period between 1928 and 1935, appointed many experts, from many other countries, to give technical help, but among them was only one Italian, an electrical engineer. (Toynbee, 129.)

26. Sir Maurice Peterson's considered conclusion was (117): 'In so far as Amharic territory proper, and in the north, might be concerned, the cession of Zeila could be construed as affording partial, though not entire, compensation.'

27. Feiling, 275.

28. Cf. above, 101.

29. Feiling, 275.

30. Feiling, 274.

31. The first public man to raise the moral issue involved in the Hoare-Laval Plan was Mr. Duncan Sandys. To *The Times* on 8 December he wrote, from the House of Commons: 'We do not yet know the nature of the Anglo-French peace proposals. How will the new terms compare with those offered to Signor Mussolini before he resorted to war? On this comparison the world will judge the answer to the question: "Does aggression pay?" '

32. Ib., 273.

33. Templewood, 183. Vansittart (543) denies that Foreign Office officials told Hoare that the Pact was 'the best thing he had

done'; it was only, he says he said, 'the best that could be done'.

34. Ib., 183.
35. Cf. above, 167.
36. This was a Five Power Conference (Britain, France, Italy, Japan, and U.S.A.) to review the 1921 Washington Agreement and the 1930 London one.
37. Avon, 301–2.
38. 52(35)1.
39. Avon, 305. One must also bear in mind that Laval could easily telephone Mussolini. There was no telephone line to Addis Ababa and the Negus himself was at the front.
40. Hansard, *Lords*, 19.12.35, c.282.
41. Templewood, 185.
42. Avon, 305.
43. 33(35)1, Appendix I. (F.O. telegram 257).
44. 53(35)1, Appendix III.
45. *Hansard*, 10.12.35, c.856. Baldwin was on this occasion repeating, perhaps unconsciously, a stroke which had proved successful in a Commons debate two years earlier, on Air Defence: 'If I were to stand here and to say where the difficulties are, and who the people are who raise these difficulties, it would be perfectly impossible ever to advance one inch with regard to disarmament. One's lips are sealed.' (*Hansard*, 29.11.33, c.1014.)
   It was on 2 May 1936 that David Low, in his famous cartoons in *The Evening Standard* took to depicting Baldwin as 'Old sealed lips', with sticking-plaster over his mouth.
46. 54(33)1.
47. Cf. above, 111.
48. Toynbee, 305.

49. Ib., 308.
50. See below, 186.
51. See below, 183.
52. With the privilege of hindsight one may doubt whether any leading article written anywhere at any time has exercised more influence over subsequent events or become more famous. Strictly speaking, however, the sting is in the heading rather than the text.
53. Cf. above, 125–6.
54. 55(35)1.
55. 5b(35)16.
56. Cf. above, 278, n.3.
57. 55(35)3.
58. Cf. below, 199.
59. 35(35)5.
60. Cf. above, p.175.
61. Avon, 309.
62. CAB 23(90B) NR, Confidential Annexes, 1923–37: Cabinet 56 (35), *The Italo-Abyssinian Dispute, Government Policy in the Parliamentary Debate, Summary of Cabinet Discussion*.
63. Baldwin's official biographers stress Swinton's closeness to him (Middlemas and Barnes, 587, 754, 815, 928, 944, 1021, 1044).
64. Cf. above, 167–8.
65. Vansittart (542) thought of resigning, but was dissuaded by Beaverbrook 'Who pointed out that there would soon be no public service if public servants resigned on issues of principle.'
66. *Hansard*, 19.12.35, c.2016.
67. Ib., *loc. cit.*
68. J. E. Wrench, *Geoffrey Dawson* (1955), 327, Dawson's diary, 18.12.35.
69. *Hansard*, 19.12.35., cc. 2034–5.
70. It was Amery's opinion (185) 'that, but for Baldwin's ignominious surrender, Hoare could have carried the House by the

incontrovertible force of his argument, if he had been allowed to deliver his speech from his place as Foreign Secretary'.

71. *Hansard,* 19.12.35, c.2008.
72. Ib., c.2009.
73. Ib., c.2009–10.
74. Ib., c.2011.
75. Ib., c.2012.
76. Ib., c.2013.
77. Ib., c.2014.
78. Austen Chamberlain dwelt on this last sentence in his speech (ib, c.2041); 'Chips' Channon put it down, slightly wrong, in his diary, *Chips* (1967) 48. Hoare had obviously already conveyed it to Neville Chamberlain (above, 188).
79. Cf. Amery's diary entry: 'It was the first practical facing of the realities which the House had heard from anyone in a responsible position, and it made a profound impression.' (Amery, 185.)
80. *Hansard,* 19.12.35, c.2015.
81. Ib., c.2015.
82. See above, p.190.
83. Templewood, 187–8.
84. Cf. *Chips,* 48.
85. Cf. Templewood, 199, and Jones, 161.
86. Ibid.
87. Herriot had resigned his Leadership of the Radical-Socialist Party on 17 December, but not his office of Minister of State under Laval. As Leader of the Party he was succeeded by Daladier.
88. Cf. de Bayac, 143: '*Sur le plan intérieur français, la guerre d'Ethiopie provoque le glissement à gauche des radicaux, vers le Front Populaire.*'
89. Templewood (188–9) is convinced there was.

90. Cf. above, p.177–8.
91. Amery (184) writes that Grandi told him, 'just afterwards', that Mussolini telephoned on the 18th with instructions for the immediate acceptance of the Hoare-Laval plan: 'Grandi asked for an hour in order first to make certain that there was truth in the incredible rumour that had only that minute reached him that Hoare was resigning.' Amery comments: 'It is tragic to think of a settlement which might have saved the world, and even the League of Nations, from the disasters which were to come about being ruined by a few hours and by Baldwin's lack of courage.' But this is to ignore the role of Caesar Cunctator.
92. Templewood, 189.
93. Avon, 262.
94. Ib., 190.
95. Paul Schmidt, *Hitler's interpreter* (Ed. R. H. C. Steed, 1951), 60.

17 The Defeat of Abyssinia (pp. 203–219)

1. See above, 191.
2. Selby, 54–5.
3. Avon, 316.
4. Ib., Avon, 316. Baldwin stated the grounds for not wanting Halifax at the Foreign Office, controversy about his Indian policy and the undesirability at that moment of a Foreign Secretary in the House of Lords. Neville Chamberlain made Lord Halifax Foreign Secretary when Eden resigned (on the issue of policy towards Italy) in February 1938.
5. See above, 191.
6. Avon, 311.
7. See above, 192.

8. Toynbee, 329.
9. Cf. above, 107.
10. See above, 110.
11. Harris, 64.
12. Cf. above, 111.
13. Harris., 75.
14. Ib., 92.
15. Ib., 111.
16. Avon, 327.
17. *Hansard*, 24.2.36, c.151.
18. 11(36)5 (p.180). Venezuela and the U.S.A. were then the two largest exporters of oil in the world, but the former exported none direct to Italy. Large quantities of Venezuelan oil were refined in the Netherlands West Indies and some of this refined oil was re-exported to Italy. The Italian capacity for refining was small.
19. 11(36)5 (p.176). The early stages of Italian industrialization were based on imports of British coal.
20. Cf. above, 127. Japan had withdrawn from this conference on 15 January. Italy on 27 February refused to sign the agreement reached by the other four Powers concerned, nominally for 'technical reasons', in fact because she was not prepared to sign a treaty also signed by two Powers (Britain and France) applying sanctions to her.
21. Cf. above, p.127.
22. Toynbee, 338.
23. Cf. above, p. 208–9.
24. See above, p. 204.
25. Toynbee, 338. Avon (329) attributes this decision to the Sanctions Committee, not the Committee of Thirteen.
26. 15(36)1.
27. The Treaty was signed by Britain, France and the U.S.A. on 25 March 1936. Lord Monsell, at this ceremony paid a tribute to the 'admirable help and co-operation of the Italian delegation' and said he hoped that Italy would eventually sign. This she in fact did on 2 December 1938, as a condition of the coming into force of the Anglo-Italian Agreement of 16 November 1938, under which Britain recognized the King of Italy as Emperor of Abyssinia.
28. Cf. above, 265, n. 25.
29. Toynbee, 339.
30. A repetition of the formula of 3 March: Cf. above, p. 211.
31. 23(36)3.
32. Cf. above, p. 94.
33. Toynbee, 355 and 472. Ecuador has another ignominious distinction, that of adding the only vote to those of the three Italian client States (Albania, Austria and Hungary) against the admission of the Abyssinian delegation to the 17th Assembly. (Ib., 525.)
34. Cf. Avon, 330, and Medlicott, *British Foreign Policy*, 148.
35. 16(36)2.
36. Cf. above, p.114–16.
37. 27(36)1.
38. Even so realistic a Germanophobe as Dr. Dalton condoned this attitude (see *Hansard*, 26.3. 36, c. 1454). The 'back garden' phrase was apparently coined by an arch-appeaser, Lord Lothian, described by Vansittart as 'an incurably superficial Johnny-Know-All' (Medlicott, *Search*, 12, n.3.)
39. For Press reactions see F. R. Gannon, *The British Press and Germany, 1936–9*, (Clarendon Press, 1971), 80–7 and 93–100.
40. 15(36)1.
41. He had been given a room at

the Foreign Office after becoming Lord Privy Seal (cf. above, 275, n.1).
42. 18(36)1.
43. 19(36)7.
44. 23(36)3.
45. 27(36)1.
46. In a speech at the centenary dinner of the City of London Conservative Association on 2 July 1936, he boasted of this, vividly reminding his audience that at his daily work in the Cabinet room he sat underneath a portrait of the first holder of his office, Sir Robert Walpole, whose boast it had also been that he had kept his country out of war except on one occasion, when he had said that the people now ringing the bells would soon be wringing their hands. (This was when war broke out with Spain in 1739.) Baldwin went on: 'War is a very terrible thing, and when once let loose in Europe no man can tell how far it will spread and no man can tell when or how it will stop. And I am quite content in the circumstances to be called a coward if I have done what I could in accordance with the views of every country in Europe to keep my own country out of war.'
47. 27(36)2.
48. Toynbee, 361, n.1.
49. Ib., 346.
50. See Walters, 382, 674 and 808. The plan was put forward by Finland and she received some material aid from the League in the Finno-Russian War of 1939–40 (see below, 227–8).
51. 27(36)3.

18 The Defeat of the League (pp. 220–225)
1. Cf. above, p.12.
2. Toynbee, 484.
3. See above, p.102.
4. 42(36) 1.
5. Cf. above, 136, 153, 207, 270, n.3.
6. *Hansard*, 18.6.36, c.1200.
7. *Hansard*, 23.6.36, c. 1706.
8. Ib., c. 1645.
9. Feiling, 265, 268, 272.
10. Avon, 445.
11. Feiling, 281.
12. Chamberlain's diary, 17.6.36, quoted Feiling, 296. To Eden he wrote a letter which conveyed the impression of an accidental lapse (Avon, 385).
13. The phrase flashed round the world, but the Shakespearean undertones must have made it most immediately understandable to those acquainted with *Twelfth Night*. Chamberlain was something of a Shakespearean scholar and quoted him to great effect in more than one political speech.
14. The full text is given in Toynbee, 461. It was on this issue that Sir Austen Chamberlain resigned from the Union's Executive Committee (cf. above, 262, n.7).
15. Cf. Toynbee, 489.
16. See above, 102.

19 Epilogue (pp. 226–231)
1. Cf. below, p. 237–8.
2. Both the term and the concept seem to have been first formulated by, understandably enough, a statesman of a country, Hungary, which had everything to gain by an Italo-German Alliance. Gömbös, Hungarian Prime Minister,

speaking on 20 June 1934, i.e. just after the first and unsuccessful meeting between Hitler and Mussolini, said: '. . . Berlin and Rome form the two ends of an Axis which, if it should find itself in a state of equilibrium, could provide a basis for a peaceful solution of European affairs.' Gömbös on this occasion said he had first put forward the idea in 1922.

3. Feiling, 250.
4. Between May 1936 and September 1939, five Latin-American States (Guatemala, Honduras, Nicaragua, Peru, Venezuela) resigned. Resignations also came from Siam, in September 1937, and Italy, in December. (Mussolini hung on to membership as long as he did in order to make what use of it he could: another way of showing his fundamental contempt for the League.) Hungary resigned in April 1939 and Spain in May. Austria and Albania lost their membership on losing their independence in 1938, as did the three Baltic States in 1940. The U.S.S.R. has the unique distinction of being the only member to have been expelled, in December 1939.
5. 'Everything that I have worked for, everything I have hoped for, everything that I have believed in during my public life has crashed into ruins.' (*Hansard*, 3.9.39, c.292).
6. *Hansard*, c.1873. Lord Avon (383) says it was 'so adulatory as to be embarrassing to all who heard it.'
7. Templewood Papers, 1755, VIII,6. (For this information I am grateful to Professor

Daniel Waley.)
8. Vansittart, 12 and 550.
9. *Hansard*, 6.4.55, c.1182.
10. Middlemas & Barnes, 1970.

20 Inquest (pp. 232–244)

1. Cf. above, 33.
2. Cf. above, 31.
3. Cf. Toynbee, 4: 'He showed a moral courage (for the like of which many English people were looking in vain to their constitutionally appointed Government) in sending half a million Italians to conduct a difficult military campaign on the farther side of the Suez Canal when the British Fleet was concentrated in the Levant, while fifty-two states had agreed to co-operate. . . .'
4. Mr. Warner (422) ends by accepting Laval's self-valuation: 'I have always had simple ideas in politics. People take me for a shyster, but they don't know me. What I do is so simple that it looks to those who don't understand like something very complicated.' (Speech on 22.2.44, to Mayors of the Lyons region.)
5. See above, p.197.
6. Amery, 426.
7. A. W. Baldwin, 291.
8. Cf. Temperley, 330–1: 'If a long view were taken there could be no comparison between Italy and Great Britain . . . as an ally. What was eighteen divisions at the Brenner Pass compared to the enormous resources and known tenacity of this country?'
9. A shrewd and not unsympathetic comment on the British attitude was made by a prominent Deputy of the Right (M. Taittinger) in the Chamber on 27 December 1935: 'The Eng-

lish have a touch of the friar predicant about them. Whatever party they belong to, they consider that they have a mission to instruct the world. One must not make fun of them for their League of Nations mysticism.' (Quoted, Toynbee, 323.)

10. Cf., above, p. 4.
11. *Hansard*, 18.6.36, c.1198.
12. Templewood, 171.
13. *Hansard*, 19.12.35, c.2116.
14. Cf. Neville Chamberlain (19.10. 35): 'I have always said that, when it came to a decision, Laval must come down on our side, though he would wriggle and jib up to the last moment.' (Feiling, 268.)
15. Cf. above, p. 206. The new Act, like its predecessor, allowed the President no discretion to distinguish between aggressor and victim and so to hinder the former and help the latter. But there was one important difference most discouraging for hopes for collective security. The 1935 Act had not required the President to extend the arms embargo to additional countries that went to war in defence of the League's Covenant and/or the Kellogg Pact; the 1936 Act made that extension mandatory. (Harris, 128.)
16. Interestingly German Military Intelligence, before the war started, 'estimated that fighting would last three years'. (E. M. Robertson, *Hitler's pre-war policy and military plans, 1933–9*, 1963, 65.)
17. This would not have been a popular sentiment. It was easy enough for Lord Phillimore, in the House of Lords, to urge the Government to 'tell the nation . . . that they have no intention

of allowing this country to be led into war except on behalf of the immediate and direct interests of the British Empire'. (Hansard, *Lords*, 18.2.36, c.624.) Another seemingly ancestral and virtually solitary voice was that of Lord Hardinge (a former Permanent Under-Secretary of State at the Foreign Office) saying 'in the present crisis there is no danger to the security of even a single British possession' (*The Times*, 27.8.35).
18. T. Jones, 193 (Jones to Lady Grigg, 13.5.36).
19. Feiling, 273.
20. Contrast Vansittart, 545: 'Germany *might* have been deterred if every valid member of the League had attacked Italy. . . . If we had attacked alone and suffered loss, Germany would not have been deterred but incited. Unless the war could be generalized the better deterrent was to keep Italy in line.' One must add that that might have proved impossible anyway. Toynbee (92) over-simplifies in saying that 'the goodly company of contemporary dictators was patently subject to the same law of dynamics . . . as a file of tin soldiers or a row of ninepins'.
21. Feiling, 269.
22. The culmination of this campaign was an Albert Hall meeting on 3 December addressed by Churchill, Sir Walter Citrine, and Sir Archibald Sinclair; the 'abdication crisis' had become public property the previous day; the abdication took place on 10 December.
23. Quoted, Robert Blake, *The Unknown Prime Minister* (1955), 447–8.

24. T. Jones, 30.
25. Toynbee, 52–3.
26. *Hansard*, 19.12.35, c.2037.
27. Cf. above, p. 282, n.46.
28. Churchill, 152–3.
29. This point was put well by Edwyn Bevan in a letter in *The Times* (30.4.35): 'The League can be a success only if the nations composing it are prepared to fight. It aims at peace, but its method must in certain circumstances mean war. Just as vaccination aims at preventing smallpox by producing the disease in a milder form, so a collective war waged against a peace-breaker who will not yield to gentle treatment is very much preferable, it is held, to a war waged by a nation for its own land. . . . It is an ironical reflection that the very same fear of war which won so many thousand votes for the League of Nations in what was termed a "Peace Ballot" is the thing which paralyses the League even in the face of an aggressor so brutal and atrocious as the Italian.'
30. Cf. above, 41.
31. Lord Cecil had helped to create one right at the start: 'The great weapon we rely on is public opinion . . . If you have a decision in the [League] Assembly of overwhelming opinion on one side you will get the whole weight of public opinion behind the one side and you will find, I think, that the nation which is in the wrong will not persist in the course which has been publicly and overwhelmingly condemned.' *Hansard*, 21.7.19, c.992
32. Cf. Percy, 133: 'The wildest misjudgment of the Baldwin of the thirties is that he fell a victim, with so many of his contemporaries, to the myth of "collective security". He never did; but I am afraid that he eventually made the mistake, in the Abyssinian crisis, of thinking he could convince his countrymen of the weakness of collective security by "trying it out", without incurring any more serious penalties than he would have suffered – and had suffered on more than one occasion – by a similar doubtful move in domestic politics.' Cf. above, 41.
33. Cf. above, 80.
34. Lord Tyrell (a former Head of the Foreign Office and Ambassador to France) told Baldwin in October, 1935, that the Union was 'the new war party in our country.' (Middlemas and Barnes, 860.)
35. Cf. above, p. 42–8.
36. Cf. Churchill's summary (155): 'Neither side usually has much to be proud of at election times. The Prime Minister himself was no doubt conscious of the growing strength behind the Government's foreign policy. He was, however, determined not to be drawn into war on any account. It seemed to me, viewing the proceedings from outside, that he was anxious to gather as much support as possible and use it to begin British rearmament on a modest scale.'
37. Cf. Lord Birkenhead (341), writing of the 'appalling frankness' speech: 'he was expressing a real dilemma, for however futile the Government's efforts at rearmament were during these fatal years, they were infinitely superior to anything that could have been expected from the Labour Party.'

Index

Index

Index

oil sanction, 109, 200
De Bono, 24–5, 228
Hoare, 298
Amery on, 233
Baldwin on, 41, 150, 233
Eden on, 96, 126
Toynbee on, 283
Vansittart on, 42
death, 228

Napier, Sir Robert (later Lord), 11
'National Government', 34, 58
national interests
British, 12, 116, 120, 153, 156, 219, 228, 237, 284
French, 141, 196, 233
National Peace Council, 49
Navy, British, 31, 127, 132, 154, 156, 157–61, 207, 237, 240, 242
French, 158
German, 156, 161
Italian, 159–60
Japanese, 157, 161
New Commonwealth Society, 49, 262
New Guinea, 22
Nile, *see* Blue & White Nile
Norway, 22, 99, 234

Obock, 11
oil sanction, proposed
Sanctions Committee, 108–11, 148, 180, 204, 210–12
oil experts committee, 204–5
British Cabinet, 145, 155, 178–90, 206–10
Mussolini's resistance, 96, 164, 169, 187, 195, 216–17, 235–6

Pacificism, 7, 43, 45, 49–50, 54, 220
Pacifism
British, 7, 40, 48–9
French, 62–3
Palmerston, Lord, 11
Pareto, 26
Peace Ballot, 37, 50–5, 75, 146, 173, 240–1
Peace Pledge Union, 49
Peace Society, 49
Pétain, Marshal, 58–9, 197
Peterson-St Quentin conversations, 145, 147, 164–5, 172, 198, 278
Pittman, Senator, 68
Plowden, W. C., 11
poison gas, 218
see also Anti-Gas Convention
Poland, 45, 77, 101, 233
Politis, K., 93
Pope Pius XI, 31
Popular Front, 57, 197
Portugal, 10, 70, 99

'Power Politics', 48
Prester, John, 10
public opinion
African, 6
U.S.A., 67–8, 111, 205–6, 235
British, 6–7, 33, 48–55, 75, 114, 119–20, 126, 128, 133, 137, 146, 154, 156–7, 190–1, 199, 208–9, 221–3, 236, 242–3
French, 174, 176, 215–16, 233
Italian, 31, 33, 121, 123, 259
Public Records Acts, 7

Radek, Karl, 257, 265
Railways
Addis Ababa–Jibuti, 9, 14, 15–16, 19, 60, 125–6, 219
proposed Eritrea-Somaliland, 16, 18, 125
in proposed corridor, 181–2
Realpolitik, 172, 237, 243
re-armament, British, 41, 47, 114, 143, 209–10, 244
German, 49, 64, 123, 137, 238
Red Sea, 8, 9–10, 12
Renown, HMS, 98, 156
République des Camarades, 57
revision of Treaties, 70, 73, 123
Rhineland crisis, 64, 156, 197, 210, 214–16, 220
Ribbentrop, J. von, 123
Riddell, Dr. W. A., 108
Risorgimento, 26
roads: Assab–Dessie, 20
Sudan-Tana, 18
Rome Agreements, 22, 60–2, 113, 138, 264–5
Roosevelt, F. D., 9, 40, 58, 67–8, 71, 79, 110, 244
Roosevelt, Theodore, 265
Rowley *see* Henderson
Rowse, A. L., 38
Rubattino Shipping Co. 11
Ruhr, French occupation, 5, 77
Runciman, Walter, 96, 207
Rumania, 99, 110, 234

Saar Plebiscite, 80–1, 85, 117
sanctions, economic
birth of idea, 66, 74
early history, 106, 133
imposition (1935), 102–5, 126–8, 131, 133–40, 153, 274
effectiveness, 104–7, 185, 187–8
impact, 31, 208, 236
lifted, 5, 216–17, 219–25
failure, 220–1
Peace Ballot, 52–5
see oil sanction
sanctions, military, 45–6, 52, 66, 74 140,

Index